The Subtlety of the Street

The Subtlety of the Street

The Discourse of Responsibility

M Peregrine Balmat

UNIVERSITY OF MICHIGAN PRESS

Ann Arbor

Published in the United States of America by the
University of Michigan Press
First published February 2026

A CIP catalog record for this book is available from the British Library.

Library of Congress Cataloging-in-Publication data has been applied for.

ISBN 978-0-472-07788-5 (hardcover : alk. paper)
ISBN 978-0-472-05788-7 (paper : alk. paper)
ISBN 978-0-472-90564-5 (open access ebook)

DOI: https://doi.org/10.3998/mpub.12350324

The University of Michigan Press's open access publishing program is made possible thanks to additional funding from the University of Michigan Office of the Provost and the generous support of contributing libraries.

The authorized representative in the EU for product safety and compliance is Easy Access System Europe, Mustamäe tee 50, 10621 Tallinn, Estonia, gpsr.requests@easproject.com

Cover image from iStock uploaded by ozgurdonmaz

"Publications by this author may also be found under Maureen T. Matarese and Mo Matarese."

This book is dedicated to street-level workers and all those served by street-level professionals, in words adapted from John Darnielle (and my large-hearted partner—Geoff Klock's—email signature):

"In the earnest hope that you find the joy, love, freedom, respect, and dignity that was always yours by right."

Contents

Digital materials related to this title can be found on
the Fulcrum platform via the following citable URL:
https://doi.org/10.3998/mpub.12350324

Tables

Figures

Vignettes

Acknowledgments

This book was written on the occupied Lenapehoking—the land of the Lenape Indigenous people—through my, and others, tacit colonialism. While I do not expect that this book will make money, and while it is not enough, a portion of the proceeds from this book will be donated to the Lenape Center (https://lenape.center/). This book would not be possible without the foundation of committed academics, student researchers, friends, and loved ones who have supported me and my work, given feedback, crossed oceans to collaborate, and paid babysitters to sit in meaningful connection with me. In particular (and in no special order), I extend my heart and gratitude to the DANASWAC community, including Chris Hall, Stef Stembrouck, Carolus van Nijnatten, Kirsi Juhila, Søren Peter Olessen, Elisabet Cedersund, Eva Hjörne, Åsa Mäkitalo, and others; the Street-Level Bureaucracy community, including Dorte Caswell (fellow DANASWACer and wellspring of advice), Evelyn Brodkin, Flemming Larsen, Bernardo Zacka, Gabriela Lotta, Flavio Eiró de Oliveira, Mark Considine, and of course Michael Lipsky (one of my favorite humans full stop); the Neoliberalism analysis working group, including Sanford Schram and Marianna Pavlovskaya; colleagues at Borough of Manhattan Community College, including Sharon Avni, Elisa Koniski, Jennifer Delfino, Hollis Glaser, benjamin haas, Robin Isserles, Brian Kelley, Rosario Torres, Ken Levinson, and Gay Brookes; exemplary undergraduate researchers, including Kyle Fraser, Kylie Lance, Daniel Antipov, Karmaria Hodge, Angie Santana, Gabriella Flores, Bryana Starr, and Bernadette Schaffer; my dissertation cohort, including Jennifer Fennema-Bloom, Katalin Kabat-Ryan, Aaron Chia Yuan Hung, Maria Hanzopolous, Zeena Zakharia, and Ameena Ghaffar-Kucher; my dissertation advisers, including Lesley Bartlett, Ofelia Garcia, Hervé Varenne, Kim Hopper, and JoAnne Kleifgen; Marchella Mazzeo and Alex (coffee heroes); Jack and Buck (my ride or die bros); Jezebel Express for her consultation on some terminology; and other early supporters of my work, including Emily Rine Butler, Kate van Tassel, and Philip Matarese. Thank you. Thank you to my parents, who have supported my work from the beginning, and who have loved me across this whole journey. Thank you to the Klocks for copious praise and for facilitating my writing by always finding a quiet place for me to work! I have so much gratitude to both my parents and the Klocks, who always make me feel celebrated for important milestones. I want to extend particular gratitude to the participants of these two studies, to the institutions that opened their doors to me, to the administrators and staff who all made me feel so welcomed and supported. Thank you to BMCC's administration, staff, and my colleagues for their unwavering support over the past sixteen years. Thanks to Penny, Adria, and Jane Kivnick. A very special thank you to early readers of the draft—Tom Bloom, Zora Tucker, and Sharon Avni for their very generous feedback and expertise, and to Christine Jacknick—colleague, best friend, reader of countless drafts, answerer of texts—thank you—we can celebrate at the diner now, my treat, obviously. Let's "get shit done" but also be good to ourselves. Thanks to my cats, who consider themselves coauthors. Finally, my particular thanks to Geoff Klock. Thank you for hundreds of meals delivered to my office, for special popcorn, for every time I interrupted your reading to ask, "Babe, what's another word for . . . ?" Thank you for keeping very late vampire hours, for bringing me coffee in the mornings, for reminding me that a lot of mediocre, white, cis dudes have unearned confidence. Without you there would be no book. Without you, the me now wouldn't be *me* now. You are my safe haven and my rapturous joy. You are my cheerleader and my ride or die, and while the book is dedicated to street-level workers and those they serve, I dedicate myself to you. I love you. I owe you a lot of dinners. You're my soup.

Preface

> There's no crying! There's no crying in baseball! Rogers Hornsby was my manager, and he called me a talking pile of pig shit. And that was when my parents drove all the way down from Michigan to see me play the game. And did I cry? . . . Yeah! *No.* And do you know why? Because there's no crying in baseball. *There's no crying in baseball!* No crying!"
>
> —Tom Hanks as Jimmy Dugan in *A League of Their Own*

This book examines how street-level workers like teachers and social workers construct responsibility with their words, particularly in institutional contexts serving marginalized people. I reveal how belief systems and tropes around work, money, time, race, and class are evoked when talking about responsibility. In writing this book, I have realized that my interest in this topic is partially fueled by my own internal and personal preoccupation with responsibility, work, productivity, and making other people comfortable. For that reason, I intentionally weave some of my own responsibility story through this book.

Many academics drift toward what we study for particular, often personal, reasons. On one hand, if I present these studies exclusive of my own thought processes, personal developments, and realizations around responsibility, that would perhaps better satisfy those hoping for an "objective" portrayal of the two talk-oriented ethnographies presented in this book. I can already hear academics opining with an eyeroll, paraphrasing Tom Hanks in *A League of Their Own* and throwing back their heads in unison, "There's no crying in [social science]" (Marshall, 1992, 1:09:17). While "crying" does not take up space in the book, I will offer some emotionally informed, interpersonal honesty and vulnerability through brief, interstitial autoethnographic writing.

Much of academia involves a wringing out of the self, if not in intention then in practice. When I finally sat down to write this book, I found that whatever written voice I had that existed outside journal articles was one with which I had no familiarity anymore, one that I did not trust, one that felt trite and irrelevant. Like that slip of paper in your pants pocket that slowly comes loose along a mile or two of city street, my voice left without any leave-taking. I looked down at my keyboard and simply noticed with some sorrow and confusion that it had gone. Sitting down to write this book, I felt unprepared for what I wanted to do. Without noticing, I had slowly fragmented over time, folding pieces of myself into dresser drawers like the putting away of winter clothes or that pair of fancy pants one hopes to remember when they fit again. I spent fifteen years peddling my intellectual wares to academic journals that I needed for promotion and tenure and that I still need in order to move my ideas out into the academy, and when it was finally time for me to "arrive" as a fully realized scholar writing this book, when I fished my lesser-used and suppressed voices and stories out of the dresser drawers, I realized that I needed to intentionally reintegrate what had been stuffed down in order to get ahead in academia and to get by in my life. I thought this book would be a vehicle for my "arrival" as a full and completed academic—Here I am! Be excited by my findings! I am a delightfully finished product!—but there is no such thing as "arriving"; as annoying as that is, we are always only travelers. There is only journey. So this is where you find me in the autumn of 2024: a forty-six-year-old white transgender man, extravagant, bedazzled, sometimes femme, usually dapper, a person carefully reassembled, missing pieces still. I am an organized mess in glitter and argyle. I am trying and sometimes failing and then trying again. I am learning how to communicate better myself by listening to others and by doing this research. This book is not *only* the culmination of fifteen years of primary research on responsibility in talk but also an attempt to authentically show up for the reader as an author, as a scholar, and as the person I am—right now.

About eleven years ago, I got divorced. It was my decision, and, as divorces generally do, it hurt and alienated a number of people. At the time, I had a hard time explaining to people what I intuitively knew to be true: I could no longer be part of this, by all appearances, excellent relationship with a nice person with whom I shared nearly fifteen years of history and memories. In retrospect, the divorce was a catalyst, a parting of ways from so many strictures that formed as a result of growing up Catholic in the Bible Belt American South, making space for radical changes that at the time were both incipient and insistent. I knew enough to go, and I had a difficult time explaining why to most people's satisfaction. This turning point initiated an unexpected blossoming of my life, opening me up to an epoch of professional and self-directed introspection that not only eventually uncovered my queerness but also my preoccupation with responsibility.

It has taken over ten years to unpack and unlearn what was conveyed through a childhood that required the extra responsibility needed to maintain the life of a younger sister with muscular dystrophy, what was conveyed through a Catholic youth and marriage. Still, I made the choices as a young person that got me here, as those choices are framed and contextualized by my small world, as I understood it. Ignatius Loyola famously said, "Give me a child until he is seven, and I will give you the man." Pre-divorce, I thrived on a dysfunctional relationship to responsibility, work, and productivity. I have since realized that my marriage (as loving as it often was), my Catholicism, and even academia itself was/is threaded with unhealthy beliefs around responsibility, productivity, and morality. It felt useful to share some of these stories with you because we do not come to what we study randomly. We generally study what we study for a reason, and as an ethnographer I want to be honest about how I see (or have seen) the world. In all my autoethnographic writing, the narratives I relate are my own perspective and interpretation, and they reflect solely my own experience of events, people, and places.

I really struggled with whether personal stories of a privileged white academic were relevant to this book, whether they detracted from the voices offered through the two focal interaction-based ethnographies. Admittedly, the mantle of responsibility that I carry is markedly different from those that marginalized people, particularly Black and Brown Americans, have had to carry. The two ethnographies in this book underscore how insidious and potentially destructive discourses around responsibility are for marginalized people. My autoethnographic reflections bring you into my life and mind for a moment, often inviting comparison and highlighting significant differences in how responsibilities are articulated to marginalized Black and Brown people in contrast to how they are articulated to and by me—a white person with significant privilege. Some stories are about my growing up, and others illustrate how, despite substantial reading, (un)learning, discussion, despite my antiracist academic passions and commitments, I was still complicit in using some of the racialized discourses used by the street-level practitioners in this book. I am likely still complicit in using other discourses of which I am not yet aware, walking as we all do with some level of horse blinkers that constrain our view. There is always more to learn. These ways of speaking and perceiving others, influenced by unanalyzed and unacknowledged ideologies, including white supremacy, are truly entrenched. Some of my autoethnographic writing provides an introspective window into my growing awareness of my *own* subtle forms of racism.

The ivory tower is characterized by a nearly unbridgeable distance that protects the elite. The researcher's vulnerability primarily exists in laying bare their analysis to the scrutiny of others; however, in not being emotionally vulnerable myself, in sharing other's stories without sharing my own, in not bringing myself to the table, I wondered if I asking something of my participants that I would not do myself. The academic may write about the vulnerability of the study's participants without ever being similarly vulnerable, occupying a position of superiority. Taking up space in this book occasionally centers me. Given my privilege and position, I struggled with whether this was appropriate. In the end, I decided to include brief interstitials exploring my experiences. I will always be at a distance from most of my study participants, given the privilege of my position, but through the brief autoethnographic vignettes included in this book, I offer a bit of my vulnerable self, sharing how beliefs around responsibility shaped my life and research; how I, too, have participated in the kinds of responsibility talk that I critique through the analysis; how those experiences shaped me; and how my own views around responsibility over time shifted.

This book covers two interactional ethnographies, and the primary data presented in this book include sixty-seven street-level interactions recorded between (1) shelter caseworkers and their unhoused "clients" and (2) between a professor and his remedial reading students at a community college. This is a discourse analysis of institutional talk, and my arguments regarding responsibility are situated in analysis of transcripts of those institutional conversations. My autoethnographic writing, indicated through vignettes, provides additional context along the way. My autoethnographic writing particularly enriches descriptions of teaching the community college remedial reading course, which I did for many years. Findings culled from the discourse data are supported by reference to ethnographic field notes and interviews. Field notes are also used to add texture to ethnographic descriptions. From these data, I describe how responsibility is linguistically constructed in the shelter and the community college settings. For those interested in my methodology, for those who are not experts in ethnography, interactional ethnography, autoethnography, and discourse analysis, and for those curious about the study's reliability, validity, and generalizability, I invite you to read Chapter 1 and to consult the methodology section in the appendix of this book.

1 | An Introduction

Autoethnography: I Am the Spirit of Christmas Present

In my family, we watch Charles Dickens's *A Christmas Carol* starring Alastair Sim (1951) each year on Christmas Eve after midnight mass. While I no longer attend Catholic mass, I still maintain the tradition of watching the film each year, and when I visit my family, we watch it together. The commitment we have to saying every line with just the right intonation, to knowing each musical cue, to mimicking the raise of a significant eyebrow (of this and every movie important to the family) likely contributed to my attention to and interest in discursive detail. After changing out of church clothes, we would light a fire (whether it was cold or not in Virginia), huddle on the couch, and begin singing the score that opens the film, strains of music that begin with low piano and French horns; the music shifts from grim and foreboding toward joyful, mirroring the shift toward Christian transformation. A choir gives us a glimpse of the film's conclusion, singing "Hark the Herald Angels Sing," before diving back down to the haunting strain that orients us to the opening of the film: Marley's Ghost. "Old Marley was a dead as a doornail," we'd chant in unison (Hurst, 1951). By the time the movie ended and the charming housemaid had encouraged Scrooge to join his nephew Fred and his wife for Christmas dinner, one or two of us would had dropped off into sleep and would subsequently try to find our way to bed still half dreaming, staying intentionally groggy.

A Christmas Carol takes us through Scrooge's change of heart, which includes a revisioning of his beliefs around responsibility. Scrooge begins by extolling the virtues of individual responsibility and applauding the punishment of the poor; the moral and social irresponsibility of joblessness earns the consequences of debtor's prisons or workhouses. When he is asked to donate to those in need, he replies, "Are there no prisons? . . . And the Union workhouses, are they still in operation? The Treadmill and the Poor Law are in full vigour, then?" (Dickens, 1843/2006, 8–9). The men collecting for the poor assure him that all those institutions are unfortunately still very active, saying, "They are . . . I wish I could say they were not." Scrooge explains, "I cannot afford to make idle people merry. I help to support the establishments I have mentioned: they cost enough: and those who are badly off must go there" (9). The men soliciting donations from Scrooge explain that "many can't go there; and many would rather die," and Scrooge replies, "If they would rather die they ought to do it and decrease the surplus population. . . . It's enough for a man to understand his own business, and not to interfere with other people's. Mine occupies me constantly" (9).

Later in the story, just before the Spirit of Christmas Present departs, Scrooge sees "something strange . . . protruding from [the Spirit's] skirts. 'Is it a foot or a claw?'" he asks. The Spirit, who is often dressed not unlike Santa Claus in velvet robes trimmed in fur, opens his robe to reveal two children crouched by his ankles who are described as

> wretched, abject, frightful, hideous, miserable, . . . meagre, ragged, scowling, wolfish; but prostrate, too, in their humility. . . . No change, no degradation, no perversion of humanity, in any grade, through all the mysteries of wonderful creation, has monsters half so terrible. (60–61)

When Scrooge is finally able to speak, he can only say, "Spirit! Are they yours?" The Spirit explains that they belong to "Man."

> And they cling to me, appealing from their fathers. This boy is Ignorance. This girl is Want. Beware them both, and all of their degree, but most of all beware this boy, for on his brow I see that written which is Doom, unless the writing be erased. (61)

When Scrooge, moved by pity and revulsion, asks whether these children have "refuge or resource," the Spirit spits Scrooge's earlier words back on him, shouting, "Are there no prisons? Are there no workhouses?"

In the beginning of the film, Scrooge's use of "idle," a word that refers both to laziness and also an avoidance of work, underscores the ideological position that a primary responsibility of adulthood is to be gainfully employed, that financial setbacks of any kind are the result of a moral failure, and that such people deserve punishment rather than help (Soss et al., 2011). With the Spirit of Christmas Present, Scrooge is asked to confront and reconsider his position on poverty and responsibility by reconsidering his own words. The Ghost is the analyst, bringing a new perspective as he recontextualizes Scrooge's words in the face of these children who are both "real" (physically manifested) and also symbolic representatives of human suffering. With his words spat back at him, it is his words and the ideology those words espouse that he must eat and digest.

While this book has no interest in Christian transformation (or religion, really), it does give us an opportunity to reconsider how we speak and how marginalized people are spoken to. It is our words, and the words of institutional workers, that we consider in this book, words communicating very similar ideologies. It is not uncommon for us to be thrust up against our own words. A loved one repeats the words we used, and we say, "Well, I didn't mean it like that." Sometimes when we are confronted with our words, we realize that perhaps we should have said something differently. I have often wished I could go back and revise the language of the past. In *A Christmas Carol*, Scrooge is made to confront the ideological force of his words: both his words and what they represent. I am, therefore, drawing on the Spirit of Christmas Present, hoping that by presenting my participants' words around responsibility in a book, we can view them freshly while also reconsidering our own discourse practices.

The Subtlety of the Street

Lipsky's (1980/2010) foundational work *Street-Level Bureaucracy* describes the common experiences of a large category of workers (e.g., teachers, social workers, police officers) who employ their own discretion at the street level, where they deliver services to the public. This book explores the subtle, mundane words that some street-level workers use to communicate responsibility to the marginalized people they serve, what I am calling the subtlety of street-level discourse. Whether the street-level workers are shelter caseworkers or a community college professor, and whether the marginalized populations comprise unhoused men or remedial reading college students, this book reveals that the way responsibility is communicated is strikingly similar in both communities of practice. While we know from street-level research that organizational requirements, influenced by trends in policymaking more generally, impact street-level professionals' discretion-based decision-making on the front lines (Brodkin, 2013; Soss et al., 2011), this book takes these studies a step further, using discourse analysis, a methodology that examines talk-in-use, to analyze street-level workers' talk about responsibility with those they serve in the moments of service delivery. In so doing, it explores how talk about responsibility changes and potentially accrues over time as the discourse responds to institutional requirements, timelines, benchmarks, and performance management.

In so doing, I share what street-level workers' constructions of responsibility look like in these two institutional domains that serve marginalized people, and why those constructions are problematic. Because these institutions—a school and a shelter—integrate business principles into their organizational management, we will explore the influence of business-oriented, neoliberal managerial structure (defined in Chapter 2) on these constructions of responsibility (Chapters 5 and 6), and I will demonstrate how neoliberally informed performance measurements, benchmarks, and timelines subtly shape the talk of street-level workers, and how references to performance management, benchmarks, and timelines point to and invoke the presence of these neoliberal pressures for workers and those they serve. I will also illustrate how cultural mythologies surface in these constructions of responsibility (Chapters 3, 4, and 6), serving as both microaggressions and moments of identity work that accrue over time. My autoethnographic writing will, in part, address how the experiences of more privileged people differ by comparison with these findings. Conclusions will discuss how street-level workers' behaviors, including the use of racialized cultural mythologies, are discourse ideologies—beliefs about particular discursive constructions—linked to systemic and institutional forms of racism, and I consider what communicative changes might facilitate needed change.

This chapter briefly introduces readers to a variety of the book's central concepts, which are further explicated in later chapters. As conversations between workers and those served constitute the primary data for analysis, we will first explore discourse analysis and interactional ethnography. We then examine my inspirations for examining constructions of responsibility, and I introduce readers to street-level bureaucracy as a concept.

This chapter concludes with an outline of the book, highlighting how subsequent chapters expand upon the topics set in motion here. My interest and appreciation for discourse, for responsibility, and for street-level work each involve both scholarly pursuit and deeply personal connection.

Discourse Analysis

Autoethnography: Becoming a Discourse Analyst

When I was a small child and we visited my cousin's family on vacation, I got to stay in my cousin's room. We'd climb under our Star Wars and Sesame Street sheets, the light switched off for bedtime, and my cousin would recite into the darkness, filling the expanse between beds pitched on opposite sides of the large room. "Echo 3 to Echo 7. *Han*, old buddy. Do you *read* me?" Unable to withhold reply, I'd respond, "*Loud* and *clear*, kid. What's up?" He'd flick on a flashlight and with the softness of footed pajamas creep over and sit at the end of my bed. We didn't need to develop rules for the game. The entirety of *Empire Strikes Back* would be recited, and whoever messed up first would lose. This included musical cues. We awarded laughter for particularly well-delivered lines or for well-deployed exaggeration. We had puppets of Bert and Ernie from my sister, using them to play out Han and Leia's steamy kiss inside the asteroid. "I *happen* to *like* nice men." "*I'm* nice men" "*No* you're *not*. You're——" (Bert and Ernie kiss passionately, heads moving in counterpoint with one another). I think in these moments I became a discourse analyst, a person who cared about and was rewarded for close listening and accurate recitation, noticing what people said and how they said it mattered. My family loves movies, and lines from movies are the intertextual glue that created (and creates) common ground and solidarity. The quotations are tethers to times when connectedness was easy and we enjoyed a bounty of common ground. Reciting a line with accuracy had and has social capital. My cousin and I later recreated the Bert-and-Ernie tête-à-tête for the family to uproarious applause. I am *so grateful* to my parents and my extended family for putting so much value on the intonational cadence of language. *Star Wars*, *Willy Wonka*, *Superman*—these movies and soundtracks I felt with my breathing. It seemed a natural next step to become a musician, to think about the how a note is leaned on and felt, the press and easy swell of a pitch, to think about the phrasing of an uttered statement, the way all music is the phrasing of an utterance, one set of measures responding to another. Questions. Answers. Elaborations. Problems. Resolutions. To this day, we can communicate solidarity and connection with the right movie line. As a person in the midst of transition, the lines of films well deployed and on key are a tether to the me of the past that less and less looks like the me of the present. The sound of the quotation, in a deeper voice, in the right pitch, with the right intonation says, "Here I am. I'm still me. We still like the same things." I am still me, even if I have a mustache.

What Is Discourse Analysis?

Definitions of *discourse* vary widely, but Austin's (1951) book title perhaps describes it best: *discourse* is "how to do things with words." *Discourse* is language-in-use, and this is an important distinction, as much early linguistic research relied on sentences and examples invented by the linguists. We can learn much more by seeing how people actually use language in a given interactional moment, whether it is a sentence, a glance, a gesture, or a text message.

While there are many different types of discourse analysis, discourse analysts share a preference for naturally occurring data, whether recorded audio or video or written text. As Heritage and Clayman (2010) argue, "Recorded interaction is a fundamental constraint that disciplines conclusions by making them answerable to what real people actually do" (13). In recording and analyzing actual institutional talk, discourse analysts avoid the pitfalls of interview data, in which participants talk about what they *think* happened. Discourse analysis provides detail and nuance generally too difficult to capture in ethnographic contexts lacking audio or video recording. Discourse analysts are, by and large, *descriptivists*, people who describe how language and discourse are used by actual speakers and communities, and in this book I will describe how responsibility is talked into being in two diverse contexts by institutional workers actively talking about responsibility with the people they are serving.

I invite the reader to watch how meanings unfold, are constructed, and then reproduced in the interactional moment, drawing on preexisting social, cultural, and historical information. I treat language and discourse as socially constructed (Berger and Luckmann, 1967), meaning words and phrases are "emergent and contingent" (Ford, 2004, 31) depending on how they are used in context. Thus, meanings emerge as interaction unfolds and are contingent on what is said and how. This approach allows analysts to see an interaction with fresh eyes vis-à-vis a broad array of available cultural information, as meanings of words and phrases change depending on a variety of contextual factors (to whom one is speaking, where they are speaking, how they said it). I am sure we can think of many examples of words and phrases that may land differently on one listener's ears versus another's. Taboo words, dog-whistle terms, political terminology, and even mundane words are shaped by who uses them, in what context, for what purpose. Constructions of responsibility in this book are indeed just that—constructions. An institutional representative puts words together just so, generating a particular vision of responsibility. What surprised me in exploring these two data sets was not only what those constructions look like but the similarity of these constructions across institutional contexts—when the subject of the talk (moving from shelter to housing and learning college-level reading) is radically different.

Discourse analysis allows us to put words and talk under a microscope, and these institutional workers have generously given us their words, their constructions around responsibility, so that we can consider whether we as a society should keep using them, in these ways, in these institutional contexts and outside of them. What makes this tricky is that the words I'm describing in this book often seem mundane. They are not necessarily charged in the same way racial, misogynist, or homophobic epithets are, and unlike many current studies of politicized language, I am not talking about the use of jargon or important political keywords like "citizenship" or "entrepreneurship." For a lot of people, these words will not seem immediately problematic, and this is because these very simple words are experienced differently *by* different groups of people and because these words are used differently *with* different groups of people. This is the subtlety of street-level discourse.

There are many different types of discourse analysis, including conversation analysis, critical discourse analysis, pragmatics and speech act analysis, and narrative analysis, to name a few. When I was a doctoral student I took a course called Homelessness and the Law, in which we read *Sidewalk* (Duneier, 1999), an excellent five-year-long ethnography of unhoused people who panhandled and sold books in Greenwich Village in New York City. The final chapter is a conversation analysis of social interaction. Conversation analysis is a specific discourse-analytic methodology with an extensive vocabulary of analytical features. I remember how baffled the law students were by the chapter, and I had this in mind as I chose the methods for analyzing this data. Several methodologies exist in discourse analysis that might adequately describe aspects of this data; many of them require an understanding of linguistic and discourse-analytic theory that would ultimately distance and alienate nonspecialists. While I hope that this book contributes to linguistics and discourse studies, I strive to remain somewhat outside the disciplinary echo-chamber in this book. If linguists and discourse analysts want to contribute to their applied fields, we need to use approaches those applied fields can interpret. Rather than asking social workers, educators, political scientists, and public policy scholars to learn a complex discourse methodology and fitting the data into that approach, this book is fully grounded in the data, describing only the linguistic and discursive concepts that surfaced in the analysis.

Interactional Ethnography

In order to ground the discourse spoken in their contexts, I use ethnography—a method that allows for thick description, field notes, and interviews. While the appendix of this book describes my methodology in more detail, I want to briefly familiarize the reader with the basics of interactional ethnography (IE), which is the approach utilized for both studies I describe. Essentially, IE combines ethnography, the method common to anthropological study, involving prolonged fieldwork in a community, with a focus on social interaction (discourse)—what people do when they communicate with each other in that cultural context. Skukauskaitė and Green (2023) explain that

> interactional ethnographers explore the multifaceted processes and practices through which people, in and through language-in-use and interaction, continuously create particular dimensions of their (language) cultures-in-the-making. (9)

IE scholars argue that through language people "engage in culturing" (9); that is, people use language and interaction to perform and construct culture. IE is grounded in the data, cognizant of the importance of collecting data over time, and fully situated in the sociocultural landscape of the community of practice. Skukauskaitė and Green (2023) explain further:

> Tracing language-in-use, or discourse, provides a grounded methodology and a point of access to explore how languaging-culturing relationships take place through the actions and perspectives of insiders, moment by moment and over time, in different configurations of actors within and across social settings impacted by layered histories, policies, and other sociocultural factors. (9)

As the name suggests, IE combines a discourse-analytic method (attention to talk-in-context) with ethnography, the latter of which can include the following: participant observation, field notes, archival data, and recorded (video or audio) interaction (researcher-participant interviews and/or participant-participant interaction). These data help generate a composite understanding of the research landscape while also triangulating findings.

The two studies in this book are both interactional ethnographies and include participant observation, field notes, archival data (textbooks in classroom; shelter policies), and interviews; however, the primary data used for analysis are recorded interactions between the street-level practitioner (shelter caseworkers or the community college professor) and the person/people they are serving. Other data are used to provide context and triangulate findings. The length of data collection in each context is relative to timescales made relevant by the contexts themselves: The nine months of data collection in the shelter corresponded to the nine-month benchmark by which time unhoused men "should" be placed into independent living,[1] and the community college course was observed during an entire semester, at which time students "should" move from reading remediation to the larger college community.

Skukauskaitė and Green (2023) argue that IE is both a way of thinking and knowing (epistemology) and a way of doing research (methodology), meaning it is a way to know and understand the world and a way to analyze data collected about a particular community of practice. IE underscores attention to what Agar (2013, 149) calls "rich points," iterative processes, and recursivity. "Rich points" are a way of bringing curiosity to the data through a grounded, bottom-up, data-centric approach that does not attempt to shoehorn theoretical positions or one particular discourse methodological approach (vs. another) onto the data prior to analysis (a priori). IE looks for patterns in meaning within the context(s) in which we are deeply immersed as ethnographers. Utilizing existing approaches may result in missing something interesting that has not yet been examined. For example, as described further in Chapter 3, while "accounts" (such as excuses and justifications) are the most common discourse approach for examining responsibility and accountability (Buttny, 1993; Scott and Lyman, 1974), if one focuses solely on accounts, one may ignore how other related discursive elements work together in context to construct responsibility in talk. This book uses a grounded approach (Glaser and Strauss, 1967), relying on a diversity of discourse-analytic literature to support conclusions without being limited by one specific approach. Similarly, theory evolves out of a grounded, emic, bottom-up approach. Therefore, while there are many theories that may aid in interpreting findings (e.g., "interpellation" surfaces in future chapters), I leave those to the discussion section in each chapter and the conclusion of the book in order to reflect their absence during data collection and analysis. This results in a systematic and rigorous analysis of social interaction that draws relevant linguistic and discursive categories directly from the data and applies theory afterward—a posteriori—in light of findings.

Ethnography and interactional ethnography are also characterized by iterative and recursive logic. Iterative logic favors data collected over lengths of time, allowing the data to unfold and affording the researcher an increasingly focused understanding of the participants, context, and discourse. Findings are honed and change according to what was learned as the researcher reviews the data over time. Recursivity allows researchers to return to data collected earlier in the iterative process, reconsidering it from newer perspectives that evolved as they learned more about the research environment. The studies in this book moved through many iterative and recursive stages, which are described further under data analysis. Like other ethnographies, my time in the field lends legitimacy to my ability to accurately interpret the data. All told, I spent six and a half years working in conjunction with New York City's unhoused people and the institutions that support them, and I have been a professor at BMCC for sixteen years.

This book comprises two interactional ethnographies in two distinct research contexts and an autoethnography. Autoethnographic writing is indicated through vignettes. These interactional ethnographic data comprise an impressive amount of discourse-analytic data: over fifteen hundred pages of transcripts, including fifty-four social work interactions (many of which are over an hour long) and thirteen classroom recordings (each one hour and forty-five minutes long). Given Seedhouse's (2004) claim that between five and ten lessons in classroom discourse research constitutes a "reasonable database," the sixty-seven interactions analyzed in this book present a nearly unprecedented window into talk over time in institutional contexts, more than enough to convincingly posit trends in street-level interaction around responsibility based on hundreds of excerpts collected across the data sets, which are then triangulated with field notes, interviews, and of course other available research literature as needed.[2]

This information presents a rare opportunity as well. Because this research requires audio or video recording of professionals working with sometimes very vulnerable populations over an extended period of time, it is difficult to obtain institutional access and participant consent. These data, therefore, provide a unique window into this level of street-level practice—where practitioners are actually communicating with those they serve. Recorded interactions between shelter workers and unhoused people that capture the entire process of housing placement from intake to placement are particularly uncommon. It also quite rare to see two separate interactional ethnographies presented in the same text for comparative study. In Chapter 2, I will describe the discourse practices that constitute the primary focus of analytic attention in Chapters 3–6.

Why Responsibility?

Autoethnography: Why I Am Drawn to Responsibility
My own sensitivity to responsibility stems at least in part from my childhood. Glyn Dearman, the actor who played Tiny Tim in the Alastair Sim *A Christmas Carol* film (Hurst, 1951) looked surprisingly like my only sibling, my sister Colleen, who lived her whole brief life with spinal muscular atrophy, a type of muscular dystrophy, and who passed away from the genetic disorder at nearly eight years old. Colleen was exceptionally fragile, and living with her was much like carrying a porcelain family heirloom that I was always worried I'd break. I was her elder sibling, and from the time Colleen was born when I was six until her death when I was fifteen, I had, while totally understandable given the circumstances, too many responsibilities: I always felt primed to defend her publicly when people stared; I was the capable babysitter who happily applied powder-blue eyeshadow; I was the extra-polite, responsible child who desperately tried to make as little trouble as possible; I quarantined alone in the basement during every cold and virus, and I understood that if I did not take precautions, I could pass my cold to her, and she could or would die. While I watched my choice of movies and had Lipton soup delivered, I was anxious to keep her safe, while also feeling lonely and resentful. I was keenly aware of my responsibility to keep her safe while she was alive, a feeling most of us became more familiar with during the Covid-19 epidemic.

While she was alive, I tried to present as little trouble to my parents as possible, but I was also a middle-class, reasonably privileged white kid, and I had my share of pettiness and emotional overwhelm. I wove profanity at school like an expert and sometimes got in trouble for it. That said, I never sneaked out of the house, tried drugs, or drank alcohol, choosing instead to write sad, angry poetry on my bed while wearing my dad's oversized sweaters—a teal knit he never got back, a cream turtleneck he wore in college. I practiced ballet in our unfinished basement where I would immerse myself in the story-worlds of *Giselle*, *Coppelia*, and Prokofiev's sinister *Romeo and Juliet*. I would dance for Colleen for hours in the living room to film scores for movies I had never seen. In private at night on rose-printed sheets, I bartered with God, begging to be disease free if I could prove my mettle by holding my breath until the end of "Walkin' on Broken Glass" or whatever song was on the radio the next day, as long as I avoided all the sidewalk cracks. I said my prayers with white knuckles and begged my grandmother, already many years passed, to keep me disease free. I kept her last card, a bounty of pink roses and lace, behind the cross that hung over my bed. I tried to be good, helpful, and responsible, and in private I anxiously frittered away hours trying to find ways to control what felt like a chaotic and precarious life.

Colleen passed away in her sleep, and decades later I can still hear the exact pitch and timbre of my father's sob while I called 911 on the other side of the house in the otherwise quiet sunlit kitchen. I remember the September chill of the early morning driveway on my bare feet, waiting for the ambulance alone in my pajamas. The subsequent weeks a blur, I have little memory of expressing grief, though I know I cried a couple times. I had a couple uncomfortable conversations with the school counselor. I said I didn't need therapy. I was fine.

I almost immediately distracted myself by becoming immersed in academics and band; I gave up ballet. I started dating a nice guy whom I fell in love with and would later marry (and much later divorce). My parents were both, understandably, grieving, and I unselfconsciously took on the role of being fine, responsible, reliable, and as successful as possible. I went from placements in low- or middle-level English and History courses to Honors and Advanced Placement. I spent hours studying, reading, and practicing flute. I kept myself at the breaking-point of busy until I was roughly thirty-two, when I finally started therapy and was able to give myself space and time to grieve and process. By that time, I had finished a double major at Virginia Tech, gotten married, acquired two master's degrees, completed a doctorate from Columbia University, and gotten a tenure-track academic job at the City University of New York (CUNY). Up until I began therapy at thirty-two, productivity, working hard, and conforming to normative societal and familial expectations were how I generated my own reliable stability.

I have spent much of my adulthood processing my relationship to responsibility. Colleen was so fragile, and keeping her healthy required a delicate balance in the house. In hindsight, the ritual viewing and recitation of *A Christmas Carol* seemed to offer a yearly window into a parallel universe where she, embodied through Tiny Tim, lived if we all did just and said the right things. "Scrooge was better than his word," those of us still awake would chant, as the film came to an end. Choral music swelled as the narrator continued,

> He did it all, and infinitely more; and to Tiny Tim, who did NOT die, he was a second father. He became as good a friend, as good a master, and as good a man, as the good old city knew, or any other good old city, town or borough in the good old world. (Dickens, 1843/2006, 83)

I do legitimately enjoy this story and the film, but it is difficult to ignore the elephant in the room. Despite thirty years standing between her passing and this book, this yearly ritual cloaks what feels like stones of grief in the glut of joy that characterizes the holiday season, and I am left absolutely choking on holiday spirit. Scrooge's decision to take on responsibility for Tiny Tim and his family creates financial, medical, and presumably emotional stability for the family. The family has no need to grieve the loss of a child, the father's wages are raised and secured, and Tiny Tim lives, presumably due to better food and access to doctors.

As I young person, I believed that the Catholic church I grew up in had a similar responsibility to take care of its parishioners. I remember watching parishioners on their knees during mass, beating their breasts with their fist, a strike punctuating each phrase of "my fault, my fault, my most grievous fault." Surely parishioners' verbalized admissions of "fault" were likely very petty sins. Certainly, mine were, exemplified by one priest falling asleep during my confessions, leaving me to wander out of the confessional quietly unabsolved to determine on my own how many "Hail Marys" to say as the priest gently snored inside. As an adult I would learn that three of our parish priests, including the reconciliation napper, had sexually abused children in my parish. Indeed, the sins of the churchgoers striking their breasts in contrition for yelling at their kids or "taking the Lord's name in vain" seem wholly trivial in comparison to the "grievous fault" of those monsters.

If growing up with my sister and family encouraged a kind of interpersonal/familial responsibility to keep each other safe and to keep the family stable, belonging to the Catholic Church made me consider: Who is asked to be responsible? Who is above responsibility? Who do we ask to be accountable? These are questions I later asked during my dissertation research in a New York City homeless shelter and that I continued asking when I took a job at Borough of Manhattan Community College (a community college within the City University of New York—CUNY—system) after graduating during the housing market and economic crash of 2008. As my new colleagues mourned the loss of their pensions and their subsequent inability to retire, we collectively witnessed the marked absence of responsibility for those who orchestrated and benefited from the housing market crash.

Isn't Responsibility an Inherent Good?

It turns out that people have a lot of opinions about responsibility. In fact, the first question people usually ask when I discuss my research at conferences is "What's so awful about responsibility? Isn't responsibility an inherent good?" However, a unique moral dimension and weight exists as part of how responsibility is communicated to marginalized people in particular, the legacy for which stretches back hundreds of years, well before Dickens was creating Scrooge, though we see it in his words as well. Personal responsibility has been a mainstay of poverty governance, dating as far back as the English Vagabonds and Beggars Act of 1495 and English Poor Law of 1601,[3] both of which emphasized the importance of individual responsibility and viewed failures at work as a lack of responsibility and a moral failing punishable by law (Soss et al., 2011; Trattner, 1998). Early Protestantism in the United States likewise moralized personal responsibility, work, and poverty (Trattner, 1998).

Vestiges of this ideology are woven into modern social policies in the United States often attributed to neoliberalism (described in more depth in Chapter 2). Clinton's overhaul of welfare policies in the 1990s emphasized that help for people experiencing poverty was temporary (harkening back to beliefs in which financial assistance contributed to "idleness") and that assistance was only given to those who could prove their deservingness through work or other "responsible" actions. Education policies like No Child Left Behind and Race to the Top funneled funding to schools with high test scores, rewarding "hard work" with financial support (Koyama, 2017; Menken, 2008). Traces of these ideologies also exist in how poor and marginalized people are talked about, what Hancock (2007) calls the "politics of disgust," and this book extends her work by explicating precisely the kinds of language frontline workers themselves use when communicating responsibility to people who are marginalized.

Before I started my dissertation, from 2001 to 2006, I taught literacy, ESL, and GED prep at a New York City transitional supportive housing residence.[4] I loved working at that residence, and I am so very grateful for the generosity and friendship of the caseworkers[5] and the people I taught and their families. During that time, the New York City shelter system began revising its policies around responsibility (DHS, 2002, 2004). While at this transitional residence, I noticed how difficult the case manager's job was, informing residents that they had assigned or unmet responsibilities and noting what punitive procedures were in place if the residents did not complete those tasks. In this context, I found myself asking new questions: How does one adult tell another adult what to do while maintaining the second adult's *dignity*? How is dignity *eroded* or lost in these moments where responsibilities are discussed? In the discourse analysis literature, there is a great deal written on "accounts," what people do to excuse or justify unmet responsibilities (Buttny, 1993; for more see Chapter 3), but there are surprisingly few studies examining what kinds of language and discourse features are used to initially tell someone that they are responsible for something.

This book was born out of noticing the strikingly similar ways people from two seemingly different professions interact with their clientele around the topic of responsibility. Why do shelter caseworkers and a community college remedial reading professor sound so similar when they discuss responsibility with the people they serve? What does responsibility look like in those settings? What similarities do they share, and why? How are they different? With both contexts revealing what I call a *gestalt of responsibility*, I illustrate how street-level workers with marginal authority speak to marginalized populations about responsibility. I argue that "responsibility"—a presumably innocuous and seemingly apolitical word—might be in fact quite political and inherently problematic, in part because discursively and linguistically *responsibility keeps bad company*.

By demonstrating how constructions of responsibility are regularly clustered around references to neoliberal organizational management and morally charged cultural mythologies, this book asks us to reconsider how street-level workers communicate responsibility, whether workers should alter how they/we talk about responsibility, and if so, how.

Street-Level Workers

The Skewering of the Bureaucrat

In the past, when I have brought my data to conferences in education or social work, colleagues in the audience have groaned, "This is just a bad teacher/social worker. I would never do this." While there may be more egregious cases, most street-level workers have engaged in some aspect of this discourse, including me. These discourses are widely used, transgressing boundaries of social class, ethnicity, mother tongue, and political party. In fact, these discourses may not even appear noteworthy to some people, primarily because they are experienced differently by different speech communities. This book addresses forms of talk that seem mundane and may therefore go unnoticed even by those who identify themselves as very reflective practitioners. While we may disagree with some of what the participants in these studies say and do, they also offered to be on this stage, so that we could together better understand institutional communication.

While the participants in this study are prone to skewering, so too are "street-level bureaucrats" and "street-level workers" in general, criticized for a rigid adherence to the rules. In the pilot episode of the popular cartoon *Rick and Morty*, Rick (a sociopathic, "mad scientist"-cum-curmudgeonly grandfather who remains obsessively immersed in work to avoid reflecting on his inner life) and his grandson-cum-sidekick Morty (a barely pubescent, easily distressed pushover who is obsessively dedicated to exacting approval and love from Rick) are attempting escape from an interplanetary space airport. The "airport," a transition place for the strangest creatures from across the universe, remains a place of institutional rigidity and bureaucracy. As they wait in roped-off queues for security proceedings, Rick mutters to Morty, "I don't like it here, Morty. I can't abide bureaucracy. I don't like being told where to go and what to do. I consider it a violation."

After creating a significant disturbance at the airport, Rick tries to program a portal at the space station to take them back to Earth. Insect-like airport security, however, is in hot pursuit. Rick tosses Morty a gun and asks Morty to "cover him" while he enters the coordinates. Morty resists Rick's request, squeaking out that he doesn't want to shoot anyone. Rick shouts back an urgent and generalizing reply, "They're just robots, Morty! It's okay to shoot them! They're robots!"

Morty shoots and immediately injures one of the security team, and the insect's cries of pain combined with visual signs of bleeding identify the insect-like beings as organic; they are unequivocally *not* robots. The wounded guard shouts, "Aaaaah! My leg is shot off!" which prompts another member of the alien security team to shout earnestly, "Glenn's bleeding to death! Someone call his wife and children!" Morty becomes understandably distressed. "They're *not* robots, Rick!" he shouts, his voice breaking and crackling. Rick rattles back unsympathetically and dismissively, "It's a figure of speech, Morty. They're bureaucrats. I don't respect them. Just keep shooting, Morty" (Roiland, 2013).

The unfortunate characterization of frontline bureaucrats as just one nameless member of a fleet of pencil-pushing automatons, "robots" systematically and mercilessly executing the whims of higher-ups, is all too familiar. Morty's frantic realization that the aliens are indeed living beings perhaps mirrors our own experiences with street-level workers who use their discretion to make the occasional exception (e.g., letting you in although you're a minute late or waiving the requirement for a bureaucratic form). In those seemingly rare moments of individuation, we are reminded that frontline workers and bureaucrats are people with lives, with pressures and requirements for what often appears to be a thankless job. As David Byrne of the Talking Heads croons, "I think of the people that are working for me. Some civil servants are just like my loved ones. They work so hard and they try to be strong" (Talking Heads 77, 1977). Byrne's observation, whether ironic or earnest, nods to the potential individuality and humanity of civil servants: teachers, social workers, and others that Michael Lipsky (1980/2010) would call "street-level bureaucrats." Every worker in this study is a person who is loved, a person who has family, a person who has been brought tokens of appreciation by those they serve.

The Wiggle Room of Street-Level Worker

Lipsky (1980/2010), in his seminal monograph *Street-Level Bureaucracy*, dispels the notion of bureaucrats as pencil pushers behind desks and windows, the expressionless Department of Motor Vehicles worker joylessly processing paperwork. He asserts that any worker who puts policy into practice and who mediates between an administrative body and a client group is a street-level worker, including teachers, social workers, and police officers, and he invites us to revise our perception of street-level workers as unwavering implementors of top-down policy. The inadequacy of resources and bloated caseloads force workers to use their discretion to choose how their meager resources are spent. These commonplace deviations from written policies materially alter policy delivery so much that Lipsky argues that "the decisions of street-level bureaucrats, the routines they establish, and the devices they invent to cope with uncertainties and work pressures, effectively *become* the public policies they carry out" (1980/2010, xiii).

Recently, when I was at the airport, heading to a conference, I brought my prescription testosterone in a medical liquids bag for carry-on. The laws have recently softened for medical liquids and prescriptions, and I had the prescription with me. One TSA agent, upon seeing the pump bottle, said, "That is over three ounces." I said, "I was told that that law now allows medical liquids over three ounces." The TSA worker replied, "It is up to the agent screening your bag." Street-level workers are not simply policy-implementing robots, but they also cannot extend fully individualized treatment to each member of their overflowing caseload. These workers experience pressure from their administration to meet institutional goals while also individualizing service when they can. Lipsky found that street-level workers tend to use their discretion in systematic ways that help make their work more efficient. His work interrogates the bureaucrat-as-automaton trope, fragmenting the monolithic vision of bureaucrats and showing how their work—and their discretionary choices—create policy in the moments of service delivery.

Making a similar argument from a sociolinguistic perspective, Erickson (2004) makes a case for "wiggle room" (178). He suggests that while sociocultural, historical, and institutional precedents exist for many social interactions (we know, for example, that lawyers generally ask questions and witnesses on the stand answer them), and while these may be produced and reproduced with little variation, there is also space within these structured precedents for "inventive resourcefulness" (178). Expanding on this, Erickson (2004) states,

> It seems to me more reasonable to say that, granting the influence of the weight of history on local social action, discursive practice in everyday life is a richer, more multidimensional matter. . . . The point is that *because local circumstances are contingent and persons*

> *are not automata, local social action inherently involves agency*, whatever the tendencies or consequences of those actions might be. (Emphasis added, 176–177)

Erickson, like Lipsky, creates space for agency, while also acknowledging the obvious importance and influence of social, cultural, and historical precedent on social interaction. Though Erickson refers to all interlocutors here, his gatekeeping encounter data underscore the need to view street-level workers and those they serve as individual actors with multidimensional identities, not robots.

While Lipsky (1980/2012) demonstrates from a macro-public policy perspective how written policies are retooled in situ through the discretionary choices of the workers, Erickson invites us to see on a micro level how the linguistic choices of those very same interlocutors can likewise show deviation from expected discursive expectations. Street-level workers are not automata. Gatekeepers individualize in spite of rules requiring equal treatment, and Erickson makes the case that discourse analysis is well suited to investigating what that looks like.

Drawing on their work, I argue that street-level workers have access to an additional layer of discretion that has been heretofore unacknowledged: discretionary talk. While street-level discretion, more generally, explains street-level choices made in situ (e.g., to sanction a client or not, to grant an extension on a paper or not), street-level discretionary talk describes the discursive choices workers make, the "wiggle room" the agency that workers have in deciding not just *what to do* but how to convey institutional information, requirements, and so on. This book is situated at the overlap between Lipsky's work and Erickson's, exploring how street-level workers in multiple disciplines socially construct responsibility in their everyday institutional discursive practice, using their discretion to create, in effect, de facto policy. Extending street-level analyses to the discourse level opens new avenues for both applied linguists interested in institutional discourse and street-level researchers, while also serving a broad community of readers interested in public policy, public administration, higher education, teaching, social work, and other street-level positions like law enforcement.

While David Byrne is right to note that street-level workers may be *like* our loved ones, I also argue that they surely *are* our loved ones. Most of us have at least one street-level worker in our family—the human resources worker, the grocery checkout person, a teacher, a social worker, a police officer.[6] So many people interface with the public every day. These workers make choices when they implement policy, and that discretion is enacted through language. Obviously, some workers have more power, authority, and autonomy than others, and while I admit that being a CUNY community college faculty member gives me more autonomy, privilege, and respect than was given to the shelter caseworkers, there is ample discrimination against community college faculty (as compared to senior colleges), and we enjoy substantially less academic autonomy than our four-year college and university peers. This book, therefore, explores different street-level work contexts with full knowledge that while not the same, workers in both places still experience "analytically similar work conditions" (Lipsky, 1980/2010, 4).

Street-level workers, like teachers and social workers, while they may feel offended by being affiliated with bureaucrats, may benefit from learning more about their relationship to the nondisciplinary part of their work. Both educators and social workers place a high premium on the ideals, theories, and practices of their discipline, as highlighted through both the literature and coursework on the undergraduate and graduate levels. Linguists like Sarangi (2010, 2011), argue that for each professional discipline (teacher, social worker, caseworker, etc.) there exists a role set, a variety of roles that one enacts as part of a job. For example, I am an educator, a facilitator, a researcher, a participant observer, a listener, a learner, and a mentor, but also sometimes a social worker. I am also a street-level worker. While the role of social worker may help explain the times when I sit with an unhoused student to discuss how to find a place to live, "street-level worker" refers more to how we manage our heavy workloads, how we put policy into practice, and what discretionary decisions we make. Rarely do you find a class in your chosen field called "Pushing paperwork and processing people: the part of the job you'll likely find frustrating and the ways you socially construct policy when you do it." Personally, I felt that teaching—even on the college level—was a sort of "calling," a vocation more than a job. I was no bureaucrat. I was a *professor*; I felt passionate about my discipline, and I loved teaching and my students (and still do). Likewise, my friends and colleagues in social work have felt drawn to the field by their affiliation with the field and their desire to help those in need. Disciplinary coursework and research appear to reinforce the idealization of those fields by, for the most part, ignoring the ways in which organizational edicts, ideologies, and assessments and the sheer number of people we need to service, often push practitioners to compromise their pedagogical and disciplinary values.[7] Organizational values and priorities may take precedence over individual credos, creating tension, frustration, and dissonance (Lipsky, 1980/2010; Zacka, 2017). In fact, attrition in street-level jobs like teaching and social work has been, in part, attributed to shifts in values and tensions between disciplinary and organizational values (Carver-Thomas and Darling-Hammond, 2019; Ravalier et al., 2021). My hope is that for street-level practitioners, this book helps us consider how we might use discretionary discourse as a way to carefully maintain the integrity of our helping professions (whether they be teaching, social work, etc.) in the face of organizational requirements. This book, particularly in the final chapter, advocates for a crucial addition to coursework for teachers, social workers, and other street-level workers (and a workshop, professional development series, or class that cuts across all street-level work) that helps not only adjust expectations but also brings awareness to the overlap between professions: Police officers do social work and teaching, and teachers police their students and do social work; social workers teach their clients and also often police their performance.

In many cases we ourselves are these street-level workers, and just as my interest in responsibility is both personal and professional, the street-level aspect of this book also involves a personal dimension, as it stems from my own realization that I (and my colleagues) were, and are, street-level workers, not unlike the shelter caseworkers with whom I worked during my dissertation data collection.

> *Autoethnography: Street-Level Worker C'est Moi*
> When I graduated from Teachers College, Columbia University, I thought I would be headed for the careers of my mentors, having given up free rides to other schools for Ivy League prestige (and debt). Instead, the housing market crashed in 2008, and jobs were scarce. I have now been a professor at Borough of Manhattan Community College (BMCC), a two-year college in the CUNY system, for sixteen years. Some days I love my job, and other days I find it impossibly frustrating. Generally, I love it more often than not.
>
> My department created a Linguistics major, and I have loved teaching in my area of specialty. Many of my students start at BMCC and transfer to another CUNY college, and every semester a few of my students get into Columbia, Harvard, or Penn. I teach Language and Culture and research-oriented classes like Forensic Linguistics, Language and Power, and Language in the Helping Professions. In my pedagogy, I aim to cultivate curiosity, radical empathy, creativity, enthusiasm, collaborative leadership and ownership, and expertise for my students and myself. The coursework is culturally

informed and, I hope, sustaining, balancing attention to white supremacy / triggering topics with attention to student content / emotional overload. My students develop expertise in primary and secondary research in sociolinguistics and linguistic anthropology, transcription, qualitative data analysis, and social science writing. The Linguistics program has been a welcome change from the developmental reading classes I primarily taught when I was hired, a course called Academic and Critical Reading (ACR) geared toward students deemed underprepared for college reading.

Teaching reading was and is important to me, and it was often fun, but it was also exhausting, heartbreaking, and sometimes demoralizing. Many students voiced shame and embarrassment around their scores on the CUNY reading entrance exam—the ACT—and their subsequent placement in a remedial, zero-credit, six-hour reading class. Students placed in ACR courses were aware of the stigma of their placement, and often they were treated differently than their non-ACR peers. Once I heard someone say to a class, "Why are you here?" When a student muttered, "Because we failed the exam," this person responded with a gentle but patronizing voice, "*That's* right. And your *mother* thought you'd pass, and your *father* thought you'd pass. They *all* thought you'd pass it, but you *didn't*." I'm reminded of Bartlett's (2007) research on literacy practices and shaming in Brazil, of which she says,

> Shaming relies upon several powerful language ideologies that individualize blame and obscure the social arrangements that produce racialized and classed educational categories of people. . . . Prevalent language ideologies legitimized shaming and placed the blame for "incorrect" speech on the un- or underschooled individual. (559–60)

Here, students' poor scores on a reading exam are positioned as disappointments to parents and individual student failures rather than the result of structural economic inequalities that are themselves the product of racist policies like school funding's connection to redlining (Lukes & Cleveland, 2021).

In my own classes, I started each semester attempting to dispel some of the shame by discussing how neoliberal education policies like No Child Left Behind and Race to the Top generated structural inequalities for public education generally and for students who did not grow up speaking Standard American English, specifically (Menken, 2008). We discussed how students had been left behind by underfunded and often structurally racist primary and secondary education systems, and I would spend time discussing the legitimacy and cultural importance of different language varieties and my own philosophical qualms about teaching Standard English, a variety that primarily persists due to the prestige and power of its speakers and their subjugation of other varieties of English.

Still, I found teaching the course very frustrating, and I'm sure taking the course was more frustrating for the students, for a variety of reasons. Some students barely failed the entrance exam, and they were livid to be gate-kept from credit-bearing classes, resenting their placement in the class. Some students in ACR had a fourth- or fifth-grade reading level according to department assessments, and we were tasked with bringing them to eleventh- and twelfth-grade levels in a single semester. Most faculty had no expertise in supporting students who had (diagnosed or undiagnosed) reading or learning dis/abilities, of which there were many. I had received no coursework that would help me better serve students with dyslexia, for example. At the time, course grades were entirely decided by a high-stakes, university-wide reading exam, and if students did not pass, they had to re-enroll in the course;[8] the course had a roughly 55 percent pass rate, though somctimes my class would be as high as 90 percent and on one occasion as low as 30 percent. The course did not give students any college credit; it met for six hours a week, and very few credit-bearing courses allowed students to take remediation at the same time. Students had little incentive to complete coursework, as none of it factored into a final grade, and they were often frustrated by my attempts to teach material, like a novel or a poem, that was not covered on the standardized final exam.

All ACR students were given a departmental midterm exam, usually just before spring break, but we only had four test versions, and we switched which one we used each semester because it was challenging to find new, appropriate tests. While we asked students not to write in the tests, they often did, and it was an unlucky faculty person's job every semester to sit and erase answers out of test booklets. The exams were graded by Scantron. I fondly remember my first time giving the midterm. I gave the exam, graded it, and then took the exam to the photocopy machine. I had an old school overhead projector in my classroom that I had never used. I got transparency paper and made transparencies of the whole exam, intending to go over the answers with my class, using the test as a tool. On the way down the hallways, a colleague of mine, one of my favorite people—now retired—stopped me in the hallway laughing, "What are you doing, Mo?" When I explained, she laughed, saying, "You can't do that. You can't go over the tests. We reuse them." This went against everything I had been taught in language assessment, but we did not have enough tests at the college level with an academic focus to spare. Some faculty, including me, would run an item analysis on the test so we could address types of questions or skills the students missed most, but we were not allowed to go over the exam with the students.

Despite serving as a gatekeeping course, most if not all faculty teaching it would argue that we strived to make it something truly enriching, interesting, engaging, and academically rigorous. We had substantial flexibility with our individual curricula, and many faculty used their discretion to teach beloved literature, critical essays, and poetry, as long as we were able to connect content with course student-learning outcomes like vocabulary development, identifying main ideas and supporting details, and inferring meaning from text. I used a wide variety of short stories, a novel, poetry, essays, and even incorporated music, art, advertising, and film. I tried to entertain myself and my students, make lemonade out of lemons.

While I strived to integrate a teaching philosophy at BMCC that drew on Bourdieu, bell hooks, Fanon, Freire, Foucault, Ladson-Billings, New London Group, Street, and Vološinov, in practice I had difficulty finding purchase for my ideals. My students just wanted to pass the class. I had difficulty cajoling them into completing homework, and most students attended only because attendance records were used as a gatekeeper to the final exam. I tried giving the curriculum over to the students, letting them decide how they would like to learn the reading skills, and while some students wanted to shape their learning, others understandably wanted to be told what to know and go home. For all the emphasis on test preparation, no one particularly enjoyed taking practice tests, and students often loved reading the course material. I positioned myself as a person resisting the CUNY requirements and routinely groaned about the university's final exam. By midterm, when students would start missing classes, I would try to reel them back in, saying, "Look, I don't wanna do this practice test, but the ACT is required for CUNY at the end of the semester, so we gotta take it and move past it. I know you can do it! But you need to *be* here, and you have to *do your homework* to learn what you need to learn. Please do the homework." Even when semesters started with literature, the last three weeks to a month were almost entirely test preparation, and I sprinkled tests throughout the semester as well.

Emotionally, ACR was hard for many faculty and students. If students failed the course, they had to retake it ad infinitum until they passed, and when they failed, they were devastated. Tissues and candy were stockpiled in my office for the day when students received their scores. I'd meet with each student the last day of the semester, get a delighted handshake from the students that passed, and hand over fistfuls of Kleenex, encouragement, and, pseudo-social work to the students who had failed—several of whom had failed for the second or third time. I choked up as they explained their roadblocks to class success, many of which involved difficulties at home or work. For me, the semesters with high pass rates would send me home soaring, and, while rationally I know that student success is determined by more than my instruction and course planning, semesters with low pass rates ended with me in tears at my desk, feeling saturated with a combination of their disappointment and my own self-critique. After that day was over, I was left with wastebaskets full of blown noses, Snickers wrappers, and the collective weight of students' and my own frustration.

Reflecting on Zacka's (2017) recent work on the common, though "morally reductive" dispositions of street-level workers, I and many of my colleagues seem like the "caregiver" type (110). I spent evenings helping secure shelter for students who found themselves unhoused, and I sat with students who asked me to support them while they called the Domestic Violence hotline. I always have granola bars, power bars, and candy in my office, and a bucket of tampons and pads. I always refer students in need to counseling, but they often followed me back to my office after class on the pretense of assignment help only to fall into tears before I could refer them to a counselor. As Zacka (2017) observes, the caregiver role is often perceived by the practitioner as a "moral mission" that requires more time and emotional availability and that often leads to burnout, resulting from the inevitable disjuncture between their successes—the people they are able to help—and their failures (106). For a while, I was burned out and running on reserves of enthusiasm and gumption, and I felt a growing fissure between my academic identity and integrity and the person I saw in the looking glass. I was working myself into the ground. We have a heavy teaching load, teaching nine classes per academic year (it has since been reduced to a four/four teaching load, with eight courses per academic year), and we had substantial service and research requirements. I created routines to manage the work, developing documents that listed common mistakes in transcription and analysis that I could use to copy and paste into student assignments and personalize as needed. I made the reading quizzes self-grading online. Between teaching 90–150 students per semester, required department and college service, and my own desire to continue research and writing, I felt completely overwhelmed.

For the first several years, I published from my dissertation research—a nine-month-long IE that examined talk between New York City homeless shelter caseworkers and their primarily hard-to-place unhoused clients (discussed in Chapters 3 and 5 of this book). My analysis explained that while "client responsibility" was emphasized and reiterated in city policy as essential to the client shelter experience, policy language like "responsible," "obligated," and "necessary" (and their permutations) was noticeably absent from caseworker-client[9] conversations. This led me to question how responsibility policy was actually communicated in these conversations. Ultimately, I found, as discussed later in this book, that shelter caseworkers used their discretion to socially construct responsibility in the interactional moment through a variety of mundane, unmarked, seemingly unimportant linguistic and discursive choices usually found among constellations of other discursive practices, including references to benchmarks, timelines, performance measurements, required tasks, and cultural mythologies.

After four years of publishing from that study, I was keen to start a new project. In 2012, two department colleagues, Chris Jacknick and Elisa Koniski, and I conducted a semester-long IE in a colleague's remedial reading ACR course (discussed in Chapters 4 and 6). We recorded and observed eleven one-hundred-minute sessions across the course of the semester, and the course ended with a high-stakes exam. While I was not looking for the constructions of responsibility from my dissertation, one day while listening to the professor during video-data recording, I could hear my dissertation data resonating like a tuning fork in nearly perfect pitch.

When I began coding the data from the community college remedial reading classroom, I saw aspects of the discursive construction of responsibility in my colleague's talk. I saw aspects of it in my own talk. I felt I was observing myself through Alice's looking glass, feeling surprise at this strange person who looked like me but who sounded like the street-level workers in my dissertation research. While I drew heavily on Michael Lipsky's street-level bureaucracy in my dissertation to explain why shelter caseworkers made the linguistic choices they made, and while Lipsky's work revealed how street-level workers, whether they be teachers, social workers, or police officers, have "analytically similar work conditions" (3), it took my being in a street-level position myself to see how the issues I described in my dissertation extended beyond the clients and caseworkers I had been grateful to know, and the shelter that had graciously and generously opened its doors to me. Street lever worker, *c'est moi*.

Outline of the Book

In this book, I present data illustrating how (1) commonly used words, such as "should," "should have," "have to," "need to," "got to," "supposed to," which I call deontic formulations, combine with (2) moralizing cultural mythologies borne out through word and phrase choices that indicate particular stances taken toward individuals being served (e.g., laziness, grit, working hard), and (3) references to organizational management concerns (e.g., timelines, benchmarks, performance). The latter two elements each chime with current research on neoliberalism and its organizational appendage, new managerialism, in higher education, social welfare, political science, and public policy. I argue that these linguistic and discursive elements often come together as a gestalt when street-level workers talk to marginalized people about responsibility, as seen in Figure 1.1. Like a constellation, this gestalt of responsibility communicates and accomplishes more than the sum of its parts.

I invite you, in this book, to consider whether we want to continue using this kind of language in general, while also suggesting that we all must be particularly mindful that such discourses have a differential

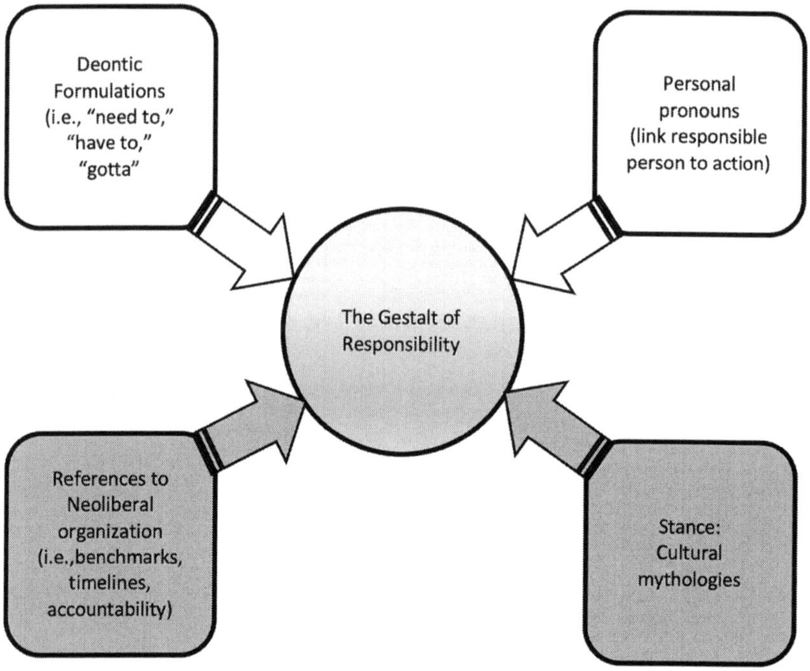

Fig. 1.1. The Gestalt of Responsibility

This diagram includes four boxes, one for each of the main aspects of discourse that collaboratively construct the gestalt of responsibility. There is a box for deontic formulations, one for personal pronouns, one for references to neoliberal organization (e.g., performance measurements, assessments, timelines, benchmarks), and one for cultural mythologies, which are often identified by stance markers. Grayscale color coding is used to highlight that deontic formulations and personal pronouns tend to be more grammatically oriented and references to neoliberalism and cultural mythological tend to be more lexical.

impact on marginalized people. The introduction to this book describes my preoccupation with responsibility as a young person. This lasting interest has coalesced here, and at BMCC I am not only a participant observer but a member of the community of practice, uniquely positioning me to describe what I call the subtlety of the street. While the analysis of policy documents and their outcomes have received attention in public policy studies (Smith and Larimer, 2017) and in discourse analysis (Fairclough, 2000), far less is known about what Brodkin (2013) calls the "missing middle" of policy implementation (9): what street-level workers *do* when constructing policy in their everyday work according to their discretion. This book speaks to how workers *do* responsibility, how they construct policy and do politics with their words.

This book introduces readers to and explores various aspects of the gestalt of responsibility. This chapter has introduced readers to me, to discourse analysis, to my interest in responsibility, and to the concept of street-level bureaucracy. Chapter 2 situates the study within the field of street-level bureaucracy research, within studies on neoliberalism and new managerialism. I then introduce you to the primary linguistic features of analysis and literature on timescales, the latter of which sets the stage for analytical work later in the book.

Chapters 3–6 examine the construction of responsibility in the shelter and educational context. Chapters 3 and 4 hang together as a pair, both examining the construction of responsibility. Chapter 3, utilizing data from the shelter context, presents the basic components of the gestalt of responsibility by examining the conversations between shelter caseworkers and the men in shelter experiencing homelessness. This chapter does not describe counterexamples. Chapter 4 expands upon the gestalt of responsibility, focusing on how cultural mythologies are employed when constructing responsibility. Drawing from Flores, Lewis, and Phuong's (2018) work, I propose responsibility-as-timescale to explain the sociohistorical baggage "responsibility" has across time (particularly the past) and space (in the United States). A timescale approach links these cultural mythologies with their sociohistorical past, including the devastating legacy of slavery and the continued structural and individual mistreatment and discrimination against Black people in the United States and elsewhere.

Drawing on the timescale literature reviewed in Chapter 2, Chapter 5 examines how talk shifts over time in the shelter context, responding to institutional performance benchmarks and assessments that shape not just what is talked about (including the gestalt of responsibility) but also how the unhoused men are addressed (including affiliative and disaffiliative discourse). This chapter explores this issue from two directions: (1) I present opening sequences between one client, Michael, and his caseworker, Ms. Innis, over nine months and (2) I use NVivo qualitative coding software to show (albeit in a crude way) how the number of tokens of responsibility increase as shelter benchmarks for housing placement approach. This chapter supports Soss, Fording, and Schram's (2012) claim that institutional performance benchmarks materially alter practice by providing linguistic evidence of such change. While several discourse-analytic studies have examined discourse in relation to time, most notably Wortham (2005), this is the first study to document how the shift of talk over time responds to timelines and benchmarks established by the institutions.

Chapter 6 both mirrors and extends Chapter 4 through an investigation of talk over time in the classroom context that shows both (1) how the gestalt of responsibility rises and responds horizontally in relation to the midterm exam and (in particular) the high-stakes final exam and (2) how cultural mythologies may accrue vertically as linguistic/discursive microaggressions over the course of the semester. The chapter primarily focuses on examining this vertical culmination of cultural mythologies over the course of the semester. The chapter concludes by discussing implications for understanding how the gestalt of responsibility functions as a form of microaggression. I conclude with a reflection that highlights my own failings, and I urge us all to find ways to grow and continue expanding.

Finally, Chapter 7 leads us through a brief comparison of findings from both contexts as they exist side by side. I argue that past and future timescales are essential perspectives that inform present talk. The lion's share of this chapter is devoted to calling out the elephant in the room—the pervasiveness of subtle forms of racism, individual microaggressions that accrue over time. Aided by responsibility language and references to performance benchmarks, we look at one final example, two campus signs that point to the potential differential treatment of marginalized people, highlighting the pervasiveness of these ideologies within institutional linguistic landscapes (Lance et al., 2023). The book concludes with (1) the proposition that a street-level approach to applied linguistics would create pathways for the practical implementation of research findings, and (2) suggestions for street-level, radically empathetic and compassionate discourse. I offer some future directions of study, as well as suggestions for administrators and street-level workers.

The Subtlety of the Street highlights the importance of attending to mundane language, arguing that subtle linguistic adjustments in these conversations may greatly impact practice. On one hand, making small seemingly semantic changes may feel purely cosmetic, not addressing larger structural institutional problems. On the other hand, small changes in wording can make people feel seen and respected (Heritage and Robinson, 2011), and giving people dignity and respect still matters. Making small adjustments to teacher and social work education not only may help manage the tension between the ideals of the discipline and the realities of the workspace but also may create more efficient and expedient results that *also* give people the dignity and respect they deserve.

2 | Situating the Studies

Comparative street-level studies are predicted upon "analytically similar work conditions" existing across different disciplines of work (Lipsky, 1980/2010, 3), inviting interdisciplinary and comparative research (Hill and Hupe, 2023). Since this book is highly interdisciplinary, I wanted to situate the studies among the various disciplines that inform them. This book, therefore, draws from a variety of different disciplines to situate the study, including research on street-level bureaucracy, neoliberalism (and its organizational appendage, new managerialism), social welfare, higher education, and discourse analysis. The literature reviewed in this chapter is, however, not exhaustive. Rather, I briefly describe the major debates in these fields in order to position the studies. The following literature review, therefore, briefly positions the research accordingly prior to describing the research contexts for each study.

Street-Level Work

In public policy studies, there is a tendency to either analyze policy from the front end (the policy) or the back end (post-implementation). We encounter front-end analyses through analyses of policy documents, and post-implementation studies may include data ascertained through surveys, interviews, observation, or statistical assessments of data. As Brodkin (2013) explains, we know significantly less about what happens on the street level, what she calls the "missing middle" of public policy (9). As noted in the introduction, Lipsky's (1980/2010) street-level bureaucracy theorizes and documents this middle space where street-level workers interface with clients, serving as intermediaries between clients and administration. Given the discretion and flexibility workers absolutely need (Watkins-Haynes. 2009), workers have space to make decisions that, in effect, become agency policy (Lipsky, 1980/2010). According to Lipsky, street-level workers (e.g., teachers, social workers, police officers, and others) respond to the constraints of their jobs, illustrating both the similarity of workers' dilemmas and how those commonalities result in a series of common coping strategies and tensions in the workplace. Street-level workers have demanding caseloads. They often have too few resources. They are generally overstretched, and this leads them to, for example, create routines and standardized ways of treating the people they serve, and they try to strike a balance between treating people like individuals and standardizing their daily practices enough to make their workload manageable (Hjörne et al., 2010).

The scholars in the field of street-level work care deeply about what street-level workers *do*. Studies in the field are wide-ranging; however, most relevant to this research are studies exploring how discretion can result in perpetuating social inequality and discrimination (Lotta and Pires, 2019; Raaphorst and Groeneveld, 2019), studies investigating the relationship between street-level practices and management approaches (Brodkin, 1997, 2013; Soss et al., 2013), and those examining sanctioning practices and accountability (Caswell and Høybye-Mortensen, 2015).

With the exception of Caswell's (Caswell, 2019; Caswell and Høybye-Mortensen, 2015) work, most qualitative studies use interview data to investigate how workers experience their workplaces. There are countless interview-based analyses of street-level work. Interviews present more accurate data about how workers *remember* an event or how they feel, but are less useful for determining what they do in situ (Brodkin, 2008). Page and Jenkins (2005), for example, interview 128 street-level workers to understand the extent to which workers do "policy work" and their relationship to institutional hierarchy and expertise. There are many such studies in street-level research that, while valuable contributions, are less helpful in situating these particular studies.

However, Maynard-Moody and Musheno's (2003) interview-based, comparative study of street-level work has had significant influence on this book. Their foundational research published in *Cops, Teachers, and Counselors* uses worker interviews to describe street-level workers' discretion across three separate disciplines. Using Lipsky's work as a springboard, they consider the "analytically similar work conditions" (Lipsky, 1980/2010, 3) of three different kinds of street-level workers. While there is not a focus on these workers vis-à-vis their specific disciplines, the strength of Maynard-Moody and Musheno's work is in the large-scale comparison between seemingly disparate street-level cohorts, which highlights their overwhelming similarities and struggles. They find that "more than enforcers of law, street-level workers—in our study, cops, teachers, and vocational rehabilitation counselors—are producers of values and character that embody mainstream notions of worth and productive membership in society" (94). In this book, I extend their findings by showing how those values and judgments are constructed in recorded conversations between street-level workers and those they serve. The inclusion of a different type of data—discourse transcripts of recorded conversations—creates an opening for seeing street-level work freshly, from a new angle. Interview data present essential narratives of workers' experiences, filtered through both memory and how they would like to be seen. For example, while drawing significantly on the influential work of Maynard-Moody and Musheno (2003), this book also contributes new findings that are elucidated a different methodology for data collection and analysis. They argue that

> the issues of discretion, control, and accountability that have so dominated the literature on public organizations rarely appear in our stories. These issues are not prominent for street-level workers. Rather, their moral judgments about citizen-clients are made in the context of face-to-face relationships that enacts the identity of both worker and citizen. (93)

While I agree with Maynard-Moody and Musheno (2003) that decision-making is a moral process that engages both identity and institutional/local requirements, this book demonstrates that accountability and control are most certainly present as verbalized concerns for both street-level workers and the clients, their relevance spoken into existence in the everyday meetings between workers and clients. Though it does not rise to salience in Maynard-Moody and Musheno's data, the discourse data in this book demonstrate the prominence of accountability and discretion in street-level work, combining with moral judgments to accomplish constructions of responsibility in face-to-face meetings. If street-level workers construct policy as they deliver services through their discretionary choices, then we need to know what they are actually saying to communicate that de facto policy. We need multiple methodologies to paint a complete picture of street-level work. Studies that gather recorded data from the actual meetings between street-level workers and clients themselves shed light on aspects of frontline work that may be missed by other methodologies. This book, focusing on spoken interaction and drawing on Caswell's contributions to street-level bureaucracy as a field, shifts the inquiry away from what workers report and toward what language is used in actual meetings with clients.

In the *Research Handbook on Street-Level Bureaucracy: The Ground Floor of Government in Context*, Hill and Hupe (2023) send out a clarion call for increased comparative research in street-level contexts, underscoring the need for broader ethnographic detail. In so doing, they argue that cases for comparative study need to be embedded in their broader contexts and that the focus should be on "contexts rather than occupations" (284) in order to capture the complexity of street-level work. They posit the following question, which this book addresses as well: "*How do SLBs, with varying individual characteristics and working in different contexts, deal with a similar public task, in a way that leads to variation in outputs related to that task?*" (285). This book considers their question from a discourse perspective, using interactional ethnography to embed the research in each institutional context to examine how street-level workers manage the verbal task of informing clients or students about their responsibilities vis-à-vis accountability protocols.

Indeed, where ethnographic research describes street-level negotiations with clients, linguistic and discourse-analytic research adds dimensions of rigor, nuance, and specificity that are wholly unavailable to other qualitative inquiries. Sacks (1992), an early architect of conversation analysis (a branch of discourse analysis), suggested analysts ask, "Why this, now?" This question asks us to consider alternatives to something that was said. Why was it said *this* way rather than *that* way, in *this moment*? The reality is that our words can have a bigger impact than we might imagine, and changing small words and phrases can also have an impressive impact. In perhaps my favorite example, Heritage and Robinson (2011) studied a large office of doctors who were reporting low patient satisfaction. After recording, transcribing, and analyzing doctor-patient discourse in the office, the researchers decided to split the group into two: one half continued speaking exactly as they had before, and the other group changed one sentence (just a few words). The control group who did not change their discourse continued ending their meetings with patients with the question, "Are there **any** other concerns you'd like to address during this visit?" (21). And the group who was asked to change their discourse asked, "Are there **some** other concerns you'd like to address during this visit?" or "What other concerns would you like to address during this visit?" (22). The discourse analysts suggested this change because the word "any" has a social expectation, or preference, for a "no" reply (even if this isn't someone's individual preference). While the doctors in the experimental group changed their discourse, they also expressed concern. If they presented patients with ample opportunity to ask more questions, patients would surely take too much time. How would doctors regulate the timing of appointments? How would they deal with all of the patients who need to be seen? However, as Heritage and Robinson illustrate,

> While the "any" intervention visits were on average 55 seconds longer (a result that was not statistically significant), the "some" intervention visits were on average one hundredth of a second shorter! Here, it would appear, the "some" question was getting additional concerns out early in the visit, which allowed for effective time management such that additional concerns could be dealt with within the confines of the normal visit length. (29)

Reading this study from a street-level perspective, we see that doctors had perhaps developed a routine for managing their large numbers of clients, a discursive strategy that wrapped up meetings quickly while maintaining a facade of inquiry and attentiveness. Discourse-analytic and linguistic analyses help us to identify *how* street-level interactions *function* and what, if anything, we might want to change. While the findings from discourse-analytic research are obviously more microanalytic than those found in ethnographic and interview-based studies, these studies not only add depth to street-level research but also can shed light on linguistic changes that can substantially impact the workplace.

There is an emerging cohort of scholars examining the intersection between social interaction and street-level practice, including social welfare scholars, sociologists, and a linguist—yours truly. Early work in this area focused on how street-level workers navigate common work dilemmas like balancing routinization (developing routines and standardized practices to make work efficient) and individualization (treating clients like individuals). Using discourse analysis, Matarese (2008) drew on Lipsky's work to explain how the paperwork and forms required to process the unhoused men in the NYC shelter system constrained the unfolding of their talk in ways that closed down space for client contributions.[1] Hjörne, Juhila, and van Nijnatten (2010) established a precedent for taking a discourse-analytic approach to examine street-level work, explaining that the dilemmas endemic to street-level practice are likely exacerbated by movements like new managerialism (an organizational approach and movement described further in the following section). Coming from a social work background, they prioritized questions like "How are dilemmas talked into being in encounters, for instance when discussing clients' eligibility for social welfare services, when considering different intervention and their effectiveness or when assessing clients' progression or regression?" (307). Many early street-level studies focused on these kinds of dilemmas of street-level workers, particularly in the welfare context.

These studies laid the groundwork for later research that examines street-level work from an organizational perspective that takes into account management approaches and even politics (Caswell, 2019; Brodkin, 2011; Soss et al., 2011). As Caswell and Høybye-Mortensen (2015) explain, "A central argument in this line of research is that new public management strategies, such as performance measures and other forms of accountability, shape the coping strategies of the street-level bureaucrats in diverse and complex ways" (34). In a landmark study examining the discretion of TANF (Temporary Assistance for Needy Families) street-level workers, Soss et al. (2011) show how "organizational routines, tools, norms, incentives, information systems and categories of understanding function as mechanisms of social control that shape the use of discretion in predictable ways" (230). Their work, which combines interview and observation, describes how workers' report that their discretion responds to organizational demands stemming from neoliberal policies. The studies in this book support their finding, showing that street-level workers do change how they speak to clients based on how close the client is to institutionally prescribed benchmarks and timelines (see Chapters 5 and 6).

Using discourse analysis, Caswell and Høybye-Mortensen (2015) extend Soss et al.'s (2011) work by describing how pressures regarding performance measurement and benchmarks in sanctioning interactions shape the discourse practices of the workers, resulting in "naming and shaming," excuses, explanations, and justification. Excuses, explanations, and justifications are, in some way, the "back end" of responsibility constructions—clients use such accounts to explain lapses in responsibility. This book builds off their foundational work and contributes to this body of knowledge by examining the "front end" of responsibility—how responsibility is constructed through the words of workers, showing how the organizational demands stemming from new managerial/neoliberal approaches shape those constructions. This book demonstrates, to quote Caswell (2019), how street-level workers "talk policy into being" in assisting unemployed people (1). Specifically, I examine how organizational constraints, stemming from neoliberalism and new managerialism, not only impact street-level workers' use of individual discourse features but also influence their use of those features over time in response to organizational benchmarks and performance measurements.

The studies in this book contribute a discourse perspective to organizational perspectives in street-level research, while also commenting on how macro-level social phenomena (neoliberalism, new managerialism, the historical legacy of racism) have a hand in shaping these discourses. This book positions street-level discourses as "sites within which individuals indirectly negotiate sociopolitical status" (Brodkin, 2011, 24). Therefore, while the book focuses on street-level social interaction, the findings are best analyzed in light of the larger sociopolitical and organizational context for policy development in the United States.

The Neoliberal Context for Policy

The influence of neoliberalism partially explains the presence of individual responsibility, performance benchmarks, measurement, and assessment that surface in concert with street-level workers' constructions of responsibility in the institutional interactions described in this book. The following section defines neoliberalism and new managerialism, for the purposes of this book, focusing on how my book contributes to understandings of neoliberalism and new managerialism in higher education, social welfare, and linguistics.

Neoliberalism is a widely overused term that today is primarily wielded by opponents of the approach. Its history is extensively covered by colleagues exploring the concept in far more depth (cf. Harvey, 2007). Developed by Milton Friedman as a response to socialism, communism, and fascism, neoliberalism[2] is an economic perspective that organizes individuals and institutions vis-à-vis "principles of market rationality," treating nonbusiness institutions like businesses and the people in them like clients (Soss et al., 2011, 2). Nowadays, the term takes on generally negative connotations, with critics calling it "economic Darwinism" (Giroux, 2014, 1), "free market fundamentalism" (Giroux, 2014, 1) and "creative destruction" (Harvey, 2006, 145). It has been attributed to trends in restructuring the state, fragmenting regulation, privatization, and standards reform (Harvey, 2007; Peck, 2010). Brown (2015) furthers this definition, showing the relationship between policy and people:

> Neoliberalism . . . is best understood not simply as economic policy, but as a governing rationality that disseminates market values and

> metrics to every sphere of life and construes the human itself exclusively as *homo oeconomicus*. Neoliberalism thus does not merely privatize. . . . Rather, it formulates everything, everywhere, in terms of capital investment and appreciation, including and especially humans themselves. (176)

Her characterization of neoliberalism highlights the connection between the policy and the personal, impacting socioeconomic life from the macro markets to individuals (*human* capital). As Foucault (1979) says in the *Birth of Biopolitics* about American neoliberalism, "Liberalism in America is a whole way of being and thinking. It is a type of relation between the governors and the governed much more than a technique of governors with regard to the governed" (218). The sticky relationship between neoliberal policy and neoliberal ideology makes it unwieldy to reckon with, like the many-headed hydra.

In applied linguistics, Canagarajah (2017) separates neoliberal *economics* from neoliberal *ideology*, defining neoliberal economics as "free market enterprise with limited regulation, the politics of neoliberal agencies assumes state protection of private property, business interests, and capital accumulation of the elite" (5). "Neoliberal ideology," on the other hand, is defined as the need for "individuals, communities, and institutions . . . to be enterprising and further their own interests without looking for outside help. Failure is explained as one's own lack of agency and effort" (5). This second quotation may remind you of Scrooge's words from the introduction of the book. This is because while individual responsibility and its moral baggage are widely acknowledged to be folded into modern neoliberal ideology, they have also circulated for centuries, folded into policies targeting the poor from the 1400s, 1600, and 1800s. Individual responsibility, then, indexes both old and new forms of poverty governance. Individual responsibility is folded into a variety of cultural mythologies, which are discussed in a subsequent subsection.

The modern institutional emphasis on accountability is also attributed to neoliberal approaches to organizational management (Isserles, 2021; Koyama, 2013; Soss et al., 2011). Neoliberalism in education stresses "organizational effectiveness, accountability, capacity building, and standardization" (Meyer, 2002, 516). In some way, accountability frameworks that assess and measure individuals' successful completion of actions along a timeline of benchmarks are the connective tissue between neoliberal economics and neoliberal ideology, as they seek "to reduce the social, political, and economic risks that governments assume by transferring these risks onto individuals through their relationships with each other and themselves" (Webb, 2011, 735; see also Olssen and Peters 2005). In short, accountability measurements (often utilizing benchmarks, timelines, and performance assessment) foist individual responsibility onto individuals seeking services (unhoused people, students, etc.), instrumentalizing and institutionalizing the ideology in everyday practice. This book addresses both cultural mythologies associated with neoliberalism and organizational policies and performance measurements (and their associated benchmarks for completion).

References to institutional performance measurements, benchmarks, and timelines are a critical aspect of how responsibility is constructed. New managerialism (also called "new public management") is the organizational administrative wing of neoliberalism in which business management principles and approaches (managerialism) are applied to the governance and administration of nonbusiness institutions: *new* managerialism (Abramovitz and Zelnick, 2015; Clarke and Newman, 1993). New managerialism is the approach responsible for instituting accountability frameworks, and in schools and social work institutions, neoliberal and new managerial approaches have been accused of contradicting the fundamental principles in both education (Beckmann and Cooper, 2004; Deem and Brehony, 2005; Fredman and Doughney, 2012; Lipman, 2011; Samier, 2002; Sullivan, 2017) and social work (Abramovitz and Zelnick, 2015; Banks, 2007; Brodkin, 1997, 2006, 2008; Kirkpatrick, 2006; Soss et al., 2011).

In Education

The negative impact of neoliberalism and new managerialism is widely discussed in education, both at the K-12 level (Anyon, 2014; Lipman, 2011) and in higher education (Deresiewicz, 2015; Giroux, 2014). Overwhelmingly, scholars are critical of the approach and for a wide variety of reasons. While Deresiewicz (2015) argues that business-oriented neoliberal policies create a "caste system of winners and losers" (n.p.), neoliberal and new managerial approaches have been particularly criticized for their negative impact on communities of color in the United States. Apple (2019) explains that, stretching back through various strands of history,

> it is almost impossible to fully understand the impulses and histories that stand behind most neoliberal "reform" efforts unless the complex politics of race and the nature of the "racial state" are taken truly seriously. (282)

In her work on public schools, Anyon (2014) finds neoliberal approaches overwhelmingly and disproportionately impact Black students, generating systemic and racialized injustices. Love (2019) extends this work by examining how cultural mythologies that intersect with neoliberalism and responsibility are applied to minoritized and marginalized students. She shows how a collection of characteristics under the umbrella of "character education" is disproportionately required of Black students and students of color:

> Critical thinking, problem solving, social and emotional intelligence, zest, self-advocacy, grit, optimism, self-control, curiosity, and gratitude are the characteristics school officials, politicians, policymakers, educational consulting firms, curriculum writers, education researchers, and corporate school reformers prepackage and sell to educators and parents of dark children. For most schools in the US, especially schools with a large majority of low-income and dark students, their mission statements, weekly blogs, and fundraising materials are plastered with these racially coded feel-good, work-hard, and take-responsibility-for-my-actions buzzwords that make up character education. (N.p.)

Love's work responds to Duckworth's (2016) Character Lab, which defines "grit" as a "strength of will," "perseverance and passion for long term goals" (CharacterLab, 2023), and Love explains how grit is measured and assessed among Black and Brown schoolchildren, arguing that such character education is "anti-Black" and ignores "toxic stress," the school-to-prison pipelines, institutional barriers, and structural racism (n.p.).

Research in higher education renders similar results. Smyth (2017) suggests that neoliberalism has created a "pathological organizational dysfunction" in universities, producing near-constant anxiety for faculty (5). Moreover, "Community college faculty . . . may be affected more by managerial and political-economic forces than their university counterparts" (Levin et al., 2006, 5). Not surprisingly, given the research on the negative impact of neoliberal policies on K-12 students, these kinds of policies also negatively impact community college students. Neoliberalism introduces dysfunction for students at the community college, fostering blame, false narratives, and ultimately an ideological departure from the open-admissions aim of community colleges (Sullivan, 2017). Isserles (2021), who also conducted her research at BMCC, explains,

> In the community college context, the *Homo oeconomicus* is the atomized student whose personal responsibility it is to retain and persist, who is glorified for demonstrating a singular version of grit while being asked to surmount increasingly difficult odds to complete their degree. (7)

Isserles's (2021) study, unique in its expert analysis of retention and persistence at CUNY, is one of several studies contributing to the emerging field of critical university studies (CUS), which examines neoliberalism in higher education and "the process of knowledge production," as connected to university reforms (Smyth, 2017, v). Smyth (2017) suggests that CUS calls for "'insider' studies that unmask the forces that sustain and maintain and enable current reform trajectories" (vii). Bringing a discourse perspective, my analysis in the community college classroom provides an insider perspective that combines participant observation of a colleague's reading classroom with my own experience as an active member of the community of practice (Lave and Wenger, 1991) and as a professor teaching the same course. Moreover, while this book takes neither critical theory nor CUS as a theoretical foundation prior to analysis, I do question and at times challenge "the basic tenets of the new managerialist discourse" (Beckmann and Cooper, 2004, 168) by examining how a professor's constructions of responsibility in a community college classroom intersect with neoliberal ideological and economic approaches. While CUNY's community colleges are recognized catalysts for upward mobility (Leonhardt, 2017), my data reveal that they may also be spaces where neoliberal discourses create negative moral categorizations of marginalized students for not being individually responsible, for not moving fast enough, for not hitting performance benchmarks required for success. Understanding how neoliberal and managerial discourses structure the daily experience of community college students is a sorely needed contribution to CUS. Finally, much like street-level studies, discourse analyses of neoliberalism in education are available but limited. This book's fit among those studies may be found in the "In Applied Linguistics" discussion forthcoming.

In Social Work

Descriptions of historical policy shifts in social work echo education. Since the 1990s, new managerial procedures, integrated into human services, have emphasized completing and evaluating target-based tasks and increasing responsibility and accountability. These new standards and systems of accountability have developed as "high profile professional scandals" caught public attention, lending support to the idea that social workers are fallible practitioners whose judgment can be poor and who thus require greater and more stringent supervision (White and Stancombe, 2003, 25). While prior to the 1970s social work emphasized public service, collectivity, and a "commitment to equity, care, and social justice," new managerialism initiated a "customer-oriented ethos, concern for efficiency, cost-effectiveness and competition, and emphasis on individual relations" (Gewirtz and Ball, 2000, 112). Likewise, Harlow (2003), drawing on Payne (1997), describes social work prior to neoliberalism as reflexive-therapeutic and socialist-collectivist, while the later perspective utilizes a "managerial-technicist" approach that emphasizes "rationality, fragmentation, technicism, and positivistic evaluation of performance [that also] denies the emotional content of practice and the significance of relationship" (38). These approaches refocus social work on corporate, task-oriented, responsibility-driven organizational paradigms for managing social and human services that refashion practice by bringing about an ideological shift of values in social work (Harlow, 2003). The modern approach favors adherence to procedures, guidelines, and checklists, which Harlow characterizes as "conveyer belt care" (35). More recently, Abramovitz and Zelnick (2015) argue that new managerialism shifts social work away from a relationship based on *care* to one with a "bureaucratic focus on the assessment of risk and rationing of resources and services, together with more top down control and moral policing" (125). They attribute social work burnout to this shift, which increases the workload and pressure on practitioners.

While many argue that the approaches instituted through new public management/new managerialism subvert the goals of social work (Scourfield, 2007; Soss et al., 2011), some scholars argue that neoliberal approaches also impact the field positively. Many scholars acknowledge that new managerialism brings some positive attributes, while still generally illustrating a dramatic shift in social services, moving away from "citizenship rights, and towards services that are increasingly targeted and means tested" (Kirkpatrick, 2006, 7). Scourfield (2007) offers a mixed review of new managerialism, suggesting on one hand that managerial discourse is an "'emancipatory' one, stressing choice, control and independence" and on the other hand that clients are obligated by contract to responsibly complete tasks, which appear to undermine the former qualities (116).

Moore (1998), likewise, points out positive attributes that managerialism brings to social work—such as keeping practitioners in check and ordering their daily practices—but also describes the dangers of the approach, which he suggests threaten the very institution of social work itself. He suggests that the model limits social work by depersonalizing service delivery, thereby homogenizing social services. Banks (2007) relabels accountability under neoliberalism "new accountability." While she presents both morally good and "morally dubious" (15) positions of workers, the upshot of her work highlights the moral and practical challenges of new accountability in social work.

Performance benchmarks, measurements, and assessments have long been identified as part of neoliberal and new managerial practices in institutions, and some scholars argue that these negatively impact practice. Soss, Fording, and Schram (2011), for example, argue that the ideological and moral principles on which neoliberalism is based (English Poor Laws), established a precedent for blaming those in need. However, our current brand of neoliberalism integrates paternalism to "discipline the poor" for circumstances outside of their control (3). In this system, the inability to meet individual responsibilities is emblematic of larger moral failings (Soss et al., 2011). Those not meeting performance standards are, therefore, often characterized as moral failures and disciplined with loss of services (Soss et al., 2011).

In investigating the use of performance benchmarks and their impact on practice through administrator data and interviews with caseworkers, Soss, Fording, and Schram illustrate how street-level concerns like limited resources and tools combine with the pressure of performance benchmarks to alter practice. They also explain that because caseworker performance success depends on clients doing what they are told, and because caseworkers understand that their job security may be tied to performance, when clients do not comply with requirements, caseworkers become frustrated and often sanction clients. Performance benchmarks, then, materially alter practice by generating more stressful work requirements and work environments, in addition to incentivizing sanctions when clients are not responsibly completing tasks. Taking this a step further, Brodkin (2011) argues that new managerialism in social work integrates performance measurements as part of an accountability system that ultimately becomes a political act when it alters street-level practice. "Under new managerialism . . . as long as performance benchmarks are met," it often is of little consequence to managers *how* they are met by street-level workers (i272). She found that workers routinely used discretion to develop routines that managed their demanding caseload, making adjustments that impact how the policy is implemented on the front lines. In line with her findings and Soss, Fording, and Schram (2011), this book also examines the relationship between performance benchmarks and street-level work from a discourse perspective.

In perhaps the most relevant study, Stonehouse, Threlkeld, and Farmer (2015) use interviews of unhoused people in Australia to examine the perpetuation of neoliberalism through an emphasis on individual risk and responsibility. While they find that individual responsibility is (re)produced by the unhoused people, these unhoused people also find that the workers are overwhelmed and that government support (and responsibility) is lacking. Using their work as a springboard, this book, in taking a street-level perspective, explores the words these overwhelmed workers use around individual responsibility. Ultimately, I reveal that workers indeed express stress and overwhelmedness, often due to institutional priorities and constraints that create increased pressure and therefore linguistic choices that degrade and dehumanize unhoused people.

It is worth briefly noting that some philosophers and economists have argued that neoliberalism is dead or dying. Fraser in conversation with Jaeggi stipulates that "as a hegemonic project, neoliberalism is finished; it may retain its capacity to dominate, but it has lost its ability to persuade" (Fraser and Jaeggi, 2018, 222). Public support behind neoliberalism wanes, and as Peck (2010) observes, what is left staggers forward neither dead nor alive, like a zombie:

> The brain has apparently long since ceased functioning, but the limbs are still moving, and many of the defensive reflexes seem to be working too. The living dead of the free-market revolution continue to walk the earth, though with each resurrection their decidedly uncoordinated gait becomes even more erratic. (109)

Whether neoliberalism and its policies are dead or walking dead, what is left of it continues to wound (Marthinsen et al., 2022). Moreover, if the moral judgment surrounding individual responsibility is sticky and persistent enough to persevere across centuries of poverty governance, it stands to reason that even if neoliberalism is dead and buried (or bludgeoned in the head, as befits a zombie), the ideology may continue unless we attend to it.

Like the Ghost of Christmas Present at the outset of the book, I urge us to take mindful notice of our words and language. Our words and the ideologies they point to have been around long enough that they too may lumber around like zombies within us, and we may not be aware of how rooted they are in white supremacy, classism, and social movements that have integrated these ideologies. People may simply not be aware of how injurious such language may be to those experiencing them (my students are always surprised and mortified to discover the ableist backgrounds of words such as "lame" and "dumb," for example).

In Applied Linguistics

As described earlier, Heritage and Robinson's (2011) discourse-analytic research on doctor-patient interaction highlights how the smallest of words ("any") can have measurable consequences, and how replacing that one word significantly improved patient satisfaction. As those who do applied conversation analysis argue, words, even the smallest and seemingly most insignificant ones, matter (Antaki, 2011). There are those who say words do not matter; semantic changes are cosmetic and meaningless. I maintain that language *is* action. Performative verbs like "pronounce," when uttered by the right person in the right place with the right people, make a marriage in that pronouncement. Likewise, the pronouncement of the "time of death" by a medical practitioner becomes "fact," although the heart failure occurred in the car on the way to the hospital. Language performs social actions, and words, in part, construct our realities. This book does not replace the need for structural change or institutional revision, but words do matter.

In Brodkin's (2013) chapter on expanding the understanding of street-level workers' roles beyond their capacity to construct policy in situ, she explains that workers should also be viewed as "mediators of the politics and processes of welfare state transformation" (17). She suggests that this extended view has the advantage of connecting more deeply with the "operational core of the welfare state" (18). She explains further:

> A political-*organizational* view puts [street-level organizations (SLOs)] at the center of analysis, offering a different perspective on how welfare states work. It links the micropolitics of SLOs to the macropolitics of the welfare state: it's a way of seeing big by looking small. (18)

I argue that through the analyses in this book, we may "see big" by looking even smaller. By examining street-level workers in two diverse contexts, both influenced by neoliberal and new managerial policies, we may see these workers as mediators not just of policy but also of politics through the minutiae of their everyday talk with clients.

There is a growing body of scholarship examining neoliberalism though a discourse-analytic lens, and this book draws from and contributes to this emerging subfield that examines the intersection between applied linguistics and neoliberal research. Several foundational texts foreground neoliberalism's rich philosophical and historical underpinnings as they relate to the field of applied linguistics, including Block's (2018) *Political Economy and Sociolinguistics*, Block, Grey, and Holborow's (2013) *Neoliberalism and Applied Linguistics*, Duchêne and Heller's (2012) *Language in Late Capitalism: Pride and Profit*, Flubacher and Del Percio's (2017) edited volume *Language, Education, and Neoliberalism*, Holborow's (2015) *Language and Neoliberalism*, and Rojo and De Percio's (2020) edited volume *Language and Neoliberal Governmentality*. I am particularly indebted to and inspired by Block, Grey, and Holborow's (2013) book, which was perhaps the first to tackle neoliberalism specifically, head on. Discourse analysis has been used to describe how neoliberalism surfaces in the linguistic landscape and in political signs (Chun, 2017, 2022). Keyword analysis (Williams, 2015), which focuses on identifying key terms from the social milieu as they circulate in a particular text, has become popular for examining neoliberalism; for example, Holborow (2015) uses keyword analysis to analyze neoliberalism in non-street-level Irish higher education.

From the social welfare perspective, Juhila, Raitakari, and Hall's book (2016) *Responsibilisation at the Margins of Welfare Services* combines Lipsky's street-level approach, keyword analysis (Ferguson, 2007; Williams, 2015) (searching for terms like "empowerment"), and ethnomethodology in the social welfare context. They draw on O'Malley (2009), who coined "responsibilization" to explain the process whereby obligations once the purview of the governments or of agencies become the individual responsibility of those seeking services. Analyzing how client responsibility is invoked in social worker-client interaction, they describe social worker interprofessional interaction and interview narratives around responsibility. They combine keyword analysis with a toolbox developed by Hall, Juhila, Matarese, and Nijnatten (2014) to show how responsibility is negotiated through accounts, categorization, boundary work, advice-giving, narrative, and resistance. Presenting an unprecedented collection of primary studies, they describe how responsibilization is constructed in a variety of institutional interactions including supportive housing services, a housing and social skills training project, an outpatient drug abuse clinic, a prison, and a probation service. Their work, unlike mine, gives more analytic attention to the co-construction of responsibility, noting more significant client involvement in generating uptake of or resistance to "advanced liberal"[3] values. Their book is impressive and expansive from a social welfare perspective, the sheer number of contexts, including worker-client meetings, interprofessional talk, and group-style case conferences, contributing to a wholistic representation of responsibilization in talk. Juhila et al. (2016), like Holborow (2015), use keyword analysis, which centers around using key terms like "resilience" to locate responsibilization in social welfare interaction. In the spirit of Paris and Alim's (2017) "loving critique," I am both deeply indebted to these scholars and these essential contributions while also gently noting that approaches like keyword analysis favor salient "big ticket" keywords over mundane language, which can limit findings. This book focuses on the subtle, everyday, mundane language that communicates responsibility, theorizing responsibility at a microanalytic level.

In a similar vein, I also acknowledge some of the earlier studies, including my own, that contribute to unpacking responsibility through the somewhat limited lens of accounts (discussed in more depth in Chapter 3). Both Caswell and Høybye-Mortensen (2015) and Matarese and Caswell (2014) use accounts (excuses, justifications, etc.) to explore accountability in social welfare settings. A person provides an account when called upon to explain some unexpected or inappropriate action (or inaction). For example:

> LUIS: Why didn't you meet me at ten?
> MARCUS: I was going to, but I overslept.

The offering of oversleeping is a kind of account. Studying accounts tells us much about how clients explain their (ir)responsibility, but it does not capture how the worker invites clients to discuss their (ir)responsible actions. Studying accounts to understand responsibility is putting the cart before the horse. Such studies do not explain how the street-level worker constructs and assigns responsibility in situ (front-end responsibility), and this focus is crucial because if we only examine constructions of responsibility where accounts are present (e.g., "I didn't go to the store because I forgot"), then we only examine *failures* of responsibility (moments when clients need to account for some untoward behavior). By examining the constructions of responsibility made by the street-level workers, we may capture all constructions of responsibility in the data, including those for which no account from the client is necessary (e.g., "I need you to get a TB [tuberculosis] test tomorrow" or "You have to keep working"). Drawing on this excellent body of work, I aim to further theorize the discursive construction of responsibility by focusing on the front end of responsibility (the constructions of responsible actions themselves), noting how it is achieved through subtle, seemingly insignificant instances language.

The Gestalt of Responsibility in Discourse

While I briefly described the gestalt of responsibility in the beginning of the book, as some readers may be unfamiliar with discourse terminology, I wanted to briefly introduce the primary components. As a reminder, Figure 2.1 illustrates the primary gestalt components.

Deontic Formulations

When I began analyzing responsibility in my dissertation data in 2006, I was looking for keywords referred to in Department of Homeless Services policy ("responsibility," "accountability," etc.). When these terms were absent in the caseworker-client conversations, I turned toward examining what language communicated responsibility outside of these terms. The analysis takes deontic formulations, ways of communicating obligation and necessity using words that specifically point to responsibility ("have to," "got to," "must," "should have," etc.), as a starting point and then examines what kinds of words and phrases regularly gather and cluster around them. Biber and Finegan (1989) define deontic stance as "the lexical and grammatical expression of attitudes, feelings, judgments, or commitment concerning the propositional content of a message," communicated through "modals indicating possibility, necessity, and prediction" (93). Some scholars have defined deontic language with more granularity. Searle (2010, 100), whose logic-based theorizing of deontic terms goes far beyond the needs of this analysis, makes a distinction between various types of "deontic powers," including "negative deontic powers," which refer to the obligations that individuals have. Couper-Kuhlen and Selting (2018) make a distinction between deontic stance (establishing authority to make decisions about what needs to be done) versus deontic status ("the mutually acknowledged underlying entitlement of one party to decide on the actions of another party") (25). However, for the purposes of

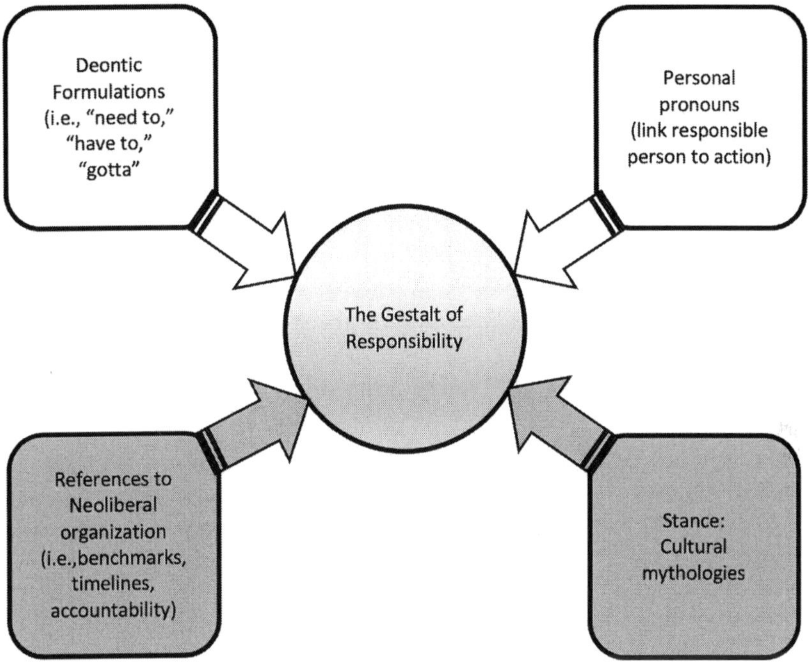

Fig. 2.1. The Gestalt of Responsibility, Reprised

This diagram includes four boxes, one for each of the main aspects of discourse that collaboratively construct the gestalt of responsibility. There is a box for deontic formulations, one for personal pronouns, one for references to neoliberal organization (e.g., performance measurements, assessments, timelines, benchmarks), and one for cultural mythologies, which are often identified by stance markers. Grayscale color coding is used to highlight that deontic formulations and personal pronouns tend to be more grammatically oriented and references to neoliberalism and cultural mythological tend to be more lexical.

this study, I am collapsing both of these into "deontic formulations," as workers' status and power are endowed by their institutional roles. These deontic formulations are the product of several component parts, including personal pronouns (e.g., "you"), deontic words (e.g., "have to," "gotta," etc.), and the object of the stance ("get a tuberculosis test").

Personal pronouns have received ample attention in the literature. Often called person *deixis* because these terms *point* to what they refer to, personal pronouns link deontic words to a responsible action, *who* should be *responsible*, and who is asking for that responsible action, potentially conveying distance or closeness of alignment (Stivers et al., 2007) between workers and the people they serve. For example, in the social work data set in this book, when a caseworker says, "You need to get a TB test," the deontic term "need" links the unhoused person "you" to the action "get a

TB test." However, if the worker says, "I need you to get a TB test," the deontic term "need" is still linked, albeit a bit differently, to client action through "you" and the action "get a TB test," but in this case the subject "I"—indicated through the personal pronoun—not only asserts authority but also places distance between the unhoused person and the worker.[4] We can contrast this with "We need to get you outta here," in which the worker aligns herself with the client through "we," making both of them responsible ("need") for placing him ("you") into housing ("get you outta here"). Personal pronouns are one way that alignment between speakers is communicated while also conveying who is responsible.

Cultural Mythologies

We cannot avoid cultural mythologies. They are truly everywhere. In my Forensic Linguistics class, I ask all my students to draw a piece of fruit as quickly as possible, using whatever their gut reaction is, and generally about 85 percent of the class draws an apple. We then discuss the "appleness" of American society: as American as apple pie, the Big Apple, apple of my eye, Johnny Appleseed, etc. I am not going to go deeply into semantic prototype theory, but essentially the theory explores semantic categories (e.g., "fruit") and indicates a particular member of the category (e.g., "apple"), which serves as the cognitive reference point for that category. In Forensic Linguistics (and at the expense of being substantially reductive with semantic theory), I explain how these semantic categories do not matter so much when they are apples, but what happens when I ask the class to draw "a scientist"? Nearly the whole class produces an old, white man with hair like Einstein. What about a "rape victim"? I ask. At this point, the class realizes the problem.

These prototypes are culturally constructed and produced and reproduced. I draw from Ehrlich (2010), who frames these as cultural mythologies, highlighting the subtle insidiousness of discourse that presents misogynistic cultural mythologies around women in rape trials. Ehrlich shows how these mythologies, in collaboration with other discourse features, substantially shape trial outcomes for the victims. When lawyers cross-examine rape victims, they "invoke cultural mythologies surrounding rape as a way of undermining the credibility of complainants" (269). She explains that these cultural mythologies are articulated through declarative statements (e.g., "We know that you . . .") and questions with embedded presuppositions that encode presumed truths.[5] Together, these generate assumptions about the rape victims that situate them according to common misogynist and heterosexist sexual and gender stereotypes. These are often used by cross-examining lawyers in combination with controlling questions to delegitimize the veracity and legitimacy of the victim's claims and to subtly influence the jury. I contend that different but similarly problematic cultural mythologies are invoked in the social interactions between the participants in these studies, complicating what constructions of responsibility can look like.

There is an extensive literature on myths and mythmaking, and while I will not be engaging deeply with that literature, it is important to briefly situate cultural mythologies as they relate to this study. Cohen (1969) explains that the word "myth" is often used pejoratively. In reviewing how myths are theorized in psychology, sociology, and anthropology, he lands on the following observations:

> Thus, I would argue one of the important functions of myth *is that it anchors the present in the past* . . . ; and it is also conveyed by dredging deep into unconscious symbolism, so that the message communicated by the myth does have an impact at a number of levels. . . . Myths were . . . explanations of the origins or transformation of things, or, as I would prefer to put it, let us say that they were originally devices for blocking off explanation. If they were valued as such, then their place in the cognitive scheme would make them eligible as means of legitimating social practices. (349–51)

Cohen's observations point to the ways in which myths highlight symbolic narratives that index the past and that short-circuit and bypass explanation, authorizing (often without good reason) the way people engage in the world. I, likewise, contend that cultural mythologies, spoken into existence, in the present, create tethers to the past.

This book examines a variety of cultural mythologies commonly leveraged against marginalized individuals. In welfare state literature, we see mythologies in what Hancock (2004) summarizes with the umbrella term *politics of disgust*. "Public identity," she argues, is "conditioned not simply by one's own speech and action but also by other's perception, interpretation, *and* manipulation—particularly for those citizens who lack political equality" (4). She describes how "socially constructed target populations" are, quoting Schneider and Ingram (1993), "the cultural characterizations of popular images of the persons or groups whose behavior and well-being are affected by public policy" (Schneider and Ingram, 1993, 443, cited in Hancock, 2004, 5). Using content analysis to investigate US welfare reform in 1996, she describes the public identity of welfare recipients through what I would call cultural mythologies around "laziness" and "fecundity," offensive generalizations "about Black women traceable to slavery" (Hancock, 2004, 6). Studies like these highlight the pervasiveness of cultural mythologies embedded into the fabric of social institutions, policy, the news, the courtroom. Educational research likewise examines cultural mythologies. Love's aforementioned work points to a variety of positive-sounding language (e.g., being gritty, working hard) that is in reality pejorative given the double standard of how the language is used: These words are disproportionately applied to and asked of Black and Brown people.

I was recently asked, "Aren't there any good cultural mythologies? Sometimes they can be good or helpful, right?" I think there are a few ways to answer this. Some cultural mythologies discussed in this book are immediately recognizable as negative, such as references to "laziness," "not working hard enough," and "taking advantage of the system." Of course, many mythologies can be helpful to one party while hurting another. In Ehrlich's (2010) study, cultural mythologies targeting female rape victims were weaponized by defense attorneys in an effort to exonerate defendants. Someone often benefits from the perpetuation of these kinds of broad cultural stereotypes.

Crucially, however, some cultural mythologies are well intentioned. While there are certainly examples of moments when exasperation and cynicism find traction in hurtful language, many examples in these chapters seem intended to be helpful. However, even the ones that seem positive are not. Certainly, "lazy" is a negative characterization or stance, and we might initially think that characterizing someone or a group as "hardworking" is good. However, as we know from the "model minority" cultural mythology, even mythologies that *sound* like praise aren't praise (Reyes, 2004). As Reyes explains,

> As the model minority stereotype later emerged explicitly during the Civil Rights Movement in the 1960s, scholars argued that the myth of the Asian American "success story" (U.S. News and World Report, 1966) was used not only to set a standard for how minorities should behave, but also to silence the accusations of racial injustice by communities of color (S. Lee 1996). Thus, the model minority myth upholds the American ideologies of meritocracy and individualism, diverts attention away from racial inequality, sustains whites in the racial hierarchy, and pits minority groups against each other. (174)

I often get the question: If the cultural mythologies around "laziness" in the United States go back to how Black people were treated and characterized during slavery, is not characterizing someone as "hardworking" just the other side of the same coin, applauding someone being "exceptional" given the more prevalent generalization of "laziness"? "Hardworking" functions to set apart, often as a note of surprise, someone who is an exception, who does not fit the more commonly applied cultural mythology. Perry (2011) explains it as follows: "When the normal state of people of color is assumed deficiency, then the departure from that state puts one into a 'state of exception'" (131). A similar case may explain the offensiveness of calling President Obama "articulate": This characterization is offense by omission because his speech is being pointed to as an exception to a "rule" (the rule, of course relating to erroneous, racist perceptions of Black people and language varieties used in the Black community) (Alim and Smitherman, 2012). The exception reifies the problem. While "lazy" is directly offensive, "hardworking" and those like it are indirectly offensive—looking like a compliment by setting someone or a small group aside as an example that does not fit, presumably, the larger negative cultural mythology, in this case the "lazy" stereotype. These cultural mythologies are being drawn upon in these chapters, and as this chapter investigates them at more depth, it is worth plumbing their depths a bit here.

I analyze these cultural mythologies by analyzing stance. DuBois (2007) says "one of the most important things we do with words is take a stance" (139). Examining stance allows us to (1) see how people position themselves and others with words, (2) show their perspectives and beliefs regarding particular ideas or people, (3) create value judgments, and (4) make evaluations. DuBois (2007) argues that stance is a "linguistically articulated form of social action whose meaning is to be construed within the broader scope of language, interaction, and sociocultural value" (139). Stances can communicate positions on emotions/feelings (affective stance) and on having/not having knowledge (epistemic stance). Personal pronouns help identify *who* the stance taker is. The object of the stance in this data tends to be whoever is in the "client" position or the responsibility under discussion. For example, when the shelter caseworker says, "I need you to get a TB test," the overall stance is linked to the deontic term ("need") through the personal pronoun ("I") and the stance object "you to get a TB test." DuBois offers the following thorough definition:

> Stance is a public act by a social actor, achieve dialogically through overt communicative means, of simultaneously evaluating objects,

> positioning subjects (self and others), and aligning with other subjects, with respect to any salient dimension of the sociocultural field. (163)

He summarizes this definition as "I evaluate something, and thereby position myself, and thereby align with you" (163). Here alignment could indicate agreement (alignment) or disagreement (disalignment).[6] While the most obvious stances refer to emotional states, and these do exist in the data, the most common stances in both data sets are those related to responsibility, cultural mythology, and time. Stances taken toward responsibility use deontic language to signal the obligation, generally nested in personal pronouns and an action (e.g., "You should've been—you were supposed to be leaving"). Stances that include cultural mythologies likewise use personal pronouns to link the stance taker with the person about whom they are taking a stance (e.g., "I'm letting you skate through the system"). Stances around time generally include the street-level worker taking a position on timelines and benchmarks (e.g., "He can't wait five months and say, 'I don't want to go'" or "This is the time in the semester when you have to work harder"). There are also affective stances that communicate emotional positions around perceptions of responsible/irresponsible behavior (e.g., "You are effing up your life. The heroin is gonna mess you up").

Time and Timescales: Looking Forward from the Present

This book is mindful of the reach and influence of time in both data collection and analysis of constructions of responsibility. The parameters for when I collected data were determined by the time-based benchmarks put in place by institutional policies: Unhoused people were "supposed" to be placed into housing with nine months,[7] and the semester timeline was used for students in the college reading course.[8] In the shelter context, I followed unhoused participants from shelter until their housing placement or until nine months had passed, and I observed the classroom for a semester.

From a data analysis perspective, there were widespread invocations of time vis-à-vis responsibility in both contexts. Street-level workers often referred to timelines and time-based benchmarks (e.g., "end of semester," "midterm," "nine months," "six months") for both unhoused people and students. The high-stakes test, if failed, can gatekeep students from the majority of classes at the college, and the individual benchmarks at the shelter, if flouted, can lead to sanctioning unhoused persons from shelter for thirty days or until they comply with requirements. These timelines and time-related benchmarks not only marked high-stakes performance assessments for those served by street-level workers but also, in the case of the shelter, marked salient assessments for the workers themselves. The shelter caseworkers' performance was, in part, reliant on client performance. In both cases, then, references to these timelines carried the weight of high-stakes assessments that could impact the livelihoods of the caseworkers, the clients, and the students. However, street-level workers did not just talk *about* time, but their constructions of responsibility also shifted *over* and *in relation to* time—over the course of the semester and over the course of individual caseworker-client cases (see Chapters 5 and 6).

Time functioned in yet another important way: Everything from the deontic formulations, to personal pronouns, to cultural mythologies, to the references to the timelines and benchmarks themselves are situated in time (when they are said) while also stretching backward and often forward in time. Workers often referenced future time-related benchmarks and policies, and the language used often harkened to past policies. Deontic formulations stretched backward to the assigned task or responsible action, as well as the policies that require them, and they stretched forward into the future as newly assigned tasks to be completed later. Even personal pronouns, which certainly stretch backward to their linguistic referents, also as part of the gestalt, connect people with future responsible actions, thereby sharing in some future orientation. Personal pronouns stretch back to their referents ("you" may refer back to "Michael," for example), and often with individuals who met over a series of months, these referents stretched back to prior meetings.

Cultural mythologies stretch backward to ideologies growing out of early English vagrancy laws and slavery that persevered in Jim Crow politics and Reagan-era "welfare queen" policies, language, and treatment. As Cohen (1969) so accurately noted, "One of the important functions of myth *is that it anchors the present in the past*" (4). Invoking these myths in the present points to their development and use in the landscape of the sociocultural and historical past, surely not isolated events but rather a litany of past events over time, threads of the past that knit together our cultural present. This gestalt is socially constructed in the interactional moment while also stretching backward and forward in time.

In Chapter 6, I argue that cultural mythologies also potentially stretch forward in time, as people carry the wounds of microaggressions around with them, as participants carry the public identities crafted in these institutional spaces into their everyday future lives. As one of my students said after reading a draft of Chapters 4 and 6, "I don't know, Professor. So many teachers have called me a lazy good-for-nothing over the years. It didn't even occur to me when I read the chapter that it wasn't true. I heard it so much, I figured I must be lazy" (personal communication, 2023). Marginalized people aren't called "lazy" once; they are called "lazy" hundreds or thousands of times, in myriad ways, from people, from policies, in social media. As Harper, a trans woman featured in the documentary *Will and Harper*, quips as they drive cross country, "The tweets are inside my head." One may endure transphobic vitriol on Twitter to live another day, but the language and the sentiments leave a mark. Some shred of them endures.

Building on Latour's (1999) actor network theory, Lemke (2000) suggests that it is useful to consider how different intersecting timescales circulate and become relevant in a particular institutional context. Lemke posits:

> Each scale of organization in an ecosocial system is an integration of fast, more local processes (i.e., activities, practices, doings, happenings) into longer-timescale, more global or extended networks. It is relative timescale that determines the probability and intensity of interdependence . . . and it is the circulation through the network of semiotic artifacts (i.e., books, buildings, bodies) that enables coordination between processes on radically different timescales. (275)

For Lemke, there are many intersecting timescales in any particular moment. Timescales are bounded by institutions, policies, and people, and many may simultaneously exist, overlap, and circulate in an institutional space. In a caseworker-client meeting, for example, a variety of timescales come together in that particular moment: the timescale of each policy and strategic plan, the timescale of each participant's lifetimes, the timescale of each participant's shelter time (how long the worker was employed, how long the man was in shelter), the timescale of the case length (which may differ from how long he was in this particular shelter), the timescales of the cultural mythologies stretching into the past—long past and more recent past, and timescales stretching into the future. Classroom settings, likewise, have a variety of timescales.

Lemke's (2000) work influenced a robust collection of studies in discourse analysis from which this book draws inspiration. Scollon and Scollon's (2004) nexus analysis, for example, offers a complex methodology that demonstrates how multiple timescales flow through a particular institutional interactional space. They aim to understand how one locale can serve as a nexus through which many discourses and timescales flow. Interactional ethnography also underscores the importance of watching talk unfold over time (e.g., Agar, 1986; Mehan, 1979). Matarese (2008) used nexus analysis to examine the way certain kinds of discourses circulated through the "nexus of practice" of the caseworker-client interaction over time. Inspired by Wortham's (2005) discourse analysis of student identities, which explored how various student identities are invoked over time, I aimed in this earlier work to understand how the timescales of performance measurements and benchmarks themselves intersected with and shaped constructions of responsibility over time in the nexus of practice: caseworker-client meetings.

The upcoming chapters, likewise, consider timescale essential to understanding street-level interaction. While Chapter 4 reveals how cultural mythologies in our talk stretch words backward in time, locking step with historical prejudices and beliefs, Chapters 5 and 6 take us forward in time in different ways. Soss, Fording, and Schram (2011) found that the social welfare caseworkers reported that performance measurements and assessments impacted their practice, and Chapter 5 in this book uses a discourse perspective to explore how performance benchmarks shape practice. Looking at both a single homeless client case unfolding over time as well as the frequency of constructions of responsibility over the course of three client cases, Chapter 5 explains exactly *how* performance measurements and assessment can shape the talk street-level workers use over the course of data collection.

If Chapter 5 considers the relevance of time passing during data collection, Chapter 6 confronts the weight of the gestalt of responsibility, repeatedly used over the course of data collection, as well as the weight participants carry with them as they leave those institutional spaces.

Chapters 4, 5 and 6 contribute the evolving work on timescale. In them I show how ideologies intersect with time, how talk about responsibility changes over time, and how constructions of responsibility accumulate over time, contributing to our understanding of how ideologies are reproduced, how work pressures change talk at the street level, and what responsibility-focused microaggressions are and how they function.

The importance of time in the data calls for a gentle revisioning of the gestalt, which may be better represented in Figure 2.2.

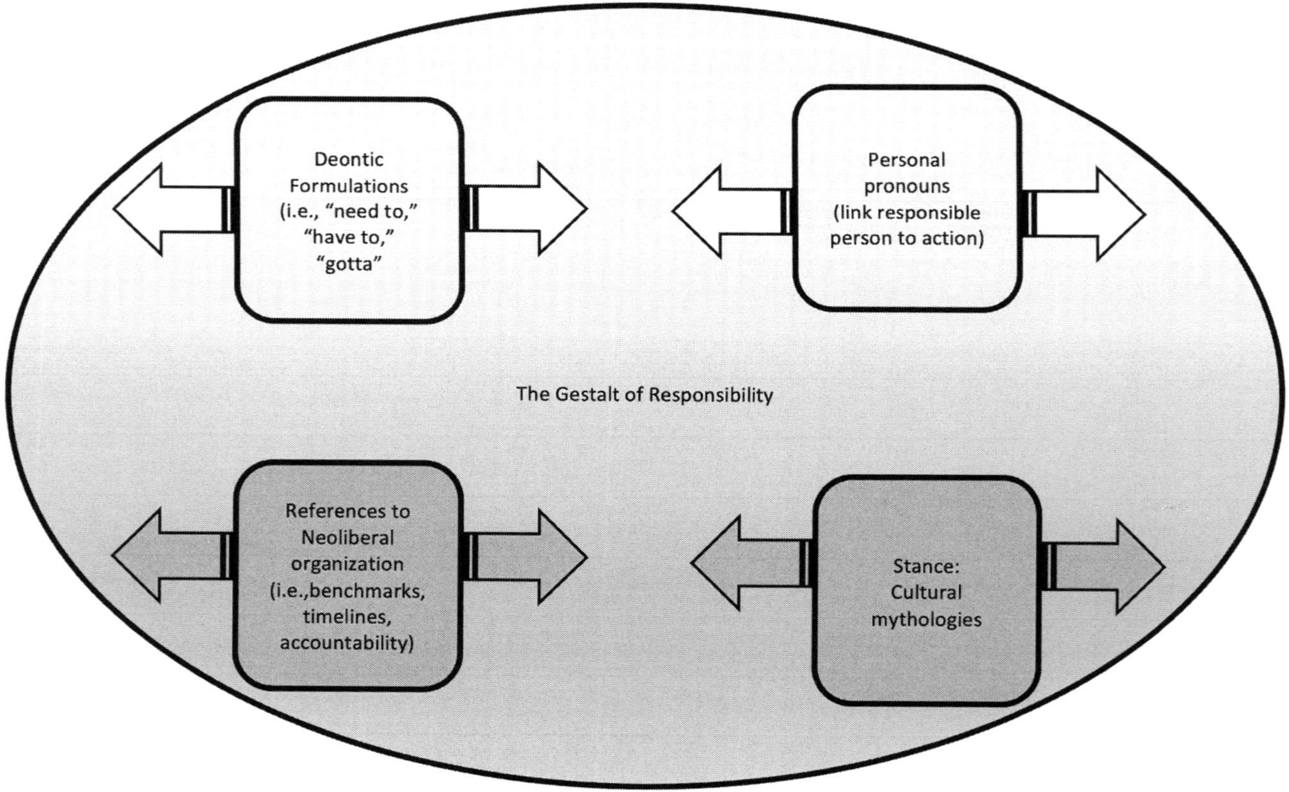

Fig. 2.2. The Expanded Gestalt of Responsibility

This diagram includes four boxes, one for each of the main aspects of discourse that collaboratively construct the gestalt of responsibility. There is a box for deontic formulations, one for personal pronouns, one for references to neoliberal organization (e.g., performance measurements, assessments, timelines, benchmarks), and one for cultural mythologies, which are often identified by stance markers. Grayscale color coding is used to highlight that deontic formulations and personal pronouns tend to be more grammatically oriented and references to neoliberalism and cultural mythological tend to be more lexical. Each of the four boxes has arrows extending to the left and right to demonstrate their connection to both past and future.

Research Participants, in Brief

This book describes interactional ethnographies conducted both in a New York City men's shelter and in a New York City community college. While this book focuses on the workers and their similar discursive practices, I want to briefly highlight the participants and what *they* share.

In Menken's (2008) study of English-language learners during No Child Left Behind, the education policy created and popularized during George W. Bush's presidency, she describes how Regents exams in New York City were only offered/translated into five languages, which leaves approximately 20 percent of English-language learners in the cold without translation support. She calls these students "the marginalized of the marginalized" (167). Both studies described in this book, likewise, involve "the marginalized of the marginalized," and perhaps even three nested "levels" of marginalization.

Most of my participants are Black and Brown people living in New York City, already experiencing racialized marginalization prior to entering a shelter or a community college. Being unhoused and being in community college (an institution often called thirteenth grade, aligning it more with high school than college) adds yet another layer to the marginal status. While homeless shelters seem like obvious spaces inhabited by marginal community members, community college are also stigmatizing and marginalizing for students and faculty. Indeed, Goldrick-Rabb et al. (2018) explain that food and housing insecurity is more commonly experienced by community college students countrywide than their peers in four-year colleges and universities.

These marginalized statuses are compounded by yet another layer of stigma and marginalization in both contexts. Most of my unhoused participants were labeled "hard to place" by the shelter. Their hard-to-place categorization signaled a variety of social, mental, physical, and legal challenges for each individual client that they carry around with them, in addition to being unhoused. They may have co-occurring mental health diagnoses and substance abuse issues. They may simply be undocumented immigrants. They may have been convicted of a crime that impacts their attractiveness to landlords or their suitability for living in proximity with others. Often hard-to-place shelter stayers were also considered "long-term stayers," individuals who had been in shelter nine months or more, and Matarese (2008) illustrated that long-term hard-to-place clients were spoken to differently than their short-term peers. By happenstance, the shelter space with the most participants also sheltered many hard-to-place unhoused men who became the focal point of this study, and I was able to track the discussions caseworkers had with these hard-to-place unhoused men, many of whom had lengthy stays in shelter, discursively over time.

Like the hard-to-place unhoused men, the remedial reading students at the community college experience yet another level of marginalization. As their CUNY placement exam categorizes them as underprepared for college-level reading, they are additionally stigmatized. Students placed in the Academic Critical Reading course are aware of the stigma of their placement. They are unable to register for most of the classes in their major, and anecdotally they are often spoken to differently than their non-ACR peers.

The participants in the two sets presented in this book share similarities in their condition outside of their marginal status: They are also the subject of street-level work. If street-level workers have "analytically similar work conditions" (Lipsky, 1980/2010, 4), then those they serve experience the various coping strategies that workers use to manage bursting caseloads. The people street-level workers serve often report feeling like a number; such impressions likely contribute to categorizations of workers as automatons, as described in Chapter 1. My research from the client side has highlighted the way in which client "resistance" may instead be viewed as client *insistence*. Matarese and van Nijnatten (2015) describe the discourse practices used by an unhoused man in shelter who rejects his caseworker's attempts to categorize him according to shelter values and categories. Instead, this unhoused client, insists on his own categories of "father" and "person with a disability" over those shelter-oriented categories offered by his caseworker (Matarese and van Nijnatten, 2015). This book does not focus on the stories of the clients, as other ethnographies of shelter life have done (cf. Desjarlais, 2011; Liebow, 1993); instead this book explores a position commonly voiced by those served by street-level workers: "I felt disrespected; I didn't like how I was spoken to." In examining how responsibility is constructed, this book provides some analytic heft to such anecdotal claims of disrespect, explaining in detail what does not work and why.

This book is unique. Bringing together a comparative study with an interactional focus, I demonstrate how responsibility unfolds in two kinds of street-level encounters. In so doing, I hope to highlight for the reader how workers introduce racialized cultural mythologies into these institutional encounters, how conversations around responsibility flexibly shift as workers respond to performance benchmarks and institutional timelines, and how these constructions of responsibility accrue like microaggressions. In so doing, these data contribute to our understanding of how street-level workers do their jobs and how performance assessments and timelines, so essential to current institutional practice, shape these encounters in meaningful ways. But perhaps most importantly, this book draws out some of the covert and subtle language of street-level encounters that can leave those served walking away feeling demeaned, misunderstood, and disrespected—language that has ties to institutional approaches that are known to create racial and class division, language that has ties to historically classist and racist ideology. Without necessarily meaning to, workers may be carrying these ideologies into their workplaces. This study asks us to be curious and reimagine these encounters.

3 | Constructing Responsibility in the Shelter

From Field Notes

Though I started working with the shelter and sampling in December 2006 and early January 2007, my first day collecting data at the shelter was in early February. It was bitterly cold. I arrived at the shelter around 7:30 a.m. each day, before work began properly. I climbed onto the New York City bus and headed for the shelter along a road that seemed more pothole than asphalt. I was so excited to begin collecting data. The bus pulled up in front of a large brick building with white columns, and on the sidewalk were droves of men waiting to get on the bus, many of whom wished me good morning. There were many men in wheelchairs waiting, and I said good morning to some of them, slapping hands with a couple of the men I knew. I then headed inside to check in, get my visitor's badge, and sign into their registry in the front office. After signing in and greeting the attendant behind the desk, I headed out the back door, toward the second building of the shelter where I would conduct my first observation and recording. In the second building, I also had to register, so I signed in and walked through the double doors to the caseworkers' offices and walked down the long, crooked space of the shelter toward Ms. Innis's office, a caseworker (offices seemed an afterthought of the building, they were so often in odd shapes with faux walls that were not like the painted concrete of the shelter). She was not yet in, so I sat and waited.

When she arrived, she ushered me into her office, and I sat down and set up my recorder for her meeting with a client we'll call Hernando, whom I had met only once when I discussed the study and consent process with him. Hernando came to the office on time and lightly settled into the chair on the opposite side of Ms. Innis's desk. He was short, lithe, and friendly. He smiled broadly, and handed Ms. Innis a sheet of paper. "For you," he said. "I got it," Ms. Innis replied, "Hernando?" Hernando, possibly trying to explain the relevance of the paper, replied in Spanish, "y" ("and"). However, Ms. Innis did not acknowledge his attempt to explain and instead said, "Hernando, I don't want to see any of that stuff right now. I need you to do stuff for me, and you keep showing me appointments." He didn't seem to understand her and offered an explanation, partially in Spanish. She then asked him multiple times, "Is your PA on?" without receiving a response, and he told her, "I don't understand, Miss." Her response was exasperated and she shouted, "PA! Public assistance! Your welfare! What are you *talking* about?!" Lowering her voice, she repeated "Listen to me" several times before saying, "And stop pretending like you don't speak English 'cause I know you do. Okay? . . . Words you don't understand, that stuff, I don't want to hear about it." Hernando apologized repeatedly and sighed audibly through his nose. I was struck by Ms. Innis's rejection of his claim to not understand her, as he obviously had limited proficiency in English, and I, myself, took a beat to understand what "Is your PA on?" meant. To a novice's ears it sounded like "Is your pee a on." I was surprised that she rejected his offer of paperwork, telling him that she did not want it and instead wanted him to "do stuff for" her. It seemed strange to me that she had not stated that he needed to do this to help move himself forward but rather for her. Who was in need here, the client or the caseworker?

Analyzing Responsibility in Discourse

The terms *responsibility* and *accountability* are often used interchangeably in the discourse analysis literature, but I suggest that they should be explored as related but separate interactional moments. Just as a conversational turn often includes a first-pair part (e.g., "Hi, how are you?") and a second-pair part (e.g., "Good, and you?"), responsibility and accountability I like to view as two parts of a whole where the construction of responsibility action comes first (i.e., "I need you to get a tuberculosis test") and accountability comes second ("I didn't get it because I was busy").

In discourse analysis, accounts[1] are the words people use to address some untoward behavior. For example, were I to accuse my friend of not getting me a coffee ("Dude, you didn't get *me* coffee?"), he might provide an account ("Ugh—I didn't know you were here today") in order to provide an excuse or justification for his behavior. Buttny (1993) argues that responsibility is commonly synonymous with being accountable. As Goffman observes, "The question of responsibility must be raised . . . for without knowing how those involved in an act attribute responsibility for it, we cannot in the last analysis know what it is that has occurred' (1971, 99). Accounts demonstrate how people address their own responsibility, often vis-à-vis other factors, addressing "unanticipated or untoward behavior. . . . bridg[ing] the gap between action and expectation . . . throw[ing] bridges between the promised and the performed" (Scott and Lyman 1968, 46). Buttny (1993) suggests "accounts involve talk designed to recast [a] pejorative significance of action, or one's responsibility for it, and thereby transform other's negative evaluations" (1). Accounts soften or "neutralise" (Scott and Lyman, 1968, 46) what is considered deviant behavior. Goffman (1981) explains that *offerings*—accounts that a speaker makes in the way of apology, explanation, or excuse—may be used to maintain affiliation and alignment with an interlocutor. In other words, accounts help people save face.

Accounts are generally broken into two common types: excuses and justifications. The former admits "the negative significance of the event, but [denies] all or some of the actor's responsibility for it," while the latter "involve claims in which the actor implicitly accepts responsibility, but denies the offensive character of the event in question" (Buttny, 1993, 16). Excuses deny responsibility and displace blame; justifications can accept responsibility but reject the premise. Buttny (1993) also discusses a less common third type—scapegoating—in which responsibility is redirected to another person.

Accounts also are used to make moral judgments of various types. In a very basic sense, people in conversation have a moral obligation to maintain conversational rules and account for broken rules (Robinson, 2016). In that perspective, individuals are held morally responsible for saying the right thing at the right time, abiding by "relevance rules" for everyday conversational participation. Whatever the cultural and discursive norms are, we are expected to play by those unwritten rules. For instance, if someone says, "I love you" and you respond in any way other than an immediate "I love you too"—perhaps you pause too long before responding or you say, "Oh, you know how I feel"—you're usually in some hot water (unless you're the dashing Han Solo in *The Empire Strikes Back*) that would require some moral work that accounts for why you did not respond in kind.

However, accounts also often involve other kinds of moral work. Scott and Lyman (1970) eloquently explain that "between the promised and the performed, between the expected and the actual, falls the shadow of deviance" (90). While accounts explain violations of social protocol (e.g., missing an appointment, misunderstanding someone), Scott and Lyman also identify a slippery slope in which untoward *behavior* leads to categorizations of a *person* as deviant, providing examples of stances like "queer," "junkie," and "troublemaker" (91). They argue that

> deviant acts are linked to an imputed mental element said to reside "inside" the action, so that presumably he knows (or can be made to know) the reasons for which he acts and the reasons for which he might restrain or inhibit his behavior. (91)

When an account is offered and accepted, they argue that the "deviance has been neutralized" (91). Buttny (1993), likewise, argues that accounts are responses to moments of blaming and/or being held responsible for actions, both of which can take on a moral component as the behavior is determined to be "good" or "bad." In not so many words, the discursive practice of accounting is linked to what many scholars call "categorizations," what this book refers to as "stance." In these moments, speakers take a position on their untoward behavior and categorize themselves vis-à-vis the circumstances.

Many scholars have examined accountability through the lens of moral categorization, analyzing how clients are categorized as "good" or "bad" by social workers, other clients, and relatives of clients (Hall et al., 2006; Juhila 2004; Slembrouck and Hall, 2003; White and Stancombe, 2003; White 2003). White and Stancombe (2003) argue that the way in which social work clients are discursively constructed is a moral act, suggesting that service providers and professionals are "moral actors" who construct themselves and their clients according to moral standards (93). Hall, Slembrouck, and Sarangi (2006) analyze moral categorizations in the child welfare context. They found attributions of blame and categorization working together to accomplish moral accountability. The discursive connection between accountability and categorization has been explored at length in social welfare research. Hall, Slembrouck, and Sarangi (2006) note that categorizations, "a set of processes which result in facts, opinions, or circumstances being established as one type of category or another," are part of how social workers substantiate claims for whatever services the person may need (15). They argue that social workers' categorizations of clients ("good" client, "bad" client, etc.) lead to subsequent accounts (excuses or justifications) that justify those categorizations.

While there is an obvious bent toward exploring the practitioner's categorizations, there is also ample literature explaining how social work clients use accounts to reject or justify social worker's categorizations. Mäkitalo (2006) finds that both social workers and clients use accounts for different reasons in social welfare interaction. She notes that clients "must demonstrate their awareness of the failure to meet particular institutional expectations" (551). In so doing, she shows how clients both need to explain themselves (account) and recategorize themselves (e.g., from "bad client" to "good client"). Moral categorizations and accounting are deeply entrenched in social welfare and are evidenced through their copresence in both social worker and client discourse. Accountability and accounts may also be used by workers to justify their categorizations (e.g., workers may provide justification for why they denied a client benefits, talk that may include both an account and a negative categorization of the client).

This is, however, by no means an exhaustive exploration of accounting literature. My reason for reviewing it, albeit briefly, is to highlight that while there is ample literature on accounts, very little research has examined how responsibility itself is constructed—the language that prompts an account. Analyzing accountability to understand how responsibility itself is constructed is a little like analyzing the "yummy" sounds people make in order to understand the ingredients of the cake they just ate. Accounts are important, and certainly part of the complex series of segments that create constructions of responsibility, but there is more to responsibility than accounts alone. While the analyses in these chapters refer to accounts, my emphasis is on these initiations of responsibility, how responsibility itself is generated through discourse. This research builds on existing accounting research, reinforcing the connection between responsibility, moral stances, and categories that index particular cultural mythologies.

What do we know about the construction of responsibility itself?[2] Well, we know that "responsibility" used to be a more flexible term with negative and positive meanings. Citing Jonas (1984), Östman and Solin (2016) make a distinction between "formal" responsibility (being accountable for what we do) and "substantial" responsibility (committing to future deeds). Drawing on Harmon (1995), Östman and Solin (2016) in their edited volume *Discourse and Responsibility in Professional Setting* note that *responsible* is often used synonymously with *blameworthy*, though Lakoff (2016) argues that "reliable" and "trustworthy" are also used (21). In order to make better sense of how responsibility evidences itself, scholars have attempted to characterize its various nuances. Östman and Solin (2016) draw out differences between moral and legal responsibility, in which moral "mark[s] out the things that are wrong for anyone" (Baier, 1970, 104, cited in Östman and Solin, 2016, 5). The legal variety refers to "a person's accountability to others because he or she has contracted particular duties or responsibilities" (5). In the shelter system, however, these responsibilities seem to eclipse each other, as people are tasked with particular actions and held accountable for them (legal responsibility), but those same tasks are ones that large swaths of society feel adults should be able to accomplish without any help (moral responsibility). This is likely also the case with literacy in the community college, in which incoming students are expected to have college-ready reading skills.

Others agree that constructions of responsibility involve a cluster of discursive features. Though he does not refer to them as constellations or a gestalt, Sarangi (2016) identifies a group of features that together explain how responsibility is constructed in genetic testing interactions. He characterizes responsibilities as they relate to roles (e.g., "parental responsibility") agency (who is responsible), accounts (excuses/justifications of why one wasn't responsible), intentionality (often established through personal pronouns), and self-other relations (as a person X is usually responsible to person Y) as established through the talk. Moreover, though his work explores intraprofessional talk in which workers describe the division of responsible labor, or "zones of responsibility," agency is also central to Atkinson's (1999) research. He describes "how actors' work and the work of others are structured in accordance with the attribution of agency and responsibility" (99). Notwithstanding terminology, Atkinson (1999) and Sarangi (2016) each emphasize the importance of a clustering of features that together generate responsibility. This book builds on this important observation, arguing that constructions of responsibility, while they may exist on their own, also exist in constellations of discourse features that take on new meaning when in concert with one another, a gestalt of responsibility.

Pomerantz (1978) argues that constructions of responsibility come in two segments that work together to formulate the attribution: an "unhappy incident" and an "attribution of responsibility." She demonstrates how an interlocutor makes a statement about an unfortunate prior incident (e.g., "I was late to your wedding"), withholding a blame-making statement that implicates an actor until after they have described the incident ("because you gave me poor directions"). These sequences, then, require a brief narrative, a statement of blame, and place to situate that blame (usually a person). The subsequent chapters of the book examine how responsibility is constructed in the present moment. While some of these constructions refer to past "failings" through segments describing "unhappy incidents" (Pomerantz, 1978), most of them include both attributions of blame and new constructions of responsibility, as the task is reassigned.

Taking this analysis of "causation and culpability" into the child welfare social context, White (2003, 183) notes that while children are generally exempt from being "blamed," the professional staff are characterized as less blameworthy than mothers, and mothers are viewed as less blameworthy than fathers. She suggests that participants either construct themselves as "good" parents who are seeking expert assistance in dealing with their child or admit that they have been irresponsible but try to positively spin the story by suggesting that their request for professional assistance shows how they want to improve as parents. While her analysis stems from an interest in solving social welfare concerns rather than linguistic ones, White adds an invaluable layer to the problem of analyzing how responsibility is constructed: the social and policy context. She explains how evidence-based practices (the belief that practitioner work should be based on results of scientific study) present social worker decision-making as objective and scientific, while in reality workers privilege the stories and accounts of some participants over others, with some having more moral weight than others. As established in the introduction of this book, street-level workers are not automatons. Rather, they use discretion to make decisions about which stories and accounts have credibility, who is blameworthy and who is not. The subsequent chapters include examples of this as well, whether it is a professor believing that students' tiredness is more likely due to late-night television watching rather doing homework or whether it is a shelter caseworker questioning the veracity of a client's account for why he missed a meeting.

Bringing institutional contexts and the larger sociopolitical context to bear, Juhila, Raitakari, and Hall (2017) explore responsibilization in social work from a discourse perspective, drawing on O'Malley (2009), who coined "responsibilization" to explain assigned obligations within a neoliberal, new managerialist era in social welfare. Using keyword analysis of social work interaction, they found constructions of client responsibility in client-worker and case planning meetings and evidence of worker responsibility in focus groups, team meetings, and interviews. Their landmark research identified constructions of responsibility in instances of advanced liberalism-adjacent vocabulary (e.g., "participation," "consumerism," "recovery"). I am greatly indebted to their work, an expansive contrastive text that focuses on specific approaches to responsibilization as evidenced through discourse.

Atkinson (1999), Juhila, Raitakari, and Hall (2017), Pomerantz (1978), Sarangi (2016), and White (2003) all seem to agree on the importance of agency, of a subject on which attributions of responsibility rest. They, moreover, agree that constructions of responsibility are complex, involving an interaction between linguistic elements, and they admit to the presence of moral weight, whether characterized by blame or a categorization of a person as "good" or "bad." White (2003) and Juhila, Raitakari, and Hall (2017) underscore the importance of understanding how responsibility is constructed in light of institutional, disciplinary, and sociopolitical demands. From these studies, I draw the emphasis on responsibility as a many-headed beast, an awareness that where responsibility surfaces, blame is rarely far behind, and that the social context is integral. Östman and Solin (2016) argue in their edited volume *Discourse and Responsibility in Professional Settings* that "explicit references to the concept responsibility are scarce in the [discourse] literature. The concept thus clearly needs to be lifted up and be dealt with on its own terms" (4). The following chapters aim to do just that. Chapters 3 and 4 explore this many-headed hydra. While Chapter 3 provides an illustration of the pieces of the gestalt of responsibility as evidenced in the shelter data, Chapter 4 focuses on one of the more problematic aspects of the gestalt: cultural mythologies as they surfaced in the community college setting.

Qualitative Views of Unhoused People and Shelter Life

It is important to begin with a useful distinction: I am presenting this less as an ethnography of "homelessness" and more as an ethnography of street-level worker talk in a shelter context. This book and this study cannot "solve" the "homelessness problem." That said, the data presented are illustrative of what some unhoused people in the shelter context experience, and these data help shape our collective rethinking of what speaking to unhoused people with dignity and respect looks like. As a friend who was unhoused multiple times explained to me, "You are representing us by showing the kind of talk we endure from shelter staff on a daily basis." Still, the takeaway from this work is *for* street-level workers and administrators *about* how they speak to unhoused people and others who are marginalized and how institutional pressures shape that talk. Even so, it is useful to briefly review ethnographic research on "homelessness."

Hopper (2003) summarized "ethnographies of homelessness . . . along three axes of interest: clinical, subsistence, and literary. In varying proportions, these concerns—with damage, with resourcefulness, and with wrested significance—have shaped our inquiries" (207). His review of the literature addresses a variety of issues that have captivated anthropologists: the "institutionalization" of unhoused men, the challenges of and strategies for living on the street, and required resourcefulness of street life, social supports outside of the shelters and invented/created resources (e.g., tent cities), ethics of street living, cultivation and assertion of identity.

Qualitative research on homelessness has traditionally been the work of anthropologists and a very few linguists. Beginning in the mid to late 1970s and early 1980s, research on homelessness boomed. Among those, many studies center around dignity. As Hopper (2003) says, summarizing Liebow's (1993) ethnography that tells the stories of unhoused women in emergency shelters outside of Washington, DC, "Liebow's tacit argument is a fiercely moral one: Forget about how they got there, no one deserved to be treated like this" (206). Liebow (1993) examines "the dynamics of shelter life" as well as "how these women remained human in the face of inhuman conditions" (1). Similarly, Kozol's (2011) *Rachel and Her Children* explores the experiences of unhoused people, ultimately toppling popular stereotypes by demonstrating how the trope of *unhoused people with psychiatric illness and substance abuse issues* inaccurately represent the reality: the largest growing unhoused community was families with children.

Some ethnographers accessed "dignity" vis-à-vis analyses of unhoused peoples' agency and identify formation. Snow and Anderson (1987), for example, aim to

> advance understanding of the manner in which individuals at the lowest reaches of status systems attempt to generate identities that provide them with a measure of self-worth and dignity and to shed additional empirical light on the relationships among role, identity, and self-concept. (1338)

Using ethnographic methods, discourse analysis of recorded interaction, and some quantitative statistical measures, they find three primary identity markers used among unhoused people in Texas: (1) distancing language, (2) solidarity language (e.g., embracing the roles of "bum" and "dumpster diver") (1354–55), and (3) language used to tell tall tales or embellish stories. Distancing often combined pronoun and deictic marker use with social categories and negative markers (e.g., "I'm not like that guy"), but also included distancing from the shelters and other helping institutions and from common social roles associated with unhoused people. Unhoused people, likewise, sometimes claimed particular roles, taking ownership of categories like "bum" and using them to create solidarity and in-group membership. Using discourse analysis of social interaction,

Juhila (2004) offers similar findings by examining how unhoused people refer to, but are at the same time critical of, their "stigmatized identities," which some clients attempt to replace with more equitable ways of representing themselves and the shelter (259). Dejarlais (1996) investigates dignity vis-à-vis a critique of the language that indexes power structures inherent in shelter roles. Shelter workers in his study, though caring, used more direct speech, while clients used more indirect speech to assert their needs while saving face. Desjerlais (1994) accomplishes similar work with unhoused people in a New England shelter for mental illness, theorizing their understanding of their "experience."

Hopper (2003), while noting the importance of studies that document unhoused people's experiences, also makes a case for more anthropologies of unhoused people that directly impact policy and practice: "I'm suggesting that it is time for the ethnography of homelessness to extend itself into the realm of defensible reforms" (Hopper, 2003, 210). We need to think about whether our work is helping solve any number of real problems. Hopper's (2003) work, whether examining unhoused people in airports or the on the streets of New York City during the yearly count, is richly steeped in the historical and sociopolitical contemporary context, using ethnography to consider "homelessness" from all sides. He makes the case for the relevance of ethnography in helping address the crisis of homelessness, underscoring that such studies should investigate questions that result in practical change. As he says, "An ethnographic corrective—to stereotypes, to psychiatric imperialism, to the presumed sufficiencies of the welfare state—is one thing; an active, engaged ethnography of how this present mess might be corrected (or improved on) would be quite another" (211).

This chapter aims to draw together an interest in protecting the dignity of unhoused people with a practical analysis of talk around responsibility by shelter caseworkers both in the interactional moment and over time, resulting in very real recommendations for changes in practice. These findings will not solve the crisis of homelessness, but they may address how we can bring dignity to the everyday experiences of unhoused people in shelter and other marginalized people, and how we can be cognizant of how institutional pressures can materially shape practice on the street level.

Responsibility Policy in the New York City Shelter System

Prior to 2002–2003, most New York City shelters addressed personal challenges (e.g., drug addiction, mental illness, co-occurring illnesses) before locating housing placements. However, due to unprecedented increases in homeless individuals on the streets and in shelters (approximately 37,319 total in 2004 according to online statistics), New York City shifted its approach. In 2002, Mayor Michael Bloomberg and Department of Homeless Services (DHS) commissioner Linda Gibbs introduced a ten-year plan for reducing homelessness in New York City. Bloomberg then accelerated the timeframe in 2004 to a five-year plan called Uniting for Solutions Beyond Shelter. I collected my dissertation data between 2005 and 2006, when these plans were in the process of being activated. This five-year plan was intended to "end chronic homelessness and reduce the shelter population by two-thirds in five years" in part by placing the current shelter population into stable, permanent housing (DHS, 2004, 1). Both the ten-year and the five-year plans, while addressing a variety of other interventions such as community-centered homelessness prevention and eviction prevention centers, also described how to reduce the numbers of homeless individuals in city shelters, making the shelters into more transitory, temporary spaces. The policies emphasized increased client and caseworker responsibility and used accountability protocols to more quickly house clients, particularly "long-term stayers" who stayed in shelter longer periods of time and often faced difficulty in finding and/or securing placement.

The plan, undergirded by philosophical positions widely acknowledged by the social welfare literature (see Chapter 1) as a dramatic shift in perspective, called for a revolutionary "paradigm shift"[3] in the culture of homelessness and shelter in New York City. We can see evidence of this shift in both public statements and policies/strategic plan excerpts below. Preparing the city for this shift, Mayor Bloomberg (2004) stated,

> I also want to stress that everyone being helped in these programs will also be expected to take as active a part as they can in the job of keeping or finding permanent homes. That is not an easy process. It can be frightening; it can require profound changes in personal behavior and habits. We will do what we can to lessen the anxieties involved. But there is also no greater personal satisfaction possible than taking charge of one's own life, and building a foundation of stability for one's self and one's own children. We're going to make sure that everyone who can, has an opportunity to experience those rewards. . . . Rapidly moving people who enter the shelter system into permanent housing will also become a major priority. This goal involves redefining the culture and practices of agencies in the homeless system. Accountability is key to achieving that paradigm

> shift. New performance standards will be set and enforced. And new client-monitoring tools will permit the staff in shelters to identify the people whose stays in shelter are lengthy, why that's the case, and help them determine if and how those stays can be shortened.

Likewise, the NYC Department of Homeless Services 2002 plan overtly referred to responsibility for homeless single adults and families:

> Individuals and families must be responsible for achieving independence, and must be informed on how they are accountable for completing service plans, and how those expectations relate to securing permanent housing. (DHS, 2002, 5)

The mission statement from 2002 includes similar references to individual responsibility:

> The Department of Homeless Services, in partnership with public and private agencies, provides temporary emergency shelter for eligible homeless people in a safe, supportive environment. In an atmosphere of cooperation and respect, we deliver services through a continuum of care, where the client assumes responsibility for achieving the goal of independent living. (DHS, 2002, 9)

Moreover, responsibility continued to be overtly mentioned in the 2004 "Uniting for Solutions Beyond Shelter" action plan for NYC shelters. The plan characterized shelter prior to the new protocols as suffering from a somewhat chaotic lack of clarity regarding roles and responsibilities:

> Individuals and providers do not at this time benefit from clearly defined roles and responsibilities that ensure that expectations are clear and best outcomes achieved, as prevention services are received and administered. (DHS, 2004, 16)

In light of that trend, DHS intended to take the following action with the 2004 NYC homeless services action plan:

> Standards of mutual responsibility will be introduced in homeless prevention programs. A principle will be established that individuals and families receiving prevention services must partici-

> pate and take responsible action to the extent they are capable. (DHS, 2004, 16)

It is worth noting here that responsibility is asked of both caseworkers and clients, though the policy singles clients out as needing "to actively participate in the development and implementation of their independent living plans" (DHS, 2004, 23). The five-year plan goes on to discuss client behavior in responsible terms, including explicitly noting procedures being developed that would sanction clients deemed able but unwilling to meet shelter regulations or those who "unreasonably refuse housing or engage in dangerous behavior" (DHS, 2002, 23). Overall, these policies outlined new responsibilities for homeless clients and shelter caseworkers, as well as new accountability-oriented performance measurement protocols for assessing caseworkers' and clients' successful completion of tasks. The policies defined benchmarks limiting clients to a nine-month stay in shelter. Those clients who exceeded the benchmark were more aggressively case-managed (meeting more frequently with their caseworkers and more strongly encouraged to complete tasks that lead to housing); therefore, long-term staying clients were among the first encouraged by their caseworkers to find housing quickly and leave shelter.

According to the policies, caseworkers were responsible for discussing the client responsibility policy with each client. This policy provided legal support to the Independent Living Plan (ILP), such that if a client did not take the minimal steps toward moving from shelter, he could receive an ILP violation, which served as a warning from his case manager. A second instance of noncompliance could result in a sanction, which would prohibit him from utilizing any shelter in the system for a minimum of thirty days or until he complied with his ILP (whichever was longer) (DHS 2002, 2004).[4] While discussing and enforcing the client responsibility protocol was part of a caseworker's responsibility, for clients it served as motivation to complete assigned tasks. Client responsibility was most often supported, motivated, and accounted for in individual meetings between caseworkers and clients, during which they discussed the client's progression along his ILP, the service plan that formed a contract between the client and the caseworker and detailed the tasks a client was obligated to complete as he moved toward leaving shelter. DHS maintains that the ILP document should be tailored to the specific circumstances of the client and be based on the client's housing and housing-related needs (DHS personal communication, 2008); therefore, case managers were meant to ensure that the unique characteristics and service needs of each client were kept in mind when developing the ILP with the client. Given the pressures on street-level workers, this can be sometimes difficult to accomplish in the face of large caseloads (Lipsky, 1980/2010) and performance assessments and benchmarks (Soss et al., 2011). The client responsibility policy requires that ILPs be renewed once a month, and the case manager and client can renew ILP goals more frequently if necessary. When clients were deemed "hard to place," they and their caseworkers often met every week. DHS policies stipulated that the ILP form a contract between the client and the shelter provider, usually including stipulations such as asking that the client comply with shelter rules and regulations, secure income through employment or cash benefit assistance, continue with any treatments he may require, and seek and accept first available and "appropriate" housing.[5] Policies require the client to meet with his caseworker in order to determine whether the goals of the ILP (as described above) are satisfied. According to the Department of Homeless Services, client and case manager personal responsibility has always been essential to overcoming homelessness, but until the paradigm shift it was difficult to enforce (DHS, personal communication, 2008). Principles articulated in DHS's 2002 and 2004 plans sought to connect responsibility and accountability to sanctioning procedures that were meant to enforce clarified rules around responsibilities and roles.

As Soss, Fording, and Schram (2011) explain, if clients do not complete required tasks, they potentially reduce the placement success of their caseworkers, who were held accountable by the administration for recurrent unsuccessful cases. In many ways, their responsibilities were tied to each other, which occasionally becomes evident in how responsibility is constructed in their discourse. These interactions between the caseworker and client, therefore, become what Scollon and Scollon (2004) call the "nexus of practice," a place through which responsibilities are discussed, ILPs are reviewed and signed, progress toward housing is made, and policy—through the discretionary actions of street-level workers—is talked into being.

When I collected nine months of caseworker-client meetings at the shelter, I assumed I would find language that more directly reflected what was stated in the policies. However, upon entering more than one thousand pages of transcripts into Nvivo, a qualitative data analysis software, I found not one use of the words "responsible," "accountable," or related permutations (e.g., "accountability," etc.). It was the lack of such language that led me to Lipsky's (1980/2010) work *Street-Level Bureaucracy* and the relevance of discretion in street-level encounters. Street-level workers are not beholden to use the language of the policy when they speak to clients. While I had originally considered discretion to be a phenomenon above language, a worker making the choice to help one client over another, for example, the language workers use is also discretionary. Street-level workers get to choose how they talk about policy. Just as street-level workers' discretionary actions add up to policy, according to Lipsky (1980/2010), perhaps their collective use of language also constitutes policy. If this is the case, it behooves us to examine the language they are using in order to ascertain whether the policy they collectively speak into action is a good one.

Fieldwork During the Day[6]

In the morning, the lobby of the shelter was chock full of men, many of them lined up for breakfast in the cafeteria to the left. At one end of the lobby was a pair of double doors guarded by security; these doors opened into a wide, blue-gray hallway that included entry points for four dormitories, entry points for several small cubicled office spaces, and a storage room. The unhoused men being sheltered were not allowed beyond those double doors during the day unless they had appointments with their caseworkers, so by the time I arrived around 9:00 a.m., most of the men had left for the day for work or school, were eating breakfast in the cafeteria, or were in the large lobby area. If I wasn't in one of the caseworker's offices recording or interviewing a client, I spent time in the common area. If the weather was pleasant, some men might gather to play dominos outside. During what was a particularly snowy, bitter winter when I collected my data, many opted to stay inside. There was always a large block of about fifty folding chairs in the common area, and in the afternoon, Jerry Springer was always on the small TV, pushing couples into revealing how a one-night stand, confirmed by DNA test, proved that "George" was absolutely *not* the baby's father. The couples would start throwing punches and pulling hair, and the unhoused men in folding chairs cheered on their favorites and chided the cheaters. Sounds of sucked teeth followed our holding our breath in anticipation. I spent a surprising amount of my downtime in the lobby chit chatting with the men, watching Jerry with those waiting for appointments, sharing in a moment of collective schadenfreude. If someone was waiting for an appointment, either the caseworker would come collect him or he showed his appointment slip to security to be allowed into the dormitory/office area at the time of his appointment. As some meetings began en route to the caseworker's office,

I often walked with the caseworkers in the morning, audio recorder in hand and field notebook under my arm, in order to ensure that I caught meetings when they actually began.

The clients' dorms were large rooms filled with, at the time, hundreds of beds, which were often partitioned for a sliver of privacy with waist-high concrete dividers, and lockers. Most of the rooms were relatively clean. Some unhoused men served in a work program that paid them for doing janitorial jobs around the building. Despite the tidy appearance of the dorms, it was also well known that even in sections of the shelter that were partitioned as "clean wings," drug deals and substance abuse occurred, according to clients. While I received a tour of these spaces when I first arrived, I stayed in public "common room" areas, the TV lobby, the cafeteria, and caseworkers' offices/cubicles when conducting fieldwork and when recording interaction at the shelter unless escorted by a caseworker and a security guard.

Speaking generally, case management[7] is different from social work, as many readers probably already know. While social work generally requires a master's in social work (MSW), caseworkers are often individuals with undergraduate degrees in human services or sociology, and some of my participants were in the process of getting a master's degree. Soss, Fording, and Schram (2011) summarize casework as follows:

> Case managers occupy a role that blends conventional features of the street-level bureaucrat with a more therapeutic role. To be sure, their jobs bear little resemblance to that of a psychologist or social work professional: They do not possess resources, expertise, or powers of diagnosis and action on anything like that scale. Case managers get little training and have few tools at their disposal. They use their discretion mainly to ration time and resources, offer small favors, control their caseloads, and make decisions about whom to penalize or "cut some slack." (233)

Casework involves more than just meetings with their clients.[8] In this shelter, case managers also met with social workers, psychologists, and administrators. They made countless phone calls to coordinate "client" care. They wrote accounts of each unhoused person's meeting, which were included in a "chart," which, much like a patient's chart at the doctor's office, reviewed each client's entire history at the shelter, including individual meetings and ILPs—a client's service plan. Caseworkers' charts were audited several times a year, during which time each chart was assessed by their supervisor, and caseworkers were given a score that revealed their achievement in keeping these charts up to date and keeping the men moving toward housing. Whenever those periods of assessment occurred, caseworkers were visibly anxious, telling me and the clients how late they would be staying after hours in order to complete the charts.

The majority of the casework staff I worked with, as recorded in my field notes, began their mornings running slightly late: clocking in inside the main intake office, being accosted in the lobby by a string of clients on their way to the cubicles in the back, grabbing the needed client files for the day from the file office, checking their email, gabbing with colleagues and staff, filling Thermoses with coffee, and changing into comfortable work shoes, which many of them kept stockpiled under their desks. Daytime casework at the shelter was often complicated by last-minute meetings or trainings of which the caseworkers were not made aware until after they had sent out the appointment slips for clients to meet with them. Therefore, sometimes caseworkers would not be at their offices during scheduled appointments with their clients, and those unhoused men often reciprocated the perceived lack of attention by missing subsequent scheduled meetings. Caseworkers also had high or challenging caseloads and occasionally forgot scheduled appointments, and unhoused people staying in the shelters missed meetings for any number of reasons. Caseworkers I worked with were often backed up and running late, pushing a 9:00 a.m. scheduled meeting to 11:00 a.m. or noon.

Fieldwork at Night

Around 5:00 p.m., caseworkers not working the evening shift, which lasted until 9:00 or 10:00 p.m., packed up to head home or to evening undergraduate or master's program classes in public administration, social work, or public health, and those who worked late were preparing for "lunch," which they took around six o'clock.[9] The shelter lobby would be moderately crowded with unhoused men preparing to get in line for dinner in the cafeteria, but the long back spaces of the shelter were also very active, as those who stayed there were allowed back in at 5:00 p.m. Some clients were showering before dinner, sleeping, or hanging out in the dormitory; others were watching evening reality TV, playing pool or dominos; and still others were waiting for an appointment with their caseworker.

Evening casework was for the most part unfettered by staff meetings and trainings. Casework began slowly in the evening and, as the time neared 10:00 p.m., became rushed and harried. All clients were required to sign in for their beds by 10:00 p.m.; otherwise they lost their bed, and it was given to someone else who was present, needed a bed, and had not yet had one assigned. However, when appointments were not kept, a caseworker would often put a client's bed "on hold," not allowing him to sign in for his bed and claim it until he had met with the caseworker. Nighttime appointments were, therefore, usually kept because of this quid pro quo arrangement. This ensured that the caseworker met with the client, but it often meant that the meeting was short because there was limited time between when the client arrived at the shelter and the sign-in time at 10:00 p.m.

These meetings generally began when the client entered the cubicle or after sitting down with the caseworker, as she did not need to retrieve the client from the lobby. However, in the evening, when a client missed an appointment, often the caseworkers checked the client's dormitory with a security guard to see if the client was around for his meeting. Upon entering the dorm, the caseworker would shout, "Female in the dorm!" and then proceed to explore the dorm space, where many clients were lying on their cots, listening to music or the news. If she did not find the client in the dormitory, she might ask the security guard to check the bathrooms. Sometimes these efforts were fruitful, and the client was found and escorted to his meeting with his caseworker. In other instances, the client was not found, and the meeting was missed, which might result in the unhoused man not receiving a shelter bed.

As the night gathered speed in the caseworker cubicles, mice appeared, running along the insides of the radiators and along the seams of the floor, causing occasional shrieks and grumbles from the caseworkers. The men's daily and accumulated frustrations and the threat of losing a bed in the evening, however, often contributed to a livelier evening in the shelter. On occasion a furious client would be escorted by DHS police and security to his caseworker, and she would listen to him roar his frustrations. Other times, an exasperated client would come to the caseworker's door, demanding to be seen when she was working with another man. She would calmly tell him that she was with another client and that he would have to wait. However, often he would insist, pacing in front of the door, talking loudly to himself and others. One time a man placed himself between the client being served and the caseworker. A client might stare at the caseworker through the door or window. When the client repeatedly asked to be seen, the caseworker would often get increasingly frustrated, often shouting to the client that she was busy with another client and that she would get to him when she was finished. Though I only saw this once, one unhoused man, as he was leaving his caseworker's office to go to his dorm to sleep, pulled that caseworker's door clean off its hinges. The level of anxiety and frustration often appeared high both for caseworkers and for their clients on the night shift. However, there were are also moments of joy. One client told me, on a night shift I missed, that two of the homeless men were married in the dorms, and the friends of the two unhoused lovers threw a small reception to celebrate.

Participants

In January 2006, when I began data collection, the shelter was below capacity, with only 750 men total. However, the shelter grew to maximum capacity during the particularly snowy winter. The men in this shelter were of varying racial and ethnic backgrounds. Most of my participants were Latino or African American. One man was Italian, and another was Southeast Asian. All of my participating caseworkers were thirty- to forty-year-old African American or Latina women.

Most of my sheltered, unhoused participants were categorized by the shelter as "hard to place," which meant that complicating factors made maintaining stable housing more difficult for the client and less attractive to potential landlords. These clients included undocumented men, people with co-occurring mental illness and substance addiction, and individuals with felonies, including sex offense. Undocumented unhoused people had increased difficulty securing housing through the shelter system because a legal, taxable income was required for housing placements. The geographic isolation of the institution—far from schools, daycare centers, and libraries—created an opportunity for sex offenders to find shelter in accordance with legal requirements. Locating and securing housing for individuals charged with felonies and/or sex offense was a major challenge for caseworkers. Individuals with mental illnesses like schizophrenia, bipolar disorder, schizoaffective disorder, and depression were frequent in this population as well, as were clients with a history of substance abuse (some of which has been cleared with the legalization of marijuana).[10]

Responsibility in Practice

This chapter brings us through the various components that make up the gestalt of responsibility: deontic formulations that signal obligation and necessity, references to performance measurements and benchmarks that point to neoliberal ways of thinking and managing institutions, and cultural mythologies. Not all excerpts include all of the components, and some excerpts are meant to highlight differences. For example, some excerpts include moralizing lexical stances (e.g., "You're effing up your life") that are not (or not as easily) tied to cultural mythologies (e.g., "I'm letting you skate through the system"; "He's not doing nothing").[11]

Client Responsibility

While the terms "responsibility," "accountability," and "obligation" (and related permutations) are used in aforementioned city shelter policies, in fifty-four caseworker-client interactions, over one thousand pages of transcript data, these terms never surface. My analyses revealed that caseworkers instead conveyed "client responsibility" through a series of commonly used Standard American English modal verbs, auxiliaries, and modal adverbs (e.g., *supposed to*, *have to/havta*, *got to/gotta*, and *need*) that connote a sense of obligation or responsibility (Couper-Kuhlen and Selting, 2018), which I call deontic formulations.

Current Responsibilities

Perhaps one of the most common[12] deontic formulations included the use of the semi-modal "need," as in the following brief examples from Ms. Clemson's meetings with her clients.

> MS. CLEMSON: **You need to comply** with them.
> MS. CLEMSON: **You need to talk to me** so that I can help you.

To take a deeper look, let us explore the following excerpt between Ms. Innis and Hernando, both of whom you met at the beginning of this chapter. In this meeting, his caseworker is explaining to him that in the future he will be required to take less methadone, which he was using to treat an addiction to heroin. Bolded text draws your attention to the construction of responsibility, a deontic formulation using "need."

Ms. Innis links Hernando "you" with the obligation "need" and the action "to wind your way off this methadone." Together, these communicate Hernando's responsibility to shift his medication over time. This type of construction was very common.

Excerpt 3.1: "You need"

Ms. Innis: Now, if you can't do it, then stay on fifty, but if you can, then-
but if you can, then come down, but **you need to gradually wind**
your way off of this methadone unless you're still using drugs
and the methadone you can't come down. When's the last
time you used drugs?

Unmet Prior Responsibilities

Supposed to also denotes expectations or held obligations (Coates 1983). In these interactions, *supposed to* primarily relayed a client's obligation to tasks in the past (was *supposed to*), particularly when paired with an infinitive verb or its particle (i.e., supposed to leave; supposed to). *Should have*, likewise, denotes unmet responsibilities. Both *supposed to* and *should have* also carry moral weight that frames the past action (or inaction) as "bad." In this excerpt, Michael's prior responsibilities are constructed by Ms. Innis through deontic formulations that harken to the past, indexical of lapsed obligations (in-house psychiatric evaluation and tuberculosis test) assigned months earlier.

Excerpt 3.2: Past Responsibilities

Ms. Innis: You **should've** been -you were **supposed to** be leaving.
I was under the assumption that you was doing what you
was supposed to do from the beginning.
Michael: Yeah
Ms. Innis: But?
Michael: Shit happens.

Ms. Innis positions Michael using person pronoun "you," using deontic formulation "should've been" and "supposed to" to construct a stance of prior responsible action. The object of the stance *leaving* earmarks the failed responsibility, and deontic evaluation *supposed to* likewise signals a failure to complete an institutional goal, reiterated by the verbal time stamp *from the beginning*. She distances herself from Michael, separating *I* from *you*. Resonating with Pomerantz (1978), lines 1–3 might be called an "attribution of responsibility," which formulates Michael as an "actor-agent performing a blameworthy . . . action" (116). Pomerantz suggests that an actor is placed in the position of the blamed person vis-à-vis the action described. This aligns with Hall, Slembrouck, and Sarangi's (2006) observation that blame and categorizations collaboratively construct moral accountability. Michael's response ("yeah") is oriented to as inadequate by Ms. Innis, given her pursuit of an account in line 5 ("but?"). Michael provides a flippant, clichéd "offering" for irresponsibility (Goffman, 1981), an account that the caseworker ultimately finds wanting: "shit happens." Much is overlooked if we simply analyze accounts. While "shit happens" is indeed an account in which Michael distances himself from responsibility by admitting to vague negative circumstances, the study of accounts tells us more about how deontic formulations are responded to rather than the formulations themselves. They tell us what Michael does with attributions of responsibility, but tells us little about the attributions themselves. While attributions of responsibility are useful they only tell half the story: examining blameworthy actions (i.e., "you were supposed to be leaving") ignores moments when caseworkers merely assign new responsibilities (i.e., "You need to go get a TB test").

Deontic formulations are one piece of the responsibility puzzle. As you might have noted already, in many of the previous examples references to performance benchmarks, requirements, and assessments were mentioned. Now that we have explored the basics of responsibility construction in talk, we will investigate the other aspects that characterize the gestalt of responsibility.

Client Responsibility as a Gestalt

After I analyzed the data for deontic formulations, I noticed upon reviewing the collection of excerpts that these formulations often surfaced in proximity to references to performance benchmarks and assessment that not only index these external assessments and benchmarks but the neoliberal organizational mechanisms that generate them. Lexical and affective stances clustered nearby, sometimes but not always indexing larger cultural mythologies.

In the following excerpt, Julio, a long-term client has missed an appointment to look at housing. This meeting transcript highlights deontic formulations, cultural mythologies, and references to performance benchmarks, which index these policies as well as neoliberal organizational approaches; however, this meeting was typed-as-heard and the recording was not viable, as such there is no underlining for emphasis here or timed pauses. Their meeting opens with a greeting from him, and what follows is Ms. Innis' first words to him after his greeting.

Excerpt 3.3: The Morality of Performance

Ms. Innis	You were **supposed to go** last Thursday. No Wednesday. I sent you an appointment.
Julio	You send appointment?
Ms. Innis	And you didn't come you didn't go last week
Julio	What day?
Ms. Innis	Last Thurs- the 9th (.). The **list**. See this **list**? You're on it. **You have to go** Julio, all these people highlighted have been here **over 360 days**. As per DHS everyone who has been here for **a year or more needs to go**. **No you have to pick a place**.
Julio	What do you mean pic?
Ms. Innis	**You have to take a room**. **You have to take a room**. This Thursday. Don't miss it, the sixteenth. See it? (points to a calendar). August sixteenth.
Julio	Thursday?
Ms. Innis	Clients that's been in the **shelter too many days**. You've been here **417 days**. **They want you outta here**. You've been in at [other shelter]. It's a lot of days to be in shelter. They want you out. So **I have to get the brunt of this**.
Julio	Shared room.
Ms. Innis	Shared. You have PA. **They're gonna come down on me** because **you've been in too many days**. See all the people on **this list**? I've already told them. You all are priority eligible clients, **more than 365 days in the shelter**. All of it adds up. **We're all under one umbrella**.
Julio	I don't have a money for rent. Me no complain for me for 3 year. Some other people here for 12 or 13 years—me no me no mucho.
Ms. Innis	Yeah but you sleep here
Julio	Yea
Ms. Innis	Yeah but that's what counts
Julio	No complain.
Ms. Innis	**You gotta go**. I'm gonna send you on a housing tour.
Julio	Sixteenth right?
Ms. Innis	I'll give you a letter for your program, but **you have to go see those rooms** but **you have to take one**, get a lease and go to welfare. I'll send you-, 16th——housing tour, 17th program, 20th meet with me in the afternoon at 6 o' clock. So next Monday at 6. All right? Monday at 6. All right?
Julio	Next Monday at 6?[13]

The gestalt of responsibility includes deontic formulations, references to performance benchmarks, and cultural mythologies. In this excerpt, we can see these unfolding together. This excerpt, and the meeting itself, begins with Ms. Innis using a past-tense deontic formulation "supposed to" to place blame on Julio ("you") for not going to his housing appointment, an "attribution of responsibility" (Pomerantz, 1978). Responsibility is constructed through a complex interplay of deontic formulations (including personal pronouns) and references to policies and benchmarks that draw from neoliberal managerial approaches. Ms. Innis follows the construction of responsibility with an institutional justification in line 5 ("The list. See this list? You're on it."). The personal pronoun "you" combines with deontic formulation "have" and the infinitive verb "to go" to construct his obligation to leave shelter ("you have to go"). Her reference to the "list" is an "environmentally coupled gesture" (Goodwin, 2007), as Ms. Innis brandishes the list of priority long-term stayers in the air. She expands on this justification by clarifying the constraints of the institution's policy. Her reference to the number of days a client can stay in shelter ("360 days") links responsibility with performance measurement, and this performance measurement is linked directly with accountability, as she references the overseer, Department of Homeless Services, and its requirements ("needs to go"). Performance benchmarks are combined with obligation.

What follows in lines 7-10 are repetitions of deontic formulations that she explicitly links to Julio: "No, you have to pick a place"; "You have to take a room"; "You have to take a room." The deontic quasi-modal *have got to* denotes an obligated subject, with the subsequent infinitive verb (i.e., to go) explaining a required action—"go-ing" (Coates, 1983; Collins, 2009; Smith, 2003). Smith (2003) notes that in American English *have got to* is often reduced to *got to, gotta, have to, or haveta. Gotta* and *have to* were common means Ms. Innis used to communicate client responsibilities (Matarese, 2008). She concludes her emphasis on his responsibility with a rare imperative: "Don't miss it." Unfortunately, he does not understand. Spanish is his first language, and he is not very proficient in English; in fact, he often has a fellow shelter resident translate for him in his meetings. Ms. Innis tries to explain the policy again, this time stating the number of days he has been in shelter as a way to highlight that he has worn out his welcome. The days once again mark a violation of the benchmarks established by the shelter policy.

Ms. Innis's reference to performance benchmarks implicates failures for both of them. Twice she uses personal pronoun "they" to position and scapegoat blame for this policy requirement with the city Department of Homeless Services ("They want you out"). In line 14, her use of person deictic marker "they" ("They want you outta here") is juxtaposed with "I" ("I've already told them"), "you" ("You all are priority eligible"), and "we" ("We're all under one umbrella"), distancing both her and Julio from the administration and aligning herself with him through the use of "we." She links Julio's "failed" responsibilities with her own, demonstrating the accountability relationship: When he performs satisfactorily, she performs satisfactorily, and when he does not meet the shelter expectations, this reflects negatively on her ("I have to get the brunt of this" and "They're gonna come down on me"). These references to performance benchmarks are not, then, neutral. They carry they the weight of not only policy benchmarks but also her own performance measurement.

While not cultural mythologies, she uses lexical stances in lines 15, 17-18, and 19-20, which all refer to judgment. In lines 15, 17, and 18 Ms. Innis positions herself as a victim of the administration that will negatively evaluate her performance. In so doing, her stance here implicates Julio through the causal "because," which links the administration's potentially negative performance evaluation of Ms. Innis with Julio's violation of shelter benchmarks for length of stay ("They're gonna come down on me because you've been in too many days"). Her metaphor "We're all under one umbrella" underscores this connection between their individual performance assessments while also reiterating that they will both be judged.

In the next example, Ms. Innis' client Michael is approaching the nine-month benchmark, at which time he will need to leave the shelter. She appears to be at her wit's end and is trying to level with him. This excerpt again stresses the impact of performance benchmarks as morally weighty judgments. Moreover, while this example includes more weighted moralizing lexical stances, they are not cultural mythologies with historical legacies.

Excerpt 3.4: Lexical Stance: "Effing up your life"

Michael °Yeah. °
Ms. Innis Cause you wanna be out there doing what you wanna do and then you gonna be back
here (.) it doesn't work like that. (0.2) Either I ↑keep telling you- you don't want my suggestions
(.) you don't wanna hear what I have to tell you, (.) come up with something. (.) you're not coming up
with nothing you're not saving no money from when you're working, you understand what I'm saying?
You're not doing anything
Michael °Okay.°
Ms. Innis What are you gonna do it's been **eight months.** You don't have a penny to show for it. (0.4) Right or
wrong?
Michael °You're right.°
Ms. Innis It's **eight months** you've been here. **eight months** you been here. **eight months** you been here. dealing
with a curfew (.) you don't like curfews
Michael [(Clears throat)]
Ms. Innis [You don't] wanna go to a drug program cause you don't wanna be locked up. You keep using the
drugs what's the-what's the poinT? You tell ↑ME! You on the methadone you using the heroin it doesn't
work like that the methadone would not work if you keep using ↑heroin once a week or twice a week or

how much ever it is. I know you're being honest with me, and I really do appreciate it but I'm gonna be honest with you. **You are effing up your ↑life**. The heroin is gonna mess you up and then you using the heroin and the methadone together it doesn't work, it's gonna counteract it, and then you be just all strung out on it it doesn't work like that. So **you gotta** really basically **it's been 8 months you need to** really make up your mind (.) and tell me what you wanna do, and tell me what you wanna do today. I'm sending you on a housing tour you can't make it cause you're working but I don't have no proof of you working because like I don't have no money to prove to anybody that you working. (0.3) You just got arrested a month ago for heroin, instead you 'en got on the methadone instead you said okay I'm gonna try to get my life together you back on the heroin. (0.4) You got a girlfriend in Puerto Rico you trying to save ten thousand dollars I don't know how you're doing all that. (0.4) So **I need you to give me** a plan of what you wanna do so I can help you execute that plan, cause my plan's is if I go my way you be in a drug treatment program. You don't want that I offered you a house where you can go to your outpatient program and you don't-but it have a curfew you don't want that, **so tell me what you want**.

In this interaction, Ms. Innis underscores Michael's proximity to the shelter's housing placement benchmark five times, and on that fifth time connects that directly with a deontic formulation "you need to" (line 19). These benchmarks carry the weight of his performance assessment. Deontic formulations "you gotta" and "I need you to give me a plan" surface in close proximity as well. Ms. Innis also uses lexical stance markers that position each of them as "honest," though the "but" in "but I'm gonna be honest with you" positions her honesty as contrastive with his (lines 16–17). It is with this honesty that she delivers another lexical stance marker that negatively positions Michael: "You are effing up your life" (line 17). She does, in fact, abbreviate the word "fucking," perhaps aware of the recording device and my presence. Shortened or not, it is a severe moral characterization that she connects to his heroin use. That said, the phrase does not index a particularly culturally loaded mythology, though the next example does.

Both Michael and Julio were categorized by the shelter as "hard to place" and "long-term stayers." Their long-term stays, well past the nine-month benchmark, fast-tracked them to more case meetings. In contrast, Luciano, in this next excerpt, was not a "long-term stayer," though as an undocumented unhoused man, he was "hard to place." This time, we can see the full gestalt surfacing in the talk between him and Ms. Innis, including the deontic formulations, references to performance measurement, and cultural mythologies.

In this extract, Ms. Innis is talking to Luciano through a Spanish-speaking security guard for the shelter who is an ad hoc translator for each party.[14] The two men speak different dialects of Spanish (Luciano is from Spain, and the security guard is speaking Dominican Spanish), so there are some moments of confusion and misunderstanding between them. Luciano explains to the security guard that his preference is to wait until his foot is healed from a serious injury, so he would prefer to stay "three to five months and then see what happens" (as translated by the security guard). Ms. Innis explains that staying this length of time is no longer possible, stating, "They are downsizing the time that you can stay in the shelter, and it's three months. Anything after that they starting to put pressure on people. That's why I asked him if he wanted to go back to Spain because I can help get a ticket and all that other stuff." After explaining the above to the ad hoc translator, she turns to speak more directly to the guard about Luciano, saying:

Excerpt 3.5: The Gestalt of Responsibility

Ms. Innis He sits here all day but he doesn't know that as he stays here the system
is changing around him. you used to be able to do that but not anymore.
See so then so his plan in his mind is to stay in a shelter for **four**, **five**,
six months and then figure out what he's gonna do. He can't do that. **He**
needs to start thinking about what he's going to do now because I can't
transfer him to another shelter because it's not an option anymore for us.
"**You have to** place these clients." Mayor **Bloomberg** is like
"**bring down homelessness and not transfer them**." Got to be placed and
so that's the problem. So all the people who's undocumented we don't
have a problem paying for a ticket to go back to their family in whatever
country that's why I offered him that because some people don't have the
money or the connections whatever. We can take care of that. the
problem is he can't wait **five months** and say 'I don't want to go' if I go
through the whole process and then he change his mind.
Then he wanna stay here. **He's not really doing nothing over here**. Ask
him, **he's not doing nothing**.

Here we see Ms. Innis justify the pressure she places on Luciano by describing the changes taking place in the shelter system. His responsibilities are communicated indirectly by Ms. Innis, who uses "he" personal pronouns rather than "you" as she conveys to the guard what Luciano should be told. Lines 3 and 4 summarize her estimation of Luciano's current plan, which Ms. Innis then rejects by saying, "He can't do that." In line 5, the deontic formulation "needs" communicates his responsibility: "start thinking about what he's going to do."

While analysis of the construction of responsibility could end there, it is worth noting the myriad references to time and time benchmarks, as well as references to policy. "System changing" and "used to . . . but not anymore" situate the conversation in a pivotal moment of institutional and systemic flux. When this interaction was recorded in mid-May 2007, the shelter had changed the benchmark for people leaving shelter from nine months to six months. Acceleration is a common feature of neoliberalized, new managerial social institutions. Fortier and Therrien (2018) argue that

> social acceleration works in concert with neoliberalism. Subjected to the constraints of market competitiveness, individuals are transformed into "entrepreneurs of the self," for whom responsibility for making one's life a success overrides societal considerations and collective action. Social acceleration therefore affects both the system and its actors, thus giving rise to a hypermodern society (Aubert 2010) characterized by a constant sense of urgency on which global capitalism thrives, while the State and its institutions, including public administration, are weakened. In this context, time must be understood as a social construction over which a wide variety of interests, private and public, fight. While multiple temporalities coexist (Adam 2004), be they financial, political, ecological or economic, this struggle ultimately leads to the reconfiguration of social relations (Martineau 2015). For this reason, issues of time and social acceleration must be considered if we are to understand the reality of social practices and institutions. (463)

Ms. Innis's description of the acceleration agenda becomes part of her justification for rejecting Luciano's plan of action. She rejects the plan he has formed, arguing that he is no longer able to stay in shelter for "four, five, six months." These time stamps signal the newly established performance benchmark that reflects this acceleration model, and these references to performance are not neutral but rather highlight external requirements that are used to rationalize the pressure Ms. Innis places on him.

She then explains that this agenda is out of her hands, displacing specific responsibility to the former NYC mayor. In lines 7 and 8, Ms. Innis uses reported speech (reporting what someone else said) and quotative "like" (when "like" is used to introduce a quotation; Romaine and Lange 1991), which shifts responsibility for the policy to the proposed speaker: Mayor Bloomberg. Rather than coming from the caseworkers, Ms. Innis positions herself as subject to Bloomberg's policy directives. In those lines, the responsibility is placed on the caseworkers through personal pronoun "you," deontic formulation "have," infinitive verb "to place," and object "these clients." The personal pronoun choice here ("these") serves to distance Ms. Innis from the cohort of unhoused men. Conley (2015), in her analysis of how courtroom talk impacts juror decisions, argues that these kinds of deictic references convey "emotional distance, lack of empathy, and negative affect toward defendants" (122). While I believe that Ms. Innis was ultimately interested in helping these men, it is possible that using "these clients" provides the distance she needs to dole out the "tough love" prescribed by the new rules. In any case, her reference to the mayor's policy displaces ultimate blame for the severity of new rules to the city and allows her to align with Luciano. She summarizes the problem: "Gotta be placed," using a deontic formulation that signals an oblique, agentless obligation to place the men in shelter into stable, independent living.

These references to city and institutional policy and pressure are bookended by a common cultural mythology that is enacted here to shift responsibility to Luciano. "He's not really doing nothing over here," Ms. Innis says. "Ask him, he's not doing nothing" (lines 15–16). Her "attribution of responsibility" (Pomerantz, 1978) situates his prior inaction as blameworthy. These final lines bring the focus back from abstract policy to Luciano's case. Using "he," she links the stance of "doing nothing" to him twice. Her characterization of his inaction resonates with a common cultural mythology of individuals in the social welfare system—"the lazy client."

Hancock's (2004) content analysis of "welfare queen" discourse and the *Politics of Disgust* draws out two popular cultural mythologies that feed into the welfare queen mythos. She argues,

> Despite the fact that African American women have worked throughout their history in the United States, they continued to suffer from being stereotyped as lazy, which originated during slavery. Mainstream Americans consistently judged poor Black women as immoral for failing to conform to the American politics value of industry, when in fact they were working and/or suffered extreme unchecked employment discrimination. (36)

In her analysis of major newspapers for the welfare queen cultural mythology, Hancock (2004) coded specifically for "don't work" and the moral judgment "lazy," tracing the prevalence of these mythologies across newspapers, many of which are considered left-leaning and newspapers of record. Her work clearly demonstrates how erroneous and baseless these mythologies are, illuminating the double standards that provided ample support to white woman and mothers seeking public assistance generally, while Black women and mothers seeking public assistance generally received scrutiny and disapproval, more often than not.

The cultural mythology of "lazy" welfare recipients is well documented across the social welfare literature (cf. Hancock, 2004), and the "lazy immigrant" myth is similarly deployed (Reyna et al., 2013) here. In this excerpt, we see "he's not doing nothing" twice employed to position Luciano as having a poor work ethic, underscoring a moral judgment. In reality, he is a relatively new unhoused man with a serious foot injury for which he received surgery, and he has difficulty getting around easily. We got so much snow that winter. He is undocumented, so finding work will require a level of hustle that his injury impedes. He both physically cannot seek work and cannot acquire legal work, prohibiting him from the legal income required to move from shelter to housing.[15] The cultural mythology of the "lazy client" surfaces again and again among constructions of responsibility in both data sets.

In earlier articles (Matarese, 2012; Matarese, 2015), I argue that Ms. Innis linguistically treats Luciano, a short-term, undocumented (and, therefore, "hard to place") unhoused man, like a "long-term stayer"—a client who has been in shelter for nine or more months. Despite the fact that Luciano has not been in shelter long, his undocumented status results in a situation in which he is unable to obtain the legal income required to leave shelter. At the time, there was an expectation that undocumented clients would eventually become long-term stayers, which may explain why his caseworker characterized him as "lazy," verbally positioning him as a long-term stayer despite his short shelter stay.

Joint Responsibilities

As noted by the responsibility policy, the research literature, and Excerpt 3.3, workers were also held responsible for their performance. Accordingly, responsibility also surfaced in other ways, in caseworker-client interaction. For example, caseworkers referred to not only client responsibilities but also their own. Importantly, however, the caseworkers do not deploy the gestalt toward themselves in the same way. In Excerpt 3.6, Ms. Innis arranges for Julio to visit a potential housing placement, and while doing so invokes her own obligations.

Excerpt 3.6: Self-Directed Responsibility

Ms. Innis:	**I have t**o send the package again downtown
Julio:	yeah you call you=
Ms. Innis	=**I gotta** call and I gotta send the package downtown, and and and **we gotta** do that first (.) it could be a week it could be two days, it could be tomorrow it could be anything.
Translator	all right

In line 1, Ms. Innis combines the deontic auxiliary *have* with an infinitive verb (i.e., to do, to leave, to take) to construct an obligatory stance for herself. The infinitive (to send) identifies the accountable action (Coates, 1983), positioning herself, through personal pronoun "I," as responsible for the stance object, sending the housing package downtown. Similarly, the perfect tense of *get* (*got*), used in lines 3 and 4, is often used to mean *have*. *Have to* and *gotta* were common means by which Ms. Innis constructed her clients' responsibilities, but here she uses both to position herself as responsible (e.g., "I have to send"; "I gotta call"). Participating caseworkers used grammatical terms to establish responsibilities for clients and themselves and, like Ms. Innis (line 3), often used "we" to construct an aligned responsible stance with clients. Caseworkers used "have to," "need to," and "got to" (and permutations) to establish their and their clients' responsibilities; however, "supposed to" or "should have" were only used by caseworkers to signal prior client responsibilities that were unmet.

Atkinson (1999) argues that "we should pay equal analytic attention to the language of the professionals as we do to their relatively powerless clients. It is not enough to dismiss the work of medical practitioners as bureaucratic, or dehumanizing, or disempowering while celebrating the perspectives of their lay clients" (76). This is certainly a common criticism of critical discourse analysis, focusing on the powerless clients and criticizing the practitioners. It is worth briefly exploring the ways in which the caseworkers are also the observed, the accountable, the blamed. The accountability system that workers are part of requires accountability from them as well (as Ms. Innis mentions above), and while the people receiving shelter have the penalty of sanction, which removes them from shelter for thirty days or until they comply with their ILP, workers also have penalties. They are obviously not as severe as what the clients experience, but probation and firing are also concerning for those who may live paycheck to paycheck in New York City while trying to fund their master's program.

In this field-note-recorded interaction between caseworker Needham and Steve, she tries to explain to him that caseworkers and the shelter itself are limited in what they can do based on the budget provided by the city. The workers and the shelter itself, she suggests, are stuck in the middle.

> STEVE: That's why we need a psych not to come in every Thursday and try to see eight hundred clients, make a little money, and then just jump. we need psych that could be available at all times in my opinion. But they make a lot of money.

NEEDHAM: Who's gonna pay for that? That's a lot of money. You know how expensive it is to pay a psychiatrist? Just that one day he's making so much money.

STEVE: Excuse me. So then we have to ask for a bigger budget, we'll have ta-

NEEDHAM: -and that's the problem.

STEVE: Listen. Somebody's got-

NEEDHAM: What you really gotta do is go to Bloomberg. Bloomberg is he is the-

STEVE: -I had seen him not too long ago in relation to another matter. He's not a very bad guy to talk to he's—

NEEDHAM: He's the source of all of this! I'm telling you he's the source of all of this. He's the one that he's sets a budget. I want to let you know that he is the source of all this. Everything you see that's going on here it's the amount of money that he gives us. We can't create. We can't steal things.

STEVE: I got him right now kinda like in a bad position when like he see me he starts going like this (puts hands in front of face) oh man this guy. But he's a very professional guy. And I admire him to degree. And, we gonna be talking about a lot of stuff cause they already agreed to le—

NEEDHAM: -But I'm letting you you know that all-

STEVE: -the grant corporations see some things that they would normally wouldn't'a said seen ten years ago so, we making progress, he's not a bad guy he's willing—

NEEDHAM: I don't think he's a bad guy either but a lot a I'm'a let you know a lot of client they blame us when they see stuff is not happening it's not us, it's what the budget that we have to work with and the stuff we gotta do with the budget we have to work with.

STEVE: Well, incite a revolution. (laughs) I'm joking.

NEEDHAM: It's not funny. We can't. We can't do- . . . . Okay be we gotta address both sides okay, that's the problem I have with a lot of Oh saying well, "staff is not doing." what you do? We gotta address both sides I don't mind you telling me what I'm doing wrong.

Toward the end, she encourages Steve to look at "both sides." "I don't mind you telling me what I'm doing wrong," but he also needs to look at "what you do."

Sometimes separate but interdependent responsibilities were constructed, as in the following example in which Ms. Innis delivers an ultimatum.

Excerpt 3.7: Joint Responsibilities

Ms. Innis: You hear me?
(.)
You have another- you have another: what's today, the fourth,
you have another week to get a TB and a psych in here.
(.)
or else I'm go[in—
Michael: [like I] said Wednesday is my slowest day.
Ms. Innis: Wednesday >I don't wan, I want you to BE here at 1 o' clock, I don't want
you to be even working.=
Michael: =No no. (.) I'll be here at 1 o' clock.
Ms. Innis: Please. You need me to come here and I'll escort you over
there so I can ensure that you'll get it done? **I need it done.**
I need to schedule you FOR it. But you need to get it done.
I need you to get a TB.

Prior to this excerpt, Ms. Innis asks Michael to reschedule his tuberculosis test and psychiatric evaluation and receives no answer. She then asks a confirmation question (line 1) and offers an ultimatum ending in an incomplete threat in line 6 ("or else I'm goin'") and later a prohibition (lines 8–9). Ms. Innis poses a question (lines 11–12), positioning him as requiring supervision to satisfy his responsibilities. Given that she leaves no space for an answer, this question appears rhetorical and closes with the deontic formulation "I need it done," ultimately positioning herself as the agent in need (line 12). "I need" . . . "display[s] 'confidence' in the request," revealing a high sense of entitlement and a low probability of rejecting the request (Curl and Drew, 2008; Drew and Walker, 2010; Vinkhuyzen and Szymanski, 2005). Her responsibilities require completion of his. Her recast (lines 13–14) clarifies the obligatory relationship: positioning herself as responsible for scheduling through a deontic marker, and using *you need* to bind him to the stance object "get it done."

Though she at first separates their responsibilities (line 13), her closing ("I need you to get a TB") positions Michael' responsibilities in relation to hers, ultimately positioning Michael as gatekeeper to her responsibilities. Constructed responsible stances were often interdependent. Lipsky (1980/2010) claims that street-level bureaucrats mediate between the client and the administration and have responsibilities to both. These excerpts show what this looks like in practice: caseworkers constructing interdependent responsible stances. Such findings resonate with Hall, Morris, and Juhila (2017), who show that for both caseworkers and clients, case management is a form of measurable surveillance.

While workers may refer to their own responsibilities, their client's obligations, or an interdependent set of responsibilities, they do not always fully employ the whole gestalt. Sometimes, the weight of performance benchmarks may be more prominently on display. In this next interaction, however, the gestalt is deployed toward her client Michael, in conjunction with a description of interdependent responsibilities. Michael has surpassed the nine-month benchmark for shelter stay, and Ms. Innis is fed up.

Excerpt 3.8: "Help me help you": Interdependent Responsibilities

Ms.Innis: I'm not telling you to get into a program, but what I'm telling
you is you're **gonna do something**. You're not gonna sit here and
continue to **heavily use drugs** the way you used to and and **just**
come in and work part time off the books and **just not doing**
anything. You know, you know, and like I said befo:re (.) you take a
wednesday off good for you because wednesday **I need to see you**
getting a psych evaluation. You've been here (.) for ↑**months**.
↑**months**. And **nothing's getting done**. And then what it **looks at and it**
reflects is (.) I'm getting- I'm **letting you skate through the system**,=
Michael = hhhh ((sniff laughs))=
Ms.Innis: =and **utilize the place just to ha**- just to make sure you have a
bed every night so you can go do what you need to do, and I can't do
that no more. You understand?
Michael: I understand.
Ms.Innis: I have 40 clients. (.3) and I'm being **honest** I can't I don't I don't have the
patience anymore I'm **stressed** I just don't have it. To let you keep
skating because when **they need something from me I have to be**
able to produce it, and if I can't produce it I'm the one that's
getting the **rap at the end of the day**. And so for on **judgment** and
being a case manager I have to case manage you. (.) **Now you have to**
help me help you. You understand what I'm saying?

Responsibility is constructed with deontic formulations and interdependently attributed obligations. Ms. Innis positions Michael ("you") in relation to his future responsibilities ("gonna") (line 2) and contrasts that with a negative appraisal of his prior actions (lines 2–5) that downgrades his current efforts ("just," line 3, 4). However, her critique culminates not by presenting Michael with a service plan violation, but by describing her own needs (line 6-7). She characterizes him as what Hancock (2004) would call a "system abuser," doing drugs, working only part time, and "just not doing anything." This cultural mythology leads directly into an invocation of her own responsibilities ("I need to see you getting a psych evaluation"), underscoring that his responsibilities are also her responsibilities. Her reiteration of "months" (line 7) locates responsibility within timetables, which Hall, Morris, and Juhila (2017) suggest are indexical of mutual commitment to policy. While this may be true, it also points to very real performance measurements that for him carry the weight of sanction and for her carry the weight of probation.

She ties his failure in responsibility to the cultural mythology of the lazy, freeloading social services client (line 9), using "skate" as a metaphor to communicate the ease of his shelter life. However, she takes ultimate responsibility for this, suggesting that his lack of action makes it look like she isn't doing her job ("I'm letting you skate"). While the critique is ultimately one of him, it is one for which she takes responsibility through her personal pronoun choices ("I'm getting. . . . I'm letting"). In lines 11–12 she underlines this metaphor by describing his misuse of the shelter. This resonates with Soss, Fording, and Schram (2011), who argue that irresponsibility in social welfare is positioned as a moral failure:

> Individuals . . . have a moral and political obligation to act as disciplined entrepreneurs. They must plan to meet their own needs, accept personal responsibility for their problems, and manage their daily affairs with prudence. The individual who does otherwise fails not just as an economic actor but as a moral and civic being (22–23).

Here, Michael's lack of action over time is tied to moral failure and cultural mythology—the "lazy client."

Ms. Innis also uses lexical stance markers to categorize herself, employing justifications tied to shelter-system benchmarks and accountability, references to caseworker burnout (e.g., heavy caseload, "stressed"), and caseworker accountability ("when they need something from me I have to be able to produce it"). Her performance management and assessment weigh heavily in her talk (though it is worth noting that Michael could be sanctioned and have to leave shelter). She positions herself and her worklife through repeated negative stance markers (lines 15–16). She categorizes herself as without "patience" and as "stressed." These negative evaluations serve as justification for why she cannot "let [him] keep skating," a reiteration of the "lazy social services client" metaphor.

Her final justification sequence invokes the institution, positioning "they" as requiring (through deontic stance marker "need") the vague performance assessment "something" (line 17). She then positions her own responsibilities as the product of administrative requests (lines 17–18). A conditional ("if I can't produce it . . .") dismisses the alternative (line 18), positioning the outcome as potential punishment ("I'm the one getting the rap," line 19). Those consequences refer obliquely to the accountability framework that measures performance. Soss, Fording, and Schram (2011) argue that performance measurement tools like outcome benchmarks "reshape the agency itself" (2), and Brodkin (2011) likewise suggests that new managerial tools like benchmarks can restructure discretionary practices among street-level practitioners. Ms. Innis's inclusion of accountability benchmarks in conjunction with constructions of responsibility supports their claims. Moreover, Ms. Innis may be drawing Michael into her troubles in order to gain compliance, a common tactic in street-level work, according to Lipsky (1980/2010).

Finally, she invokes her role as case manager (line 20), and makes her managerial role the verbal object of her deontic formulation. She reiterates their interdependent responsibilities: "you have to help me help you," positioning Michael as ultimately responsible (through deontic stance marker "have to") for the stance object: helping her.

The six caseworkers in my data used similar client-responsibility talk (e.g., *you gotta, you need to, you should have*), related positioning, references to shelter policies and performance benchmarks for the client, and cultural mythologies. However, only three workers used *self-directed* responsibility language and references to stress and burnout. Notably, these were generally the participating caseworkers who had the most hard-to-place clients.

Client Responsibility as Cultural Mythology

While many workers use the gestalt of responsibility in their talk, there are a few moments where the cultural mythologies and the performance benchmarks were invoked without deontic formulations (e.g., "I need you to do X") that situate those myths and timelines in attributions of responsibility. In this excerpt with Xavier and Ms. Innis, there were constructions of his own responsibility.

Xavier, an older Black man in his sixties, had been staying at the shelter for some time. His previous caseworker had apparently found Xavier appropriate housing, went on vacation for the New Year's holiday and, to everyone's surprise, never returned to his job. He just left, and his clients were distributed across the already overworked casework staff. Xavier was assigned to Ms. Innis, who inherited him as a "long-term stayer" or

"9-month-stayer," which means he had exceeded the amount of time he was supposed to be in shelter, according to Department of Homeless Services policy and strategic plans. Xavier began a program of aggressive case management with Ms. Innis, which included being assigned to attend case conferences, which meant that he must sit with his caseworker, the administration of the shelter, and DHS once a week and discuss his progress in leaving the shelter.

Caseworker Innis met Xavier for the first time in his first case conference as a nine-month stayer. In that case conference, he told the members present that he would be leaving the shelter the following Monday (case conferences were held on Tuesdays). After this case conference, Xavier met with Ms. Innis individually for the first time. This was my first recording with Xavier and Ms. Innis. It was here that she learned that he had not found a place to live at all. Instead, he confessed that he was simply sick of the shelter system and planning on leaving whether he had a place to go or not. Both Ms. Innis and Xavier were visibly frustrated.

Xavier met with Ms. Innis three times while he was on her caseload. In these three meetings, they developed a strategy for securing him housing, and he was placed in a shared room. This excerpt was from their first interaction in which Xavier was describing his frustration with the explanation he had been given about finding a place to live during his case conference. Many client meetings post-case conference began in a "huff," with the caseworker annoyed with how the client behaved in the conference and the client enraged by a variety of uncomfortable aspects of the case conference. When Xavier met with Ms. Innis, neither was very cheerful. She called on him to explain where he was moving. The excerpt that follows is part of his explanation.

Excerpt 3.9: "Just playing devil's advocate"

Xavier: All the time I'm going there they say the sa:me thing. Blah
blahblahblahblah. Oh **Bloomberg**, yeah. It ain't
Bloomberg. (.) Come on. I ain't jum- you- they got
you jumping through hoops, I ain't jumping through no hoop.
Ms. Innis: Okay, well unfortunately. This is my job, so I have no
[choice
Xavier: [I'm not talking about you.
Ms. Innis: hhhhhhh ((laughs))
Xavier: I'm talking about her,=
Ms. Innis: =right,
Xavier: Cause the pressure's on her, right?=
Ms. Innis: =right [the pressure's on basically all of us.]

13	Xavier:	[okay technically technically] okay,
14		>technically technically < when you come in the door that's when you're your
15		umm (.) what- what's that the I-P-O: or whatever,=
16	Ms. Innis:	=I-L-P,=
17	Xavier:	=I-L-P, that's suppose to
18		take your place, so by the time you're **nine months** due **you're supposed to** be=
19	Ms. Innis:	=But **it's not supposed to** be n-=
20	Xavier:	I [↑know.]
21	Ms. Innis:	[lemmie] lemmie explain something to you. It's only **supposed**
22		to be **three months**.
23	Xavier:	right=
24	Ms. Innis:	=**that you're supposed** to be in the shelter.
25	Xavier:	Exactly,
26	Ms. Innis:	you been here **nine**.
27	Xavier:	right.
28	Ms. Innis:	Okay. um so (.) the pressure is on now because this is not- (.) What
29		happened is(.) it took (.)people started to make this into a home.
30	Xavier:	[exactly]
31	Ms. Innis:	[They]started living here 26 years, 10 years, 5 years, 4
32		years, and it was never supposed to happen. [Things fell
33		through the track.]
34	Xavier:	[mmmhmm XXXX]
35	Ms. Innis:	Right. Things fell through the crack.(.) fine. so now the
36		pressure's on us. Yes, the **mayor** do have a **five.hh year plan**
37		to bring down homelessness and yes **he's cases on our**
38	Ms. Innis:	cause he wants to look good. So: **heads will ↑roll**.
39	Xavier:	Mm-hmm
40	Ms. Innis:	So we have to put the pressure on you guys unfortunately
40		**you've been here for nine months**, so: now the pressure's on.
41		it's not like you've been here for **si:x**,=
42	Xavier:	=No, I can handle [the pressure].
43	Ms. Innis:	[Right]
44	Xavier:	I can handle the pressure. I can take care of myself.
. . .		((Xavier explains how he is rationally considering his options))
56	Ms. Innis:	Okay so but what their thing is is you been trying and you been working,
57		(.) I'm gonna play devil's advocate. Just to be on the (.) on the both sides so
58		you can understand where we're both coming from. I'm not here to push
59		you out because I just got you on my caseload, so so I don't know what
60		previous case managers have done for you .hh or who's held up on your
61		paperwork or what the situation [is,]
62	Xavier:	[Mm hmm]
63	Ms. Innis:	Right? So I can't (.) judge that. I can't judge them based on what they've
64		done, I can only do what I've done. And you know you just got on my caseload,

>as usual< but you got on my caseload **as nine months.=**
Xavier: =right
Ms. Innis: or—**a nine months stayer or longer**. Correct? (.) So now the question is is
they've been there through the whole thing with you=
Xavier: =Right
Ms. Innis: I haven't. (.) So I really don't know. I really couldn't jump in and say listen
well this is what he's been doing. Just because we only been working together
a couple of weeks.
Xavier: Right.
Ms. Innis: But on the other hand you've been here for **9 months**. So what are you going to do
differently in the **next three mo:nths** (.) or **the next month** to really get you outta
here. Because its gonna turn into a year, then it's gonna turn into fifteen months,
and then it's gonna turn into—>you understand what I'm saying?< and then it adds
↑ up. **So if they don't put the pressure on then (.) we gonna give you the time to slide**.
just playing devil's advocate. And that's basically what they look at. Regardless of
whatever you're doing. You're not doing enough.

This excerpt highlights how cultural mythologies and references to shelter policies can *stand in for* the deontic formulation that conveys responsibility. Xavier begins by taking a dismissive stance ("blahblahblah") toward the city mayor, who had recently accelerated the move from shelter to housing. He refers to this because the administrators in his case conference used Bloomberg as a scapegoat for the pressure they were putting on him. Xavier characterizes the shelter and its bureaucracy, using a circus metaphor (line 4), creating disalignment with Ms. Innis by negatively characterizing her as satisfying needlessly bureaucratic tasks and positioning himself outside that bureaucracy (lines 1–4). He uses "you" and "I" to distance himself from Ms. Innis (Conley, 2013). Ms. Innis provides an account of her adherence to the shelter policies and rules, taking a negative stance ("unfortunately"). In lines 7, 9, and 11, Xavier makes an affiliative shift by moving the critique to Ms. Innis's administrator ("I'm talking about her"), and Ms. Innis repositions the stance object of the pressure ("her") to "all of us," collectively distributing the pressure among administration, caseworkers, clients, and staff for responsible action. This is in line with Soss, Fording, and Schram (2011), who find that caseworkers rely on the compliance of their clients to satisfy job performance requirements.

It is in the following lines that the institutional accountability framework is repeatedly invoked in connection with hypothetically oriented constructions of responsibility. In lines 14–18, Xavier tries to reconstruct shelter policy: "When you come in the door that's when you're umm what-

what's that the IPO or whatever . . . that's supposed to take your place, so by the time you're nine months due you're supposed to be." He uses personal pronoun "you" and deontic stance markers "suppose to" and "supposed to" to construct a hypothetical, past-tense, generalized client responsibility, which he connects with performance benchmarks measuring client and caseworker accountability ("by the time you're nine months, you're supposed to be").

Here he tries to recite the policy, demonstrating knowledge and awareness of the protocol; however, Ms. Innis responds with implied disagreement through the pre-sequence (Schegloff, 1978) ("lemmie lemmie explain something to you") and a correction of the benchmark timeline, which she follows with a generalized deontic formulation ("that you're supposed to be in shelter"). "You" (line 24) likely refers to "clients" given that she positions Xavier in the subsequent utterance within the accountability framework ("you been here nine," line 26). She places him amid the acceleration framework and refers to the time benchmarks for shelter stay to locate his violation of current policy. This correction on the accountability timeline could be viewed as an indirect speech act that, while seeming like a statement ("you been here nine"), instead offers an oblique critique of perceived irresponsibility.

She uses a narrative account sequence to justify the pressure (line 28), including a micronarrative (line 29–35) that describes clients living in shelters for years, about which she takes a negative stance ("it was never supposed to happen" line 32) and a second micronarrative (lines 35–38), which connects this to the city mayor's policy and his desire "to look good." Her evaluation "heads will roll" (38) provides a hyperbolic metaphorical consequence for their collective irresponsibility. Both narratives function to provide reasons for the current performance benchmarks that are part of the accountability framework and the subsequent pressure she is placing on him. In lines 40–41 she shifts from a collective, general stance to a specific one: "you've been here for nine months . . . it's not like you've been here for six." Again, placing him along the timeline situates his performance as negative vis-à-vis performance standards. While her negative stance ("unfortunately") potentially affiliates with Xavier, her reference to his extensive length of stay ("you've been here for nine months") may be understood yet again as an indirect speech act that obliquely critiques his irresponsibility.

In her last major metaphor, Ms. Innis offers to play "devil's advocate," invoking a performance metaphor that allows her to disaffiliate with Xavier, while ultimately maintaining an affiliative stance (lines 57–80). Here she works in a border space that acknowledges her inexperience with his case, while acknowledging from an administrative standpoint that he has gone beyond established accountability benchmarks, the reference to which carries the weight and threat of sanction. In line 74, she poses a question to him before positioning him as a future client in the "clients stayed in shelter for years" narrative (lines 29–35), using repetition to highlight the importance of time and benchmarks. This resonates with Matarese's (2012) claim that caseworkers used hypothetical statements to posit predictions used to motivate clients to progress and comply. Using "so" (line 78) Ms. Innis positions the pressure put on clients as a result of their violation of shelter stay benchmarks. She uses a conditional statement to again connect the pressure to a moral cultural mythology, the "system abuser," also described in Hancock (2004). In mentioning "time to slide," she characterizes the potential for losing traction on uphill progress; "sliding" is regression and is akin to abusing the system, particularly because the system requires forward progress at all times. In some way, "laziness" and "system abuser" are one and the same in their lack of forward momentum. She concludes her "devil's advocate" stance by summarizing the general perspective of the administration (line 79), recapitulating the administration's stance, which positions any client's responsible action as "not enough." In this case, while "supposed to" is used in a hypothetical and in a general way to refer to general practices and requirements early in the transcript, there is no explicit deontic formulation that Ms. Innis uses that connects Xavier with his assigned responsibilities. Instead, this gestalt of responsibility, the cultural mythologies, the references to performance measurement and timelines all communicate "Do more, make progress. Always."

I am reminded of a great comedic moment by Paul F. Tomkins when he describes his teenage job working retail at a hat store (Hats in the Belfry). People would come in, try on hats, buy nothing, and then leave saying to him, "You must have so much fun working here." The reply to which he narrated as follows,

> Oh, must I? You are not the boss of me, this other teenager is. I'd never had a boss before. Never had—this is a whole new world of getting yelled at. You know, like I couldn't even imagine what this was like. Hats in the Belfry, that was the first place I ever heard the phrase "If you've got time to lean, you've got time to clean." A human *being* said that to me. To my *face*. "If you've got time to lean, you've got time to clean." Why are you talking like that? Are we in the army? So leaning, just totally out of the question for eight hours?! Never a possibility of leaning? You know, I'm not a *horse*,

right? I can't just lock my knees, and I'm good for the day. (Tomkins, 2018)

If the system doesn't keep pressure on, it gives homeless clients "time to slide." If you got time to lean, you got time to clean. "Time to slide" connects performance with time, while also implying laziness. This phrase, so part of the American cultural mythos with historical ties to Calvinism (Weber, 2001), informs modern perspectives around work and moral "goodness." Tompkins is, however, white, and it is worth emphasizing again that Black and Brown communities face these mythologies in significantly more punishing ways, so much so that Tricia Hersey (2022) explicitly pushes against this mythology in her book *Rest as Resistance*, which illustrates the ties between capitalism, white supremacy, and the neoliberal "grind."

The gestalt of responsibility is a constellation of discursive features that generally involve some combination of deontic formulations, references to performance and time, and lexical stance markers that point to cultural mythologies. These collaborate, amounting to more than the sum of their parts (as in Excerpts 3.3 and 3.8). Sometimes one element or another is absent, making the trust of the interaction slightly different. In Excerpt 3.4, the weight of Michael's performance failure takes the foreground, while in 3.5 with Xavier, in not using explicit deontic formulations, the focus is both an educational correction and an indirect way to signal that Xavier's days at the shelter are numbered. Responsibility is offered through connecting Xavier obliquely to the larger narrative of the shift in the shelter system. Sometimes these involve the caseworkers invoking their own responsibilities (3.6, 3.7, 3.8), and other times they are directed solely at the clients.

Discussion

The Positionality of Street-Level Caseworkers

These street-level workers are situated between administration and clients, and here we see them serving as intermediaries between the administrative body and client, having responsibilities to both (Lipsky, 1980/2010). Moreover, while caseworkers constructed client responsibility, they also invoked their own responsibilities as justification for asserting client responsibility. Caseworker Innis and other caseworkers often entangled constructions of client responsibility with invocations of caseworker responsibility, which, given the dual focus of the shelter policy, is not surprising. She and her clients' interests and responsibilities were not mutually exclusive; rather, they were intertwined and interdependent. Due to the interdependence of obligations between them, social interactions concerning her clients' (ir) responsibility encouraged descriptions of her own responsibilities within an accountability framework. Ms. Innis and other workers position themselves in this middle space as both victim of administrative demand, needing the client's progress for performance success ("you've got to help me help you"), and facilitator of client support.

The examples demonstrating the inextricable relationship between caseworkers and clients highlights their alignment with the plight of the clients. Whether they do, as Lipsky (1980/2010) suggests, sometimes refer to their own work troubles to gain their clients' compliance, they discursively construct their job success as depending on their clients' success, which is in line with Soss, Fording, and Schram's (2011) interviews with social welfare caseworkers. Therefore, while it may feel easy to criticize the social workers for callous behavior, their jobs are often on the line too, and they serve more people than they can handle.

Bhabha's (1994) "third space" helps theorize the social construction of policy in Ms. Innis's talk. The "third space" is a hybrid place where meanings "have no primordial unity of fixity; that even the same signs can be appropriated, translated, rehistoricized and read anew" (Bhabha, 1994, 28), "where the negotiation of incommensurable differences creates a tension peculiar to borderline existences" (312). Street-level workers exist on the borders between the public and the institution, translating policy. Policy discourse is processed, (re)packaged, and (re)constructed by caseworkers as they talk to those they serve. "Accountability" and "responsibility" are produced through mundane language ("have to," "gotta," "need," "supposed to," and "should have"). Words that surface in everyday parlance take on new shades of meaning when injected into policy delivery. Implementing policy vis-à-vis discretion occurring within conversations is inherently different from the policy itself, and this borderland third space is activated, allowing for the translation of policy into something digestible. As Lipsky (1980/2010) identifies, the ample discretion provided to street-level workers allows policy implementation to look and function differently in situ than it does on the pages of policy. Ms. Innis's ability to "play devil's advocate" and "be on both sides," for example, highlights her occupation of the middle space in negotiating and constructing meaning. Constructions of responsibility, as elucidated through this case, are revealed to be complex, dynamic, interdependent.

While serving in this middle space, street-level workers also serve as interpreters and enactors of policy and politics (Brodkin, 2013). The references to performance benchmarks and assessments connect the street-level workers to neoliberal and new managerial politics, while references to cultural mythologies situate the workers as craftsmen contributing to what Hancock (2004) calls "public identity." If indeed street-level worker's discretionary choices create policy in situ, then this chapter highlights that this produced policy includes a gestalt of responsibility that connects responsible action with policy, performance, assessment, and cultural mythologies.

Social work and education researchers agree that neoliberal approaches in these fields generate inequalities, and exploring how these cultural mythologies attach to constructions of responsibility helps highlight that inequality can be systemic, institutional, and linguistic. Deresiewicz (2015, 12) argues that neoliberal policies in universities create a "caste system of winners and losers," and Soss, Fording, and Schram (2011, 3) likewise note that neoliberalism in social welfare "discipline[s] the poor," particularly Black Americans experiencing poverty, for circumstances outside of their control. Hancock (2004) looks specifically at the cultural mythologies surrounding the welfare shift in the United States prior to and during the Clinton administration (Personal Responsibility and Work Opportunity Act), noting how the cultural mythology of the "welfare queen" was/is a racialized repurposing of earlier cultural mythologies that morally judged the poor. The unhoused people in this study are men who are Black, men who are Latino, men who are immigrants, and it is important to acknowledge the racialization of these cultural mythologies and their ties to white supremacist (e.g., slavery, Jim Crow) and racialized anti-immigrant movements. The way responsibility is linguistically constructed is both inclusive of neoliberal organizing practices (e.g., performance benchmarks and incentives) and mythologies that exist in collaboration with (but also outside of) neoliberalism. Accordingly, these findings speak to the challenges of a neoliberal framework in these institutions while also speaking more broadly to issues of inequality, questioning, *Why are marginalized people spoken to this way?*

The Positionality of the Unhoused Men

Lipsky (1980/2010) suggests that people are translated into "clients":

> People come to street-level bureaucracies as unique individuals with different life experiences, personalities, and current circumstances. In their encounters with bureaucracies they are trans-

> formed into clients, identifiably located in a very small number of categories, treated as if, and treating themselves as if, they fit standardized definitions of units consigned to specifics bureaucratic slots. The processing of *people* into *clients*, assigning them to categories for treatment by bureaucrats, and treating them in terms of those categories is a social process. Client characteristics do not exist outs of the process that gives rise to them. (59)

The translation of individuals *into* "clients" is a discursive maneuver. Street-level workers use language to position and categorize *people* as *clients*. In the shelter data set, this surfaced in a variety of ways. The word "client" feels inherently neoliberal, connected first and foremost to business parlance. Though not appearing in these examples, case managers sometimes called the next man in the queue into their office using last name, first name, sometimes even saying "comma" (e.g., "Balmat comma Peregrine"). In the reordering of names, people become positioned vis-à-vis their case files. Workers also address those they serve in relation to specified roles and tasks, rather than seeing unhoused people more holistically. Unhoused people were also positioned as "clients" vis-à-vis documents, as in Excerpt 3.3, in which Ms. Innis says to Julio, "See this list? You're on it." Direct reference to the unhoused men as "clients" also shifted the men away from personhood by positioning them vis-à-vis their institutional identities, as when Ms. Innis says to Luciano, "gotta place these clients," where she indirectly refers to Luciano as a member of the group "clients" in Excerpt 3.5. Conley (2015), in examining how jurors distance themselves from defendants in death penalty cases, explains how personal names are more intimate and less distancing, whereas labels like "the defendant" or "these clients" is more distancing. Conley argues that this kind of distancing language may be part of what jurors use to separate themselves from defendants enough to choose putting them to death. Similar kinds of distancing work are being done here by Ms. Innis as she talks about Luciano as one of "these clients." The deontic formulations also themselves subtly convert people into "clients." As the caseworkers assert "I need you to," "you have to," and "you got to," with the support of very real sanctions, they position the unhoused men in a subjugated, responsible position in relation to themselves. The use of cultural mythologies, likewise, position the unhoused men vis-à-vis damaging cultural stereotypes.

It may be useful to consider this translation from *person* to *client* as a form of *interpellation* (Althusser, 1971). Althusser describes a variety of "ideological state apparatuses," sub-ideologies enacted through institutions broadly defined (schools, families, etc.) that together promote a unified macroideology that ultimately supports the "ruling class" (81). While there may be forms of control that are ignited primarily through violence and repression, ideological state apparatuses, as the name implies, subjugate through ideology. He explains that beliefs in the ideology give way to adherence to and engagement in institutional engagement and rituals (e.g., someone who believe in God goes to church, etc.). He ultimately suggests that ideology "recruits" or "hails" (86) individuals, interpellating them as subjects. While I would argue for a more social constructivist approach to ritual and interpellation, the concept contributes hegemonic heft to Lipsky's (1980/2010) claim that workers translate individuals into clients. In so doing, we see not just this shift from "person" to "client" but also that this shift puts "clients" in a subjugated institutional position vis-à-vis the worker. In this data, deontic formulations interpellate unhoused men into a subjugated "client" position. Who is beholden to the caseworker? Likewise, workers' use of cultural mythologies like "lazy" or "freeloader" interpellate unhoused men vis-à-vis historically and morally loaded ideologies. This gestalt of responsibility, then, may interpellate people into institutional roles—in this case "clients," and, in the subsequent chapter, "students."

There are, however, exceptions worth noting. In Excerpt 3.4, for example, Ms. Innis, after describing all the housing scenarios that Michael has rejected, exasperatingly pleads with him, saying, "Tell me what you want." The personal pronoun "you" individuates this utterance, focusing on Michael's specific desires. In general, workers' ability to use their discretion means that their interpellation of unhoused men as *clients* may also shift in relation to their goals. Ms. Innis also interpellates herself as a subjugated intermediary, subject to the shelter administration in Excerpts 3.3 and 3.8. In relating her own fears about performance assessment ("I have to get the brunt of this," "They're gonna come down on me," "I'm stressed," and "when they need something I have to be able to produce it, and if I can't produce it I'm the one that's getting the rap at the end of the day"), she interpellates herself as a "victim," highlighting her own medial position between the clients and administration and her subjugated position vis-à-vis shelter administration.

The gestalt of responsibility integrates several problematic elements. The deontic formulations sit in constellation with more obviously insidious cultural mythologies and with performance benchmarks. The gestalt is not sullied by cultural mythologies only. References to benchmarks carry the weight of future unpleasantness, even threat of sanction. These references to performance in the conversation potentially point not only to the presence of these benchmarks and their relevance in conversation but also to the looming pressure and the potential for sanction these benchmarks represent. The upcoming classroom context (Chapters 4 and 6), without sanction, carries the threat of failure, of having to repeat the course or leave college. These references to performance, then, are not themselves weightless or neutral; they are looming performance measurements with consequences, scapegoats that justify the caseworker's pressure on the clients, displacing responsibility to the institution—to those who ultimately create such requirements

When I turned to my newer data set in the developmental reading course for community college students, I found strikingly similar constructions, supporting my conceptualization of the gestalt. While I went into data collection at the community college without an interest in examining responsibility, it became clear that there were similar ideological issues at play in how responsibility is constructed. This next chapter examines this context. Although this context does not utilize an explicit responsibility policy, constructions of responsibility sound surprisingly similar. Chapter 4 explores in more depth how cultural mythologies surface in the gestalt.

4 | Constructing Responsibility in the Reading Classroom

While the previous chapter introduced the gestalt of responsibility, this chapter takes us into a remedial reading community college classroom, focusing on one aspect of the gestalt: the lexical stances that point to cultural mythologies. Chapter 3, in the interest of establishing the components of the gestalt in general, left some questions unanswered. Does anyone ever say anything nice? Do "positive" cultural mythologies exist? Are there constructions of responsibilities that focus outside of the parameters of institutional demands? By exploring how the professor constructs responsibility in his classroom, this chapter seeks to answer some of those questions by digging deeper into not only cultural mythologies but also street-level discretion. In this investigation, we will look more closely at cultural mythologies around the construction of responsibility surrounding two classroom topics. The first is directly tied to performance benchmarks and measurements: talk on the topic of remedial reading course high-stakes assessments (or steps en route to the high-stakes assessment). The second conversational context is a semester-long discretionary assignment developed by the professor: the reading of *Fahrenheit 451* by Ray Bradbury. I present these two contexts to explore how bonded these cultural mythologies are to institutional performance benchmarks and assessments when responsibility is constructed. Do they occur in discussions around less institutionally required topics? The chapter ends by considering the relevance of time and timescale in the gestalt of responsibility and in these two research contexts.[1] In so doing, we begin to consider how stances around cultural mythologies intersect with relevant timescales. I will also present some negative cases that interrogate other ways responsibility surfaces in the classroom.

Social Context for Study

Like the New York City shelter system, the NYC educational system experienced a wave of federal policy shifts in accordance with neoliberal principles. While the social welfare system saw Aid for Dependent Families with Children (AFDC) shift to TANF (Temporary Assistance to Needy Families), inserting performance benchmarks and increased accountability into receiving social safety nets (Trattner, 1998), the educational system saw No Child Left Behind (NCLB) and Race to the Top (RttT), both of which hurt marginalized communities (Lipman, 2015; Menken, 2008). NCLB and RttT focused on standardized test scores and linked school funding to test performance incentives. Menken (2008) examined the way in which standardized testing under NCLB left English-language learners behind. Ravitch (2009), an educational historian, has called RttT "Bush's third term in education," and Lipman (2015) suggests that Obama's RttT educational policy not only doubled down on the neoliberal agenda of the Bush Jr. era but disproportionately impacted "schools serving low-income students of color" (57).

In higher education, and particularly at CUNY community colleges, the neoliberal focus shifted toward accelerated learning, persistence, and retention programs (Sullivan, 2017) and to a restructuring of community colleges based on (primarily quantitative) research conducted by the Community College Research Center, a center at Teachers College, Columbia University, that is populated by researchers who (to my knowledge) have never spent time as faculty in a community college. The CCRC has been conducting large, grant-funded research on community colleges for decades, informing federal, state, and citywide policies that impact community colleges across the United States (Bailey et al., 2015). They have conducted studies on the role and macrostructure of community colleges, the transition from high school to college, developmental education and remediation, student persistence, and completion, among other topics. However, while some of their findings are useful (e.g., shifting the structure of courses away from "cafeteria-style" education), many of their studies also recommend acceleration and other neoliberal educational mainstays. Their work paints a narrow portrait of community college life, student challenges, teaching, and learning, obvious to anyone actively teaching in a community college (Isserles, 2021). Notwithstanding, their research has led to a series of state and federal policies that do not properly reflect the community college experience, and those studies generate challenges for faculty and staff on the ground who are asked to make changes based on poor data. In fact, at CCRC's twentieth-anniversary celebration, First Lady Jill Biden challenged the CCRC to conduct more qualitative research, asking it to examine the lived experiences of community college students. Moreover, CCRC has consistently relied on CUNY community colleges as sources of data without offering to collaborate with community college faculty researchers, a relationship that exploits the community college, its faculty, and its students.

In addition to the studies conducted by CCRC, increasing numbers of community college faculty and administration have published studies about community college remedial/developmental skills (Levin and Calcagno, 2008). These studies, however, are neither ethnographic nor discourse analytic. Instead, they primarily focus on large-scale enrollment numbers and do not consider the experience of students inside these classrooms. This is particularly egregious considering that developmental reading classrooms include a particularly marginalized and heterogeneous population of students, coming from a variety of linguistic and dialectal backgrounds. This chapter and Chapter 6 use an interactional ethnographic approach to explore how an instructor of a remedial reading course constructs responsibility with his students over the course of a college semester.[2]

From Field Notes

> If they give you ruled paper, write the other way.
>
> —BMCC

One of the weird things about BMCC is its placement. Though it is a college primarily serving marginalized students, including students from approximately 170 different countries and from approximately 37 different language backgrounds (BMCC, 2024), it is in Tribeca, one of the most expensive, affluent neighborhoods in New York City. Our proximity to the World Trade Center and the financial district is ever-present. You can regularly see people clustered outside of Hugh Jackman's coffee shop and people feasting in Robert de Niro's Tribeca Grill. Tribeca is home to celebrities and host to the Tribeca Film Festival, one theater of which is actually located inside BMCC.

Walking up the long cement incline to the large, brick multi-city-block college building, I shout a passing "Good morning" to colleagues and students on my way into the main building, and they shout greetings back. A large abstract statue of a torso casts a shadow on the ground, which upon closer inspection is called *Icarus*. This art piece at the entryway to the college appears to warn against the dangers of reaching too high at a college that, upon entering, proclaims that students can "start here, go anywhere." I go through the security turnstiles, scanning my ID, and go up the escalators to my office on the sixth floor. Most of my colleagues would head up to the fourth floor to our department, where many offices have an unparalleled view of the Hudson River and New Jersey. Outside of the view, the spaces are set up not unlike those at the shelter, many offices partitioned by cheap, impermanent walls that keep few conversations private. Offices for three or more people use blue-gray cubicle space dividers. I, however, do not go to the fourth floor. Instead, I have a random solo office about two floors away from my office that I scored on a lark. There is no window, no natural light, and no direct heat or air conditioning, but I can decorate it how I like. I am right on the main hall, and I enjoy my proximity to the Social Science, Social Work, Criminal Justice, and Speech departments. En route to my office, I start to sweat through my suit. One or more of the escalators is always broken, and I laugh inwardly thinking of Mitch Hedberg's joke about how escalators never break, they just become stairs. In any case, I nearly always get to my office a little drippy, and often there's a line of sleepy students ready who have all signed in and are ready for office hours. I throw my coat off, hit the private, gendered faculty/staff bathroom, fill my water at the water fountain. The clock turns over from 10:59 to 11:00, and we begin office hours.

Vigilantes take the law into their own hands because they perceive law enforcement to be inadequate. In similar fashion, my partner, a comics and film scholar, often jokes that teaching at BMCC is "vigilante education." He says, "You have to be like Batman." The resources we have do not work, and what we are offered is often tied up with red tape. We have money for student researchers but no place to put them. We have money for student tutors but the funding isn't settled for several weeks into the semester, and when they finally start, they have to sit in the hallway outside of closed study rooms that neither they nor I can reserve. A provost signature is required to make any and all color copies.

Many semesters have begun with my ID card not being properly coded with the right classrooms, at which time I have to call campus security, who seem deeply skeptical of anyone's right to be in the room when they arrive to unlock my classroom door. However, if security is occupied, or if they are on the other side of campus, or (likely) if this is happening to ten other professors at the same time, classrooms are sometimes opened upwards of forty minutes after class should have started. During these times, I have often taught in the hallways for the entire session.

During several semesters I have had to call media services at the beginning of every class session the entire semester because whoever used the classroom prior to my class ritually mangled the hookups for the computer and projector. One semester, in my partner's film class, the audio cord that links the computer to the speakers appeared to be missing. My partner, frustrated but pressing on with the film (without audio), pulled down the projector screen, only to notice that whoever had been in the room before him had used the computer's audio cable as the pull-string for the projector screen. In any case, I have media services on speed dial on my cell phone. It is higher up on the list than my parents' numbers (sorry, Mom and Dad).

Autoethnography: I Want to Show You My Determination

Personal responsibility permeates many aspects of academic life, department meetings, the senate floor, among teachers and students, and even surfacing in hallways and bathrooms (as discussed in Chapter 7). One place I notice responsibility most is in emails sent by students who have missed, in some cases weeks and in other cases months, of class. Students at BMCC face all manner of difficulties, including housing and food insecurity. Some students experience serious health issues or are taking care of family who are sick, and other students are parents and caregivers. Students have family living in all parts of the world, and when war breaks out or when an earthquake hits, they are understandably distracted. Each semester, I have a few students who fall out of conversation with me and the class. They stop attending (whether in person or online), and all communication ceases. Emails from me to check in on how they're doing go unanswered.

In my classes, one set of assignments related to course readings has inflexible due dates, and major assignments (papers, transcription and analysis assignments, etc.) are entirely flexible, which allows students who email at a late date an opportunity to pass the course. Generally, in the last third of the semester, weeks after midterms and sometimes directly before or during finals week, I will get emails from several of the students who went missing, asking if there is time enough to make up work. I check their grades and assignments to see where they stopped, and depending on when they disappeared, I let them know what their chances are of passing. Each semester, there are a couple students who withdraw just prior to finals week who perhaps stopped coming in the first several weeks of the semester, but generally students who attended and participated who simply have not done the major assignments are able to catch up and pass with a D or C.

While I have not collected official data on this, I have noticed a trend with these emails, one that harkens back to the self-flagellating "my fault, my fault, my most grievous fault" I described earlier. Emails from students often begin with a description of their difficult semester, which may either be vague or include specific events/situations. Many of these involve a performance of trauma that I imagine must be painful to have to invoke and even more painful to exploit in order to get readmitted to courses/the college. It is worth noting that students who are put on academic probation are asked to appeal their probation, in part, by submitting a letter that explains why they have fallen short in the classroom or in college more broadly. There is precedent, therefore, for students reproducing their trauma in their narratives.

At this point in the email, some students ask for what they need: an extension, an incomplete grade, help catching up on assignments. Other students, however, continue the email by offering a negative evaluation of their performance: I know that I haven't been the most attentive student; I know that falling behind is completely on me; it is my fault that I am behind in your class. They take on responsibility for falling behind, often using the factive predicate "I know" to present their appraisal as "fact." What follows is a student email written to a colleague of mine, which the student (and colleague) consented to share (parentheticals have been added for clarity and identifying information has been deleted as needed).

> I am a part of your XXXX class. I have had a rough semester trying to complete my classes; however, it was stressful to a point where I wanted to give up. It's been hard and tough to go and complete work when I was unmotivated with myself. However, I am more determined than ever now to do better for myself. And I know that starts with your class, I want to do better, I want to show you my determination to pass your class. I just need some guidance from you in what I can complete in your class to

> maybe be able to receive a C. I want to complete the [research article] annotations if that is okay with you to receive a grade for it, and also my analysis I want to complete however I'm unsure what the analysis is and I need help understanding what exactly I need to do, is it a paragraph, can we talk about this is class tomorrow to see what I need to complete please and thank you. Thank you for your time.
>
> Sincerely,
>
> XXXX

In this student's email, we see multiple references to grittiness, self-knowledge, and evaluation. After describing their difficult semester in more general terms, the student explains their inaction as lack of motivation, which they offer to counter with renewed "determination." They even use the factive predicate "I know" to demonstrate their self-awareness. They use "I want" multiple times to underscore their desire not only to do better but to display determination. The student then asks for guidance.

I get countless emails like this every semester. Students perform their awareness of their perceived failure to be gritty in the face of homelessness, domestic violence, caring for a chronically sick sibling or parent, the death of a close relative, losing nine family members to Covid in the spring of 2020. They often punctuate these statements with acknowledgments of their failure of responsibility: I know I should have done better/worked harder. Each time, I gently email back to remind students that we are all humans, and that college is just one part of their lives, and that it is unrealistic to think that anyone can prioritize school above everything else all the time. I remind them that they do not need to berate themselves or self-criticize for me. I do not need doctor's notes to prove sickness, and I do not need explanations for missing class. I trust my students, and as much as possible I structure my courses in a way that allows them to be adult-scholar-researchers who make adult choices. I do not want to police my students, and I want to remove, to the extent that I can, my function as an "officer" and as a "boss." Creeping neoliberalism has tentacles everywhere.

Responsibility in the Community College Classroom

Having already spoken about the Academic and Critical Reading (ACR) course in this book's introduction, I will just remind the reader that students taking this course were required to do so by an entrance exam that labeled them as requiring reading remediation. ACR was a gatekeeping course that students had to pass in order to take most college courses, and professors tried their best to balance test preparation and skills development with intriguing readings that generated critical thinking. From a street-level perspective, these courses and indeed the position of the professor allowed more discretion. We could choose what kind of readings we wanted to use to suit the requirements and learning outcomes of the course. The epigraph to this subsection comes from *Fahrenheit 451*, which the participating professor assigned to his students. The book, a love letter to reading and books, as well as a cautionary tale that warns against naive acceptance and fascism, set the tone for a course devoted to critical thinking and critical reading. In *Fahrenheit*, reading is a moral imperative.

Neoliberal Organizational Concerns

As in the previous chapter, the professor in this chapter sometimes constructed responsibility in simpler ways. Without belaboring an introduction to deontic formulations described in Chapter 2, Table 4.1 includes samples of the deontic formulations that typified overt constructions of responsibility in this classroom.

Constructions of responsibility in the community college reading classroom looked surprisingly similar to those in the social work context, with some notable exceptions. While they were produced through personal pronoun choices, deontic formulations, infinitive verbs, and

TABLE 4.1: Constructions of Responsibility Around Testing

	Examples of deontic formulations in the community college course
1	So how many of you have more than two TVs in your apartment. (**Gotta**) raise your hands.
2	All right? Okay. So remember for:: Monday? The handout? And also remember that **you need to** be reading the next twenty pages in *Fahrenheit 451*.
3	Communist government. But a dictatorship. O:r in many cases **you should write** these words down if you don't know them? A totalitarian government.
4	This was homework. **Everybody should have** the answers.
5	**You hafta keep** going back and asking those questions

objects, the classroom context more often included imperative commands that assigned responsible actions, though most of those did not include deontic modals and verbs and so were excluded from this analysis (e.g., “Look it up”). Imperatives may be more prevalent in this context because ACR was a very difficult class for which to plan. While my Linguistics courses include a detailed course schedule, including daily readings and assignments, holding students to a course schedule in ACR was difficult, if not impossible. Though I always gave my students a projected course schedule, our ability to get through a particular reading really depended on the students: how many students attended regularly, how many students did the homework (work, which did not count toward a grade for much of our time teaching the course), what the skill level of the student group was overall, and which skills were the most troublesome. Accordingly many professors did not give the students a semester course schedule at all but instead assigned students work the day of, perhaps giving them a week or two in advance. Imperatives may surface more in ACR because in this particular class, and others like it, the assignments and “to-dos” were not established ahead of time and were often modified in the moment.

Constructions of Responsibility Around Performance

In Excerpt 4.1, the instructor is reviewing a test the students have taken, and he uses the student’s correct answer as a model for how students should interact with the test.

Excerpt 4.1: Willingness to work

T: B. B. Good Bahar right? They all require very similar soil and climate conditions. Okay **make sure you go back**. When there’s factual questions. This is a matter of strategy. **Are you willing to take the time**, **make the effort, and look for the answer in the test**. **Look at the question, look at the answers, look for the words** that match up, Inferencing you can’t do that. Right? **You have to think larger**. **You have to read** what you have and then **connect it**. But factual questions? Just **go back** to the passage. And also **do** the process of elimination if the answer doesn’t get you right away. **Eliminate** those that you have a strong feeling are negative? then (.) **choose** from what’s left. How bout number four, Beryl?

S: “As it is used in the passage, the underlined word fabricated most nearly means” manufactured.

After positively evaluating the student's answer and reading the answer to the class, he provides the class with strategies for locating facts in a text. Using a directive in line 2, he offers a recommended general reading practice (Lance et al., 2023): "make sure you go back." Lance et al. (2023) explain that commands were often used in Covid signs in the New York City linguistic landscape to suggest generalized Covid safety practices. Similarly, many of the commands used by this professor urge the students toward general practices for being good readers or test takers.

The type of test question the student is answering is a "fact finding" question, and the professor makes the argument that factual questions require strategy, noting that the fact-finding questions are comparatively easier than inferencing questions where the information is not directly stated. A series of commands mark the strategy for locating facts, including "look[ing]"—at the questions, at answers, and for keywords (lines 5–6). He follows this with constructions of deontic responsibility (lines 6–7): "you have to think larger" and "you have to read what you have and then connect it." "Thinking larger" is a morally weighty critique of thinking too "small." These two sentences utilize personal pronouns to link deontic responsibility "have to" with the target of assigned responsibility "you." This description of responsibility includes and closes with imperatives: "connect it," "just go back," "do the process," "eliminate those," "choose from what's left." These constructions of responsibility, however, are also tied to a characterization of grittiness (lines 3–4): "are you willing to take the time, make the effort, and look for the answers in the test." In positioning test success as "willingness," the instructor links reading and testing success to the cultural mythology of hard work and perseverance. In reality, some students who work hard to learn the skills, attend every class session, and do all the homework will not pass the final exam. This excerpt, like those in the social work contexts, points to a gestalt of responsibility that combines deontic formulations, imperative commands, personal pronouns, and cultural mythologies.

While sometimes students are positioned as "unwilling," other times they are characterized as "lazy," a cultural mythology applied to a room almost entirely composed of students of color. Hancock (2004), in her book *The Politics of Disgust*, separates "lack of work ethic" into two different codes—"don't work" and "lazy," thereby showing how characterizations of people's *actions* are tied to *moral judgments*. In the following excerpt, the instructor invokes this combination of mythologies while reviewing inferencing, a skill that teaches students how to draw conclusions that are not directly stated in the text.

Excerpt 4.2: If you're lazy

T: TIME! All right there's a good one. TIME. That's fine we assign numbers for that we don't really count time. That's kind of made up or who ever made up these rules. Twenty four hours in a day. It's all garbage, right. (Inaudible) But what do we count? What do I have to count in class here?

Ss: How many students

T: HOW MANY STUDENTS! What if I'm a farmer and producing cotton? Should I just sell different amounts for the same amount of money?

Ss: nooooo.

T: So I need to weigh things in a scale. Or if I make uhh I don't know I make the trees that they they grow the trees that they put in these uh urban parks over here. XXX XXXX. Now remember **we're at the point of the semester** where **simple answers aren't good enough**. You **have to keep asking why**. **Keep digging more and more**. okay? That's what you're going to be **tested** on most. That's what thinking inferences are about. Have some knowledge, add what you know, come to a conclusion. **If you're lazy**, it doesn't happen. **If you're satisfied with the surface**, it's not gonna happen. You can all read and understand on the surface but that's not the challenge. The challenge is to keep asking questions. **You should keep asking**. Move on to number three. Oh wait do we have the answer for ten, by the way?

Ss: (Inaudible)

T: Ten. Good. Okay (Inaudible) I forgot it's your answer. I'm more than ten. much, more. °all right.°

Responsibility is constructed through both imperative and deontic formulations. He urges them in lines 12 and 13 to "keep asking why" and to "keep digging more and more." In line 17, he uses "should," a deontic formulation, to suggest future action. Like the social welfare examples, the gestalt of responsibility here combines these constructions of responsibility with references to timelines, performance assessments, and cultural mythologies. He connects the work required from students to the timeline of the semester: "at the point of the semester" (line 11) and the high-stakes performance measurement that serves as a gatekeeper to the majority of the classes on campus ("that's what you're going to be tested on most," line 13). These performance benchmarks carry the weight of potential failure, money lost, a college career forestalled by a reading exam.

The "simple answers" he refers to in line 11 index less complex reading skills such as finding the main idea or supporting details, and he explains that given the timeline of the semester, students need to stretch beyond these skills. While these "simple answers" surely refer to a simpler skill set, it is hard to not also see the phrase as a characterization of student effort in light of the moral judgment that comes after it. The conditional "if you're lazy, it doesn't happen" indirectly positions the students as "lazy" through the conditional "if," which embeds consequences in a phrase that also warns against the hypothetical dangers of "laziness" (Fergyson et al., 1986; Fillenbaum, 1986). These hypothetical dangers, however, seem less hypothetical when nested alongside descriptions of student behavior that point to "simple" work. As Hancock (2004) points out, a lack of work is tied to a judgment of morality. While nested in a conditional, the reference to "laziness" indexes a presupposition of potential student laziness. Likewise, the conditional, "if you're satisfied with the surface, it's not gonna happen" warns the students about the dangers of complacency and not going deep enough in the text. Going "deeper," however, requires more work, so this excerpt too points to the need to be gritty, persevere, and work harder for the deeper textual meanings.

In the final example in this subsection, we again see the gestalt of responsibility emerging as a constellation of interrelated and collocated features, features that through their repeated proximity to each other highlight a way of "doing" responsibility. This transcript marks the first class back after spring break, and the classroom is full again for the first time in weeks, students returning to class after various setbacks that kept them away from the classroom.

Excerpt 4.3: Work Harder

= ((Students laughing))
T: There you go we're all sniffing. That's good. Okay. But you're all here which is a **good** thing (1.) Okay? Some: of you are **making a rare appearance** and uh **welcome back**? Its **good to see you again**. An:d, we ha:::ve what **three three and a half weeks of class left**. (3.) So this is the time your teachers tell you things like, "**Well you gotta kick it in to a higher gear, you gotta start working even harder than your working**," so when the teachers tell you do you pay any attention?
S1: No=
S2: =Yes
T: $No, there's an [honest answer.$ Ok (2.) °alright°]
Ss: [students laughing]
T: But its good advice (3.) The last **part of the semester**, you guys are all **facing the exact same thi::ng** at **the end of the semester**. You gonna have to **take the ACT**, sit for the test, do your best hopefully pass and get to move on. (2.) Well this is the **time** of the semester that, (.) yeah I want you- I hope you all start **working even harder than you were working** but it's also the **time to assess what you've done** so far, to **really look yourself in the mirror, HONESTLY, to see how hard you've actually worked**? Have you done all the assignments, do you go over the work after we finish it, have you gone to the reading lab, have you gone online, worked from home? If

the answer to all those questions (.) is no, **it's not too late** to start. So I'm not here to **criticize you, chastise you, chide you, I'm here to encourage you not to stop at this point and if you haven't really st:arted its ok::: to start now, when teachers tell you to kick it in to upper gear (4.) what they really mean is you got three weeks to work as hard as you can (1.) to accomplish your goal, but you're in control of that**. We'll continue doing what we do in class, we're gonna focus on inferences probably for the entire period and last two weeks we'll start doing some practice.

This excerpt begins with a lightly censorious welcome, the instructor both noting the presence of sniffling students with colds and students who have long been absent. What follows is a well-intended call-to-action wherein the gestalt of responsibility unfolds. The gestalt begins by situating the call to responsible action in time with "three and a half weeks of class left" (lines 4–5). The instructor then references the hypothetical speech of professors at this time of year, and in so doing combines deontic formulations "gotta" with two similar cultural mythologies "kick it into a higher gear" and "start working even harder than you're working." The hypothetical instructors in this scenario initiate "gritty" mythologies, encouraging students to double down on their efforts.

The professor then repositions the hypothetical teachers' advice as his own, saying, "but it's good advice," harkening to Schegloff's (2001) paper that describes the use of "no" to shift from joking to seriousness. He moves from the "smiley voice" in line 10, which gives permission for students to laugh in line 11, to a no-nonsense, getting-down-to-business tone. Having reoriented the conversational tone, the instructor then restates the argument in more specific terms, referencing the time benchmark in the semester as a way to situate responsibility ("part of the semester" line 12) as they prepare for their performance assessment ("facing the exact same thing," "take the ACT," lines 13–14). He reiterates the timeline ("time of the semester") as it relates to the cultural mythology of working harder. In some way, this harkens back to Ms. Innis's response to Xavier from the Chapter 3: "Whatever you're doing, you aren't doing enough."

At this point, the discussion of responsibility shifts toward accountability, as he asks students to "assess what you've done so far" and to "look in the mirror HONESTLY" (lines 16–18). The intonational emphasis on "honestly" here indirectly suggests that self-assessments tend to be generous. When asking them to assess "how hard you've actually worked," the word "actually" likewise suggests a disjuncture between the assessment and the reality. The instructor then lists assigned responsibilities, telling students that there is still time to complete currently unmet responsibilities. He closes by once again emphasizing the timeline "three weeks" and the cultural mythologies "kick it into upper gear" and "work as hard as you can" (line 23), which underscore the relationship between time, performance assessment, responsibility, and cultural mythology. The moral coda that concludes this topic shifts the focus of responsibility from the cultural mythology "working hard" to "individual responsibility," when he states "you're in control of that."

As a capstone to the pep talk, the instructor reminds students that he is not criticizing them, using a sequence of three intonationally stressed, synonymous words to underscore his goodwill and intentions. He contextualizes his comments as "encourage[ment]" (line 21), explaining to the class that it isn't too late to start preparing for the final exam.

In these examples, cultural mythologies are utilized in conjunction with deontic formulations and references to performance assessments. In order to understand the link between performance assessments and cultural mythologies, I briefly provide examples of how responsibility was discussed when class time was devoted to the course novel, which was not included on the high-stakes final exam.

Discretionary Concerns: Becoming Readers

Incorporating reading materials unrelated to the test was, for many faculty (myself included), a way of salvaging some sense of professionalism, a feeling that our areas of expertise were being used for learning *content*. Including a novel, short stories, or poems could be a form of resistance, a discretionary action afforded by the power, prestige, and privilege of the position. This professor also intentionally utilized this book to teach the value of reading and critical thinking. In this class, the professor taught *Fahrenheit 451*, and reading the novel was woven throughout the semester. This subsection examines the constructions of responsibility that occur as part of this discretionary topic and the cultural mythologies that surface alongside them, comparing these to similar constructions in the performance assessment talk described earlier in this chapter.

The Discretion of the Professor

As street-level workers we utilize discretion, which allows us to construct responsibility how we see fit. Instructors can make decisions about what to teach and how. One morning, as the participating instructor and his students discuss the vocabulary word "autonomy," the class started generating examples of jobs and professions that provided flexibility and autonomy. One student said "teacher," to which the instructor agrees, mirroring her comment:

> TEACHER. An' this is one of the main reasons, not the- the main reason? One of the main reasons why people become teachers.=They like autonomy. Right¿ No boss. Yeah I know we're being filmed here, but that's different. Right, okay. No boss here. Yeah there's a curriculum we have to follow, there's goals we have to meet, but nobody comes in and tells us how we have to teach each day.

One student chimes in, saying, "But there are a lot of responsibilities." "Oh, say that louder," the instructor says. "But you have a lot of responsibilities." The instructor positively evaluates the student's contribution saying, "Good." And then connects responsibility to autonomy, commenting, "Cause that's what goes along with autonomy, doesn't it. Good."

Notably, teachers have "bosses" and more oversight than professors. In ACR, this professor exercises his autonomy by teaching a novel that is both relevant to the course topic and one that he loves: *Fahrenheit 451*. The novel emphasizes the importance of books, reading, and critical thinking, making it perhaps perfect for a college level reading course.

In Excerpt 4.4, we find constructions of responsibility that only tangentially relate to the high-stakes final exam, instead focusing on cultivating a culture of readers who engage in the practices that readers engage in. In the excerpt, the instructor is discussing the first several pages of *Fahrenheit 451* with his students, introducing the protagonist, Montag's, job as a "fireman," which in the context of the book is a person who sets books, which are illegal, on fire.

Excerpt 4.4: "We should get into the habit"

Okay. So. A fireman. He doesn't put out fires? He burns books. So part one, the
title is "The Hearth and the Salamander." **Anybody bother looking up**- a
salamander's a little creature, but in mythology, **anybody look up**
what a salamander is?
(5.0)
All right we should get into the habit- particularly, I even put that word
on the board in the list of vocabulary? If you can't figure out what it
means, **look it up.** <**look** **it** **up**>. look it up in the dictionary. Go online. So
in mythology a salamander is a creature that's immune to fire. That
can't burn. So when a fireman wears a shield of a phoenix? Phoenix,
the bird that- another mythological creature?(   ) flies out of the fire,
salamander can't be burned. Good thing for firemen to be wearing.
The hearth. What's a hearth.

In this excerpt, the gestalt of responsibility is generated through the use of a deontic formulation and cultural mythologies. In lines 2–4, the instructor says, "Anybody bother looking up," and he stops short of finishing his statement, recasting the question with some context: "a salamander's a little creature, but in mythology, anybody look up what a salamander is?" As we have learned from Heritage and Robinson (2011), the word "any" when used in a question anticipates a "no" answer. Here the expected "no" is reinforced by the term "bother," which recognizes inconvenience and extra work involved in doing the task. The phrase "anybody bother" signifies both the cultural mythology of grittiness (doing extra work even though it is frustrating or difficult) while also creating an expectation through "any" that no one did the task. Even the recast "anybody look up what a salamander is" creates an expectation that no one looked up the information. The lengthy silence (line 5) from the students draws attention to some trouble around answering the question.

This becomes a teachable moment, then, where the instructor explains what readers "should" do, using a deontic formulation to communicate future responsible habits students should cultivate. This is followed by a series of commands "look it up" (said three separate times) and "go online" (line 8). The instructor then defines the creature for the students. The instructor uses his discretion to include the book in the curriculum, and uses the teaching of the book as an opportunity to discuss the practices expected of college-level readers in general.

In an earlier moment of class, the instructor similarly says, "All right, so this is the first sentence if the book. Oh by the way, anybody bother looking up why this book is called *Fahrenheit 451*? Does anybody care?" On one hand, one might critique the attitude presented in this statement. On the other, it is worth remembering that because passing the course was contingent on a high-stakes multiple choice exam, students at this time were not required to do any class work in order to pass. I remember my own frustration, described earlier, of students not doing their homework. On a good day, about half to three-quarters of the class would do homework. It was hard to plan class sessions because it was unclear who did the reading/assignment, and it was hard to help students move forward when so few did the assignments. "Does anybody care," while critiquing the students by expecting a "no" answer, also gives voice to the professor's daily exasperation of having to cajole students into completing assignments that while not required will help them develop important reading skills. Such a statement aligns, perhaps, with Ms. Innis's (Chapter 3) claims to being overworked and "stressed," indicators of job-related exasperation.

In the next excerpt, the instructor is addressing this very issue, describing the responsibilities students have in general. While the term "responsible" and its permutations surfaced rarely in the social work data, they do surface in the education corpus.

Excerpt 4.5: Should the Teacher Read the Textbook to You?

T: Yeah, it is easy to fall asleep then, because (.) it's not making any sense to you. It's boring. It's one of your favorite words, It's boring to sit and listen to somebody talk about a subject and you have no knowledge of it, or you have very little knowledge of it. So you're asked to read before the teacher talks about it. In most cases. So that when you come into class, and the teacher starts talking about these ideas, what we want to happen as teachers is for you to say "oh yeah, I remember that. I just read that last night." But what the teacher is saying is gonna reinforce what you've already read. **After all should the teacher just come in and read the textbook to you?**
((Dave shaking head "no"))

Dave: No,

T: That's not how college works, it's your **responsibility** to do that. That's why you're in this class in part, isn't it, to help you be able to do this more effectively. S**o that you can read** what may seem strange to you, but to still understand it, an' make your life a little bit easier in class. "One of the characteristics of society, the existence of segmentation." What do you think that word means, "segmentation".

In a similar vein to the last excerpt, the instructor is explaining why reading ahead of class is helpful. While there are no deontic formulations in this example, there is a description of what Lance et al. (2023) call statements of "general practice," which do not include immediate actions to be performed but rather descriptions of how one should behave generally. In this case, the professor describes the general responsibilities of a student, inside and outside of his class. In lines 6–7, he asks what seems like a rhetorical question, "after all should the teacher just come in and read the textbook to you?" Indirectly, the professor invokes the cultural mythology of "not working hard" by suggesting that some students prefer not to work for their learning by relying on the professor read the textbook to them. Given the cultural norms around student learning, the question in lines 6–7 may position the students for a "no" reply. In so doing, he asks students to assess the responsibility of instructors as compared with students. One student shakes his head "no" and then says "no," and the instructor validates his answer, explaining that, as a general practice, it is students' responsibility to read the textbook. This excerpt, then, underscores the division of responsibilities in the classroom, while also utilizing the time to explain what is expected of college students. Though this is not an overt aim of the course, the instructor uses his discretion to weave this goal into the course. It appears that even when the class discussion focuses on non-test-related topics, the cultural mythologies are present, but what about deontic formulations?

In the next excerpt, the class is once again discussing *Fahrenheit 451*, and the instructor is encouraging the class to ask questions.

Excerpt 4.6: "That's like reading CliffsNotes. That's cheating."

T: Can make you stop and think. Even if you don't really know clearly
what's going on. Alice you said that you had trouble, you didn't
quite understand everything that you read. Okay? And I said to you:,
It's okay? What did I suggest that you do. <You write do:wn,>
STU26 Questions.
T: Your questions. Cause on the second day of class, what did I fill the
board with?
STU26 Questions.
T: Who, what, when, where, why. **You hafta keep going back** and asking
those questions. Even if you don't have answers to the questions.
cause that's why we're doing this. It's one of the reasons we're doing
this. Is that when you come and talk to each other, instead of **just**
some professor giving you all of the answers, you can get the answers
among yourselves. (It's) much better. **You'll learn much more that**
way. Cause I could just come up here and tell you what the book is
about. But will you have accomplished anything if we do it that way?
That's like reading Cliff's Notes. That's cheating. So even if it's a
struggle for you, and that's perfectly okay, okay? **Just keep fighting**
your way through. But write down the questions. I put about, what
about twenty words on the board, the other day? Make sure you can
define those words. Same way we do the vocabulary exercises, you
have to use everything we read to build the vocabulary as well.

In this interaction, the instructor is once again using his discretion to center the lesson around the novel. In this context, we once again see the gestalt of responsibility rear its head through the confluence of deontic formulations and cultural mythologies. This final excerpt shows us that the gestalt of responsibility can surface in and around testing talk *and also* when the discussion is centered around discretionary topics like the novel. The instructor begins by describing a student's difficulty with the text, using that experience as justification for constructing responsibility through a description of general responsible reading practice "you hafta keep going back and asking those questions" (line 9). The deontic formulation "hafta" (have to) communicates the obligation to keep questioning, which he connects to a cultural mythology. He encourages students to "come and talk to each other, instead of just some professor giving you all the answers." "Just" and "some" both downgrade and generalize the professor, so that the lesson extends beyond this classroom, and "giving you all the answers" alludes to the cultural mythology of laziness wherein students take the easy route and do not do hard work required of a "good" student. He explains that students can get the answers themselves, and he takes a stance on this approach, calling it "much better," which upgrades ("much") the already positive assessment.

The professor equates receiving information solely from the professor (rather than working for it) with "reading CliffsNotes," a summary of the novel with thematic analysis that provides students with information about the text without reading it. He takes a stance on this, positioning the easier route as "cheating." This may refer to "cheating yourself" or using an inappropriate shortcut common in school settings such as copying answers, plagiarism, and so on. I wonder how the students interpreted his use of "cheating," but we cannot know. The cultural mythology links once again to laziness, as students are cast as (potentially) avoiding the hard work of reading by waiting for the professor to tell them about the book. The professor says, "I could just come up here and tell you what the book is about" (lines 15–16), suggesting that taking an easy route is "cheating." By saying this, he applies an overtly moral stance to students who rely on the professor to communicate the text. He closes by invoking the cultural mythology of "grittiness," asking students to "just keep fighting your way through" "even if it is a struggle for [them]." One student, whom we'll call Alice, makes incredible improvement through the semester and is often called out by the professor as an example of hard work and dedication. She scored a 54 on the final exam, sixteen points below the passing grade. While hard work certainly works for some, it is not always indicative of who will pass. Moreover, many students may make great strides in improving their reading given where they started, but they may be unable improve enough in one semester to pass the final exam. The commands at the end of the excerpt reinforce the responsibilities described earlier in his talk. Whether the topic relates to the course end-of-semester final or to discretionary course readings, the construction of responsibility functions quite similarly.

Counterpoints: What About "Nice" Cultural Mythologies?

Harkening back to the question at the outset of the chapter about positive cultural mythologies, let us consider one final excerpt. Professors tried to encourage students by preparing lessons that were engaging, but students at BMCC experience a variety of hardships that might influence class attendance, including not being able to afford a metro card for the subway or having last-minute shift changes at work. Given that attendance in ACR did not ultimately contribute meaningfully to the final grade, and given that students often triage coursework as it fits into their lives, keeping a class filled was a challenge for professors. As was his routine, the professor gave students thirty to forty minutes to arrive and begin working in their vocabulary book, but on this day, the class size remained small with only two or three total students, so he decided to commence with class and end early after reviewing the vocabulary assignment.

Excerpt 4.7: Hard Workers

1 T: Want to just go over them? Make sure you have the right answers? Obviously
2 we don't have a- a full class today? But I think what we will do is after we go
3 over the vocabulary? (then) we can do some more practice
4 on the test and maybe I'll have you read a longer piece? You can read that
5 answer questions and we can call it a morning okay?
8 But **I appreciate you guys showing up. It says a lot about how hard you work**
9 so just we'll go through it together ( ).
10 ((T goes back to working with Alice))

Across the course of the semester, the professor consistently praises the students, making note of when they've mastered something by encouraging the whole class to notice the student's improvement and success. In fact, a general search for most frequently used words in this data set reveal that "good" is the first and most frequently used stance marker in the data set. This professor uses positive evaluation often and encourages the students regularly. In this excerpt, he acknowledges that the class is not filled and lets the students know how much he appreciates the presence of those who came. In this example, we see an example of the exceptionalism found in the "model minority" cultural mythology (Reyes, 2004). In singling out the few students who worked hard, he not only creates a challenging standard to live up to for the students who are present but also draws awareness to those that did not show up that day and characterizes them negatively by point of contrast. His statement of appreciation is followed by a characterization of students as hard workers that serves as a linguistic counterpoint to the lazy "other" who did not show. It is possible that all cultural mythologies present problems, even the ones that seem "nicest."

Discussion

Cultural Mythologies and Interpolation

If the caseworkers in the shelter are interpellating “men” into “clients” through deontic formulations that tell them what to do and translating “clients” into certain “types” of clients vis-à-vis cultural mythologies, is the professor doing the same (“lazy,” “hardworking,” students who favor getting work finished over the quality of the work)? While the professor uses fewer deontic formulations (favoring commands), he certainly still uses them to create institutionally situated, responsible relationships, thus positioning *people* as *students*, which in this context situates them as receivers of information, direction, and encouragement with certain responsibilities. Whether the professor discusses student test taking or being a reader, he further interpellates these *students* as certain types of students. While those types may include “hardworking” and “successful,” they may also include those who search for simple answers, who are satisfied with surface-level thinking, who could be lazy, who should start working harder, who do not assess themselves with honesty, who could not “bother” looking up definitions. This second level of interpellation becomes more complicated when we consider the historicity of some of the cultural mythologies he invokes.

If the previous chapter establishes the gestalt, this chapter asks us to consider more deeply both cultural mythologies and discretion. At the outset of the chapter, I describe some ways in which I have heard remedial reading students shamed by those in charge. This professor is not going quite so far, though the mythologies are still problematic. The cynicism of “did anybody bother,” “does anybody care,” presents negative expectations of the students, categorizing them as lazy. Likewise, suggesting students might be “satisfied with the surface” presupposes their disinterest in critical thinking. Asking them to “think larger” implies that they are thinking small. The multiple references to “not rushing” speak to the presupposition that students are interested in speed over quality, and the repeated references to working harder underscore the hustle-and-grind attitude that suggests that, as Ms. Innis says in Chapter 2, “whatever you’re doing, you aren’t doing enough.” This position calls for grittiness in the face of adversity and pulling oneself back up when setbacks occur. Love (2019) and Hancock (2004) describe how these mythologies are disproportionately applied to Black and Brown people. These uses of language are racialized even if speakers are unaware of them.

Discretion

Street-level workers, given their substantial workload, use discretion to manage their work, and those discretionary choices become de facto policy (Lipsky, 1980/2010). This chapter speaks to several facets of discretion worth considering more deeply. The first concerns acknowledging the relative amounts of privilege that come from being street-level workers at disparate degree levels, working in unique institutional systems. The professor in this context has tenure and job security. While there are neoliberal policies influencing student "momentum" (e.g., how many classes they should take and when, etc.), and while there is a high-stakes exam that constrains his practice, he is not operating with the same level of constraints on his everyday work as the caseworkers in the shelter. Casework is constrained by the client and worker responsibility policies established by the city government, and they are at very real risk of losing their jobs if they do not meet performance assessments. The professor's day-to-day work is far more flexible; as they discuss in class, the professor has "autonomy." He is not required to turn in lesson plans, and he is not required to submit reports on individual students and their progress. Had this study been conducted in an adjunct/part-time faculty member's class, I imagine there may have been even more similarities between the shelter case manager speech and instructor speech. Adjunct faculty are contingent on student enrollment and need; they have little job security and even less discretion. I have observed them being handed a textbook and asked to follow it. When I had contingent positions, I was sometimes given an online class fully prepared by someone else and merely asked to "run" it. The professor for this study, in contrast, has more job security and therefore discretion, allowing him to include other topics and readings (e.g., *Fahrenheit 451*). Notwithstanding differences in oversight and discretion, the professor still incorporated aspects of the gestalt of responsibility into his talk that were strikingly similar to those used by the caseworkers in the shelter talk study (Chapters 3 and 5).

If the discretionary actions (and words) of street-level workers socially construct policy in the interactional moments of service delivery, what kind of policy are street-level workers making in these social institutions? At least some of these policies-talked-into-being are based in racialized ways of viewing marginalized people. If there is discretion in the workplace, then we have choices about what kinds of language to use. We have choices about whether to foster deficit perspectives or whether to promote culturally sustaining pedagogy (Paris and Alim, 2017) and liberatory linguistics (Hudley et al., 2022). This is considered further in the conclusion of the book.

Looking Backward from the Present

While Lemke's timescales (see Chapter 2) locate the ways in which different scales of time may be found in a particular interactional moment, Bakhtin's (1981) conceptualization of chronotope is more expansive, combining space (locale), time, and personhood. Agha's (2007) work theorizes chronotopes for discourse studies, explaining that "a chronotopic depiction formulates a sketch of personhood in time and place; and, the sketch is enacted and construed within a participation framework" (321). For Bakhtin, all words and represented signs are chronotopic, and histories and space-times are engaged when, for example, a particular word is used in a particular conversation or social interaction (Agha, 2007). As each of us is a member of individual subcommunities, we may be aware that certain words used *within* our subcommunity resonate differently when used by insiders as opposed to outsiders. This is often the case with taboo language or words that have been reclaimed by marginalized communities. When these signifiers are used in an interaction, they bring with them time, place, and person. The use of such terms by insiders carries forth a different sociohistorical context than it does when the same terms are used by outsiders.

Flores et al. (2018) explore chronotope through a raciolinguistic lens, that is, a critical lens that considers relationships between language, race, and power (Alim, 2016). In so doing, they highlight the relationship between, on one hand, the words used by teachers in the classroom and, on the other, *collective* and *historical* times, places, and people that these words engender. Presenting data demonstrating a fissure between schoolteachers' beliefs and their actions in a bilingual school in Philadelphia, they show that while teachers may be ideologically progressive and while they may believe in, for example, the legitimacy of the Spanish language and dialects, those beliefs may not find purchase in the classroom and may in fact run counter to their actions and behavior. Flores et al. identify a double standard when comparing how teachers police marginalized students' language in the classroom when compared with other examples of the same linguistic/discursive features spoken by more privileged speakers.

In order to explain the disjuncture between teacher ideologies and actions, the authors work to explain the relationship between the teachers (in the current time and space of their actions) and what they say in the interactional moment (words that have historical resonance for marginalized members of the school community). They argue that the position that teachers *listen* from in this institutional context, what they call the "institutional listening subject position," is a future one in which the listener is someone who will negatively judge the students for their language (16). In their study, it is less that the teachers themselves view the students negatively (although that can also be the case) and more that they have anxiety about future negative assessments and listen to students from that future position. Viewing the teacher as an institutional listening subject allows the authors to move away from examining individual teachers' language attitudes and toward seeing these attitudes with reference to their institutional position. Their work allows for a radical revisioning of teacher attitudes as (at least in part) structural—baked into large-scale sociocultural histories and institutional positionings. This perspective is less concerned with individual people's choices (although they certainly matter and are damaging) than with interrogating how teachers' listening position operates within an institutional context.

What might we gain from viewing the street-level workers as institutional listening subjects? Each of these street-level workers expressed a strong commitment to helping people in need. By viewing these workers as institutional listening subjects, we can shift the conversation away from individual street-level worker attitudes and toward an institutional perspective: the caseworker nine months down the line who is required to sanction an unhoused man, the shelter administrator who may see that man's lack of movement toward housing as worker and/or client laziness, the professor who fears watching half his class fail the high-stakes final, the future teacher or employer who will reject someone because the applicant's reading or writing is "poor." The "institutional listening subject position" allows us to see the individual workers, their attitudes, and their racializing discursive choices vis-à-vis their own institutional positioning. This book's conclusion will consider in more depth the institutional listening subject position of street-level workers as it relates to both discretion and discourse.

Flores et al.'s (2018) work also creates an opportunity to view institutional language use as chronotopic—each word situated in its sociohistorical, cultural, personal, situational, and political contexts. Integrating their work, I argue that the gestalt of responsibility, and particularly the cultural mythologies, are chronotopic, pointing back in space-time to racializing language connected to the American slave trade, to the classist origins of the social welfare "laziness" myth in Britain, to the shift in the use of these myths to discriminate against Black applicants for public assistance. These myths, when levied against marginalized people through discourse, ring backward in time. The gestalt of responsibility is not only a constellation of words used in the moment but also a series of interrelated chronotopes that allow us to see the cultural, historical, and social time stamps embossed on the language we use in these institutional contexts. Drawing from the previous chapter, then, our words, with their rich cultural baggage, not only interpellate *people* into *clients* and *students* but also position these students and clients vis-à-vis cultural mythologies that interpellate them still further: not just *students* but *students who do not work hard enough*, *students who are not honest with their self-assessment*, *students who are lazy*, *students who are sloppy*. Interpellations like "lazy, dishonest, sloppy," when applied to Black and Brown people, ring differently, harkening back to white supremacist language commonly applied to Black people during and after American slavery (Daykin, 2006; Hancock, 2004).

While this chapter introduces how cultural mythologies stretch back in time and space, time is also explicitly referred to in social interaction, as it relates to performance measurements in both contexts (references to the semester midterm and final, references to the nine-month shelter benchmark, etc.). The subsequent two chapters explore in more depth how talk changes over (Chapter 5) and through (Chapter 6) time.

5 | Gestalt of Responsibility over Time in the Shelter

While street-level workers regularly use discretion in formulating routinizes and other strategies that manage the intensity of their workloads, new managerialism further complicates their work. Benchmarks within new managerial policies are used to measure the performance of both clients and workers. This new managerial architecture of benchmarks and performance management puts responsible action "at cross purposes" in social welfare (Soss et al., 2011, 231–32). In fact, Brodkin (2011) argues that new managerial governance "assumes that as long as performance benchmarks are met, it is not necessary to consider *how* policy work is done" (272). She continues by arguing that the confluence of organizational criteria, individual discretion, and performance incentives create an environment that requires workers not just to "respond" to these changes but also to make adjustments that "have systematic consequences for how policy work is done and, ultimately, what is produced as policy on the ground" (272–73). Ultimately, while we know that benchmarks impact practice and that street-level workers shift accordingly, we still know relatively little about what these adjustments look like. This chapter seeks to interrogate the issue further by considering it from a discourse perspective, examining how street-level caseworker talk shifts over the course of a client's stay in shelter. In so doing, it reveals that the way street-level workers put policy into practice changes with the ebb and flow of client compliance and progress vis-à-vis established benchmarks. My previous work has shown how time is indexed in social welfare interaction, that is, made relevant as a topic of talk. Matarese (2012), for example, examined the ways in which short-term, undocumented, homeless clients were discursively treated like long-term, documented clients who exceeded the benchmark for shelter stay established in policy. Caseworkers invoked responsibility, benchmarks, speed, performance incentives, and work stress with long-term clients who were considered hard to place. I found that one caseworker discursively treated short-term, undocumented clients like long-term clients, invoking "imagined time," a hypothetical space in which these short-term clients become long term given the perceived future difficulty in finding housing placements for undocumented clients. That study highlighted the way in which time itself was made relevant. This chapter, in contrast, captures how a lack of compliance and a nearing benchmark change not just *what* is said but also *how*. The focus in this chapter is less on constructions of responsibility than on how performance benchmarks can shape the way caseworkers talk to clients. Time is not the *subject* of the talk but rather *the guiding force* that changes it vis-à-vis established timelines and benchmarks. While many studies exist that examine individual moments of social work interaction, this chapter departs from that body of research by examining how talk evolves and changes over time.

Framing for Chapter

The length of data collection in each context is relative to timescales made relevant by the contexts themselves: The nine months of data collection in the shelter corresponded to the nine-month benchmark by which time unhoused men "should" be placed into independent living,[1] and the community college course was observed during an entire semester, at which time students "should" move from reading remediation to the larger college community.

This chapter uses two methods to capture the shift in talk over time. First, I use interactional linguistics (Couper-Kuhlen and Selting, 2018) to analyze the opening sequences between one unhoused man in shelter and his caseworker over six months, showing how affiliative constructions (e.g., pleasantries, politeness) are increasingly exchanged for disaffiliative constructions over time. To a lesser extent, my analysis also shows increasing constructions of responsibility, benchmarks, and performance. Stivers (2008) posits that affiliation is signaled through a variety of discursive features including minimal encouragers (e.g., uh-huh, mm-hmm, oh yeah?), assessments (e.g., the professor frequently uses "good!" after a student answer), signals of alignment (e.g., this could be topical agreement or providing the socially anticipated response), indirect forms of question that help save face, and through (often shared) laughter. Disaffiliation is displayed through topic shifts, directness, the introduction of uncomfortable or delicate topics, threats to face (e.g., an accusation, a threat, a statement that makes a person look bad), and uncomfortable pauses before responding (Makri-Tsilipakou, 1994). This chapter also presents a simple count of constructions of responsibility across three client cases, drawing codes from NVivo. Each of the three caseworker-client dyads (the three longest-staying clients) shows how the discourses shift over time as clients approach shelter-relevant benchmarks for progress.

During data collection, the benchmark for housing placement was accelerated from nine to six months. For this chapter three client cases are used. The opening interaction sequences between Michael and Ms. Innis over a nine-month period make up the lion's share of the analysis. The three cases reviewed at the end include two cases of Ms. Innis's (Michael and Julio) and one case between Ms. Clemson and her client Otto. The three clients chosen for this analysis were the three who had the longest shelter stays during my data collection, each one staying beyond the shelter-mandated benchmark. I coded the discourse of those three caseworker-client dyads over the course of their shelter stay. Each of these three clients became a long-staying homeless client during the duration of his shelter stay. Julio (all names are pseudonyms) had a seven-month shelter stay, including thirteen meetings with his caseworker, all of which were recorded and transcribed. Michael had an eight-month shelter stay and nine total meetings with his caseworker, all transcribed. Finally, Otto was in shelter over nine months, and I have the final three months of his meetings transcribed and recorded, totaling five meetings.

A Case Study of Talk over Time

This portion of the analysis examines opening sequences to illustrate how Ms. Innis shifts her affiliation toward Michael over time vis-à-vis his (non) compliance. Each excerpt begins just as the meeting opens. In the interest of space, as they met a total of nine times over six months, some meeting openings are not presented here. The first caseworker-client meeting is often the longest, requiring the completion of an intake form, which includes a general history of the client and information relevant to helping him find housing. The intake assessment is a form, generally completed on the computer, that collects historical information about the client and establishes his position in the process toward housing (i.e., where he lived prior to the shelter and whether he has a job and has been saving money, which would help with a security deposit and rent for a new residence).

Michael was Ms. Innis's client from April to September, but he first came to the shelter in late January. He is a Latino man who was in his forties at the time but looked much older. He regularly used heroin and alcohol, landing him in jail multiple times during his shelter stay, and his case was punctuated by nearly six months of delay before getting his required psychiatric evaluation, the second step in the housing application process. In this first opening excerpt, Michael has been called into Ms. Innis's office. He enters and sits down next to Ms. Innis, who had been preparing intake paperwork for his case file. She begins by establishing the discursive norms for the intake assessment that constitutes this first meeting.

Excerpt 5.1: Opening Statement, Meeting 1

Ms.Innis: okay. >I have to do an intake on you<, (.) umm (.) I'm going to ask
you basically a lot a- >a couple a < questions .hh I'm gonna try to run
through this as quick as possible, see how everything'll work. okay?
Michael: oka[y.
Ms.Innis: [Get you outta here, get you in your bed. I feel the same wahy yohhhu
dohhh. ((laughs)) (0.11) What building you came from, Intake?
Michael: na. (.) I was:, (.) I was supposed to be at [XX shelter name.]
Ms.Innis: [mm-h[mm.]
Michael: [and they sent, [you know.]
Ms.Innis: [Okay.]
Michael: but I never went.
Ms.Innis: °Oh okay. Oh° ((mumbling under breath-indistinguishable))
((mumbling)) today is Fri:day:. seven ((writing down the date)).
Michael: (0.7)
Ms.Innis: you been saving your money?
Michael: ((outbreath)).hhh no.
Ms.Innis: okay, why not?

While she establishes an asymmetrical participation framework for their interaction (she is the questioner and he the answerer), she also uses various affiliative strategies to soften the bureaucratic task at hand and develop rapport. As these excerpts will show, Ms. Innis's affiliation toward Michael, represented through these opening sequences, shifts over time.

Affiliation is first indicated through Ms. Innis's downgrade of the bureaucratic intake questioning itself, from *a lot* to *a couple a* (line 2). Stance expressions emphasizing brevity (e.g., *run through, as quick as possible*), combined with her downgrades, soften intake questioning. This is an affiliative move that demonstrates a respect for his time and her desire to allow him to get to sleep (the meeting time was approximately 9:45 p.m.). Her affiliation work with Michael is more overtly presented in lines 5–6 (*I feel the same way you do*), a topical stance meant to establish solidarity and rapport (Makri-Tsilipakou, 1994). Her in-talk and following-talk invitation to laughter in lines 5 and 6 (Glenn, 2003) additionally functions to develop rapport through affiliation, despite Michael's lack of reciprocation.

Turn-taking here is also affiliative. While the majority of the intake interaction involves short, closed questions with brief answers, the opening sequence here provides space for Michael to answer confirmation checks and questions (lines 4, 7, 17). Her backchanneling (e.g., mm-hmm) (lines 8, 10), demonstrates her involvement while also passing on potential turns at talk, allowing him to maintain the floor. Overlapping backchanneling talk (lines 8, 10) here, moreover, shows Ms. Innis's involvement in his talk. Despite power differences and conversational asymmetries inherent in the structure of their institutional talk (Drew and Heritage, 1992; Thornborrow, 2002), Ms. Innis does substantial affiliative, rapport-building work with Michael.

In terms of bureaucratic language and constructions of responsibility, the intake form itself shapes the majority of this first meeting, prompting caseworker-asked questions and generally brief client answers. As Matarese and Caswell (2017, 2018) claim, these forms are part and parcel of neoliberalism and new managerialism in social welfare discourse. Moreover, in lines 13–14, Ms. Innis takes note of the date, marking his place on his timescale. These are, however, relatively small nods to the bureaucratic, institutional process in comparison to what comes later.

The next excerpt examines their third meeting, in the third month of his shelter stay. Michael had not yet completed those tasks assigned to him in his first two meetings, and the tone of the meeting began to shift. Not only was he deemed noncompliant, but he was also significantly closer to the newly established six-month benchmark, at which time he "should have" (according to policy) moved out of the shelter and into independent living.

Excerpt 5.2: Opening Statement, Meeting 3

Ms.Innis: Excuse my messy office.
(0.4)
Ms.Innis: Michael. I'm gonna give it to you straight, and I'm gonna give it to you like
this. (.) this w[eek is it.
Michael: [wel-,
Ms.Innis: >I'm gonna give it to you<, <this week is it.> (.) ain't no more dippin,
dodgin and hidin.
(0.2)
Ms.Innis: >you losing weight?<

10 Michael: ((whispers)) °y[eah. °
11 Ms.Innis: [why?
12 Michael: I'm suffering. (.)
13 Ms.Innis: <what are you suf-fer-ing from.>
14 Michael: depression.
15 Ms.Innis: <what are you depressed about?>

It is clear that between the first and third meeting, Ms. Innis's attempts to establish rapport and solidarity are overshadowed by the bureaucratic requirements that Michael has not yet satisfied. Her affiliative work in this excerpt is limited to a minimal pro forma apology (line 1), which is not taken up by Michael. His silence (line 2) highlights a dispreferred response and disaffiliation.

The silence is broken by Ms. Innis's utterance (lines 3–4), which reveals a shift in footing and alignment (Goffman, 1974), as well as a disaffiliative stance first indicated through her invocation of Michael by name. Clayman (2001, 441) suggests that a speaker calling his or her interlocutor by name signals "deeply felt opinions and personal feelings, particularly when such opinions or feelings are oppositional in character." Three pre-sequences (phrases that lead toward or warm someone up for a statement) follow her invocation of his name (line 3), perhaps preparing him to receive a bureaucratic ultimatum (line 4): *this week is it*. Ms. Innis's use of pre-sequences (Schegloff, 1978, 2007) presupposes Michael's rejection of her critique, and the stance of the pre-sequences suggests that she is serving him honesty (*gonna give it to you straight*). The honesty, given the negative stance implied by calling him *Michael*, can likewise be perceived negatively.

He is not given the opportunity to provide an account, however (line 5). Instead, she repeats the pre-sequence and the ultimatum (line 6–7) and follows it with three negative stance markers, *dipping*, *dodging*, and *hiding*. These words characterize Michael as an irresponsible client, who is avoiding meetings and responsibilities. Her negative stance is met with disaffiliation from Michael, who does not respond (line 8). Receiving no answer, Ms. Innis initiates another question (line 9), which may be interpreted in this context as a negative stance marker, as weight loss could imply heroin use. Ms. Innis then continues to disaffiliate through a disagreement-implicated, other-initiated repair (line 11), a term developed by Schegloff (2007) to describe postexpansion requests for more information that concurrently imply speaker disagreement with an element of their interlocutor's statement. Additional disagreement-implicated repairs (lines 13, 15) signal continued inadequate and problematic responses from Michael, as well as Ms. Innis's disaffiliation with him. This disaffiliation is also signaled through her emphasis on *from* (line 13) and *about* (line 15), both of which highlight the inadequacy of his minimal responses and perhaps skepticism regarding his excuses (lines 12, 14).

In sum, this opening sequence may begin with affiliation work, but unlike the previous excerpt, there is no involvement backchanneling or affiliative laughter. There are no bids for respecting Michael's time. Instead, Ms. Innis shows disalignment from Michael by naming him, using negative stance markers regarding his noncompliance, and using disagreement-implicated other-initiated repairs. The time lapse and benchmark are briefly and obliquely acknowledged in *this week is it*. As Michael's noncompliance persists, Ms. Innis's affiliation with him is replaced with increasing disaffiliation, thus changing how bureaucratic requirements are contextualized in the talk itself.

The opening sequence of their fourth meeting reveals similar discursive practices to the prior excerpt, though how the bureaucratic tasks are constructed in talk vary.

Excerpt 5.3: Opening Statement, Meeting 4

Ms.Innis:	Have a seat, Michael. What do you what do you->What are you doing
	to try to get up outta here, Michael?<
Michael:	What am I trying to do right now? (.) I've been very, very busy.
	that's one. Two, the guy that I was working with as a driver, you know the
	driver that was working with me? (.) He got fired. He got arrested, because he
	was stealing money. He was doing embezzlement, so now, I'm doing my truck
	my route and helping the guy that's driving also do his route. So that's wh[y—
Ms.Innis:	[Are
	you driving now?
Michael:	I wish I was, (.) I don't have my license. . . . . ((brief narrative exchange about his
	job excluded here)) I'm busting my ass helping them out (.) And, you know.
	they're gonna treat me you know? like shit? Na, fuck that. (.2) but you come
	out losing?,
Ms.Innis:	((under breath)) °all right.° What do you want to do to get outta here? What are
	we [doing-
Michael:	[What do I wanna do to get outta here? I'm trying to do anything.
Ms.Innis:	<Anything like what, Michael?>

In this opening sequence, Ms. Innis again begins with a pro forma invitation for Michael to sit, which while a directive, is a pleasantry that is noticeably absent in future meetings. Her affiliation wanes when she introduces Michael's lack of progress on bureaucratic tasks. Those tasks are contextualized in questions, the stance of which implies that he is not taking the necessary steps to leave shelter (lines 1–2), which she underlines by concluding the question with his name, taking a disaffiliative stance (Clayman, 1998).

Ms. Innis orients to the necessities of the institution, couching bureaucratic task talk in her disaffiliative stance toward Michael's noncompliance. Her opening question both disaffiliates and indexes his lack of progress toward meeting the goal of leaving shelter. Her question "what do you what do you," is subsequently recast (lines 1–2) in a request for an update on the specific actions he is taking to leave shelter.

His response, a narrative account (Buttny, 1993) used to justify his noncompliance, is treated as trouble by Ms. Innis, who provides a minimal acknowledgment so quiet as to sound self-directed, or what Goffman calls backstage (1959). She offers a slight recast of her original bureaucratic question (line 14), which may be seen as a dispreferred third-turn evaluation. Her recasting of the question shifts from present action (*what are you doing*) to desired goal setting (*what do you want to do*). In so doing, she moves from his present inaction to shoring up new goals. Through "we" talk we see a small attempt to affiliate (line 15), and through her use of *we* she joins their institutional responsibilities at the shelter (as established in Chapter 3), highlighting the collaborative nature of their work together. Though the preferred response would be to affiliate, Michael orients responsibilities toward himself using "I," rejecting Ms. Innis's bid for affiliation (line 17) and answering her question using an extreme case formulation (Pomerantz, 1986), which provides Ms. Innis another opportunity to disaffiliate with him by requesting (through a disagreement-implicated other-initiated repair) a specific example (Pomerantz, 1986) in slowed, emphasized speech (line 18).

Despite her use of *we*, Ms. Innis overwhelmingly disaffiliates with Michael. The focus of her talk is on his progress (through *doing* and *get up outta here*), which may obliquely imply a timeline but in no way overtly invokes it. In the next opening sequence, Ms. Innis's continued disaffiliation with Michael, and the focus of the meeting from the first moment, is bureaucratically oriented.

Excerpt 5.4: Opening Statement, Meeting 6

1 Ms.Innis: Michael.
2 Michael: #↓Ye::s#?
3 Ms.Innis: Look, you see this ((waves his chart in the air))? (.) It's too thin.
4 Michael hh. ((laughs through nose))

Ms.Innis: You're laughing. I'm not joking. Do you see [my face?]
Michael [okay.]
(.)
Ms.Innis: Okay. (.) I'm tired of scheduling you (.) for (.) psych-=
Michael: =Yeah, but
what happened I got locked up. (.) I was locked up for- for thirteen days,
(2.0)
Michael and I lost all my property, I don't have nothing now,

Meeting 6 is the first meeting in which there is no affiliative work in the opening sequence. The meeting begins not with a greeting or an offer to sit but rather with Ms. Innis invoking Michael by name, potentially indicating oppositional feelings toward him (Clayman, 1998). Here a preferred response would be to align with her goals and agenda. His dispreferred response betrays exasperation and perhaps resistance vis-à-vis sarcasm through an elongated vowel and a creaky, affected vocal tone (line 2). In line 3, Ms. Innis utilizes the directive *look*, often "used in repeated directives and challenges" (Schiffrin, 1987, 327), as a pre-sequence (Schegloff, 2007) that is marked because it highlights Michael's lack of attention. The pre-sequence preempts his rejection of her main argument: He has not completed any assigned tasks and is therefore still not compliant (line 3). She conveys this message through the veiled criticism *it's too thin*, which implies that his file is thin, or empty, because he has not completed the tasks necessary to adequately fill his case file folder. The critique introduces an overtly negative stance, reified by the name use and the directive. Still, the obliqueness of her critique (a criticism of the file size rather than specific incompleted actions) may be viewed as an initial softening of the overall negative stance.

Michael invites laughter (line 4) by treating her critique as laughable, which could be seen as a bid for affiliation, asking Ms. Innis to laugh also. She, however, rejects his interpretation. Given her response (line 5), his laugh could be a conversational misfire or an act of resistance (if he could in fact read the facial cues Ms. Innis refers to). In not sharing in his laughter, Ms. Innis persists in disaffiliating with Michael (Glenn, 2003). By verbally disagreeing with his treatment of her statement, she rejects his interpretation of her statement (line 3) as laughable, while critiquing his ability to interpret her paralinguistic cues. Not only does Ms. Innis not affiliate or offer any pleasantries, but she overtly rejects Michael's offer for affiliation.

Institutional topics are once again introduced by Ms. Innis at the beginning of the meeting (*it's too thin*) (line 3) and in line 8, where she sets up a description of a sequence of activities (she schedules him for a psychiatric evaluation, and he does not show up). As in meetings 3 and 4 (Excerpts 5.2 and 5.3), she refers to his noncompliance by referring to his progress. Unlike Excerpts 5.1, 5.2, and 5.3, there is no attempt to affiliate, even in a pro forma way (*excuse the messy office, have a seat*). His lack of compliance and the pressure of the DHS-mandated benchmark is reflected in increasing disaffiliation and an increasingly negative stance.

Meeting 7 illustrates a final culmination of interactional practices that together index noncompliance over time, as well as the persisting need to accomplish required institutional tasks.

Excerpt 5.5: Opening Statement, Meeting 7

Ms.Innis: You got the- you got the psych evaluation? ((from outside the office))
Michael: No cause you never gave me the appointment.
(.)
Ms.Innis: Michael, you know your psych evaluation was for Friday. I was [busy.
Michael: [yeah
but I need a paper to come here eh- or else they ain't gonna attend me.
Ms.Innis: Did you try to see me on Friday?
Michael: Yes, I will.
(0.4)
Ms.Innis: Michael, you need a psych ev—listen, Michael, (.)
<and I'm going to be very honest with you. (.) Get your
shit together. (.) Honestly.>
Michael: °Yeah.° ((client acknowledges, shakes head))
Ms.Innis: I'm serious because, (.) we have not- done
anything we haven't done.
↑anything.
Michael: ((client sniff-laugh)) h. °right°
Ms.Innis: > I don't even have a package to put together to say
if somebody call me right now to give you something
give you anything< I don't have ↑anything.
Michael: I got some (.) medical things for today from my program.
((hands her some paperwork))
(1.0)
Michael: My blood test.
(0.6)
Ms.Innis: You're positive for Hep C?
Michael: Yeah ((breathy))

In this meeting, blame and responsibility are negotiated, passed back and forth by Ms. Innis and Michael, and Ms. Innis's stance is generally disaffiliative. She begins the meeting by condensing her greeting into a "bureaucratic request," "thereby showing a preference for institutional talk over social" (Clayman and Heritage, 2002 as cited in Shon, 2005, 835). Michael provides a dispreferred response, excusing himself and accusing Ms. Innis (line 2), after which follows a silence that marks her turn as dispreferred and disaffiliative. Ms. Innis does not apologize but instead shifts blame back to him through a dispreferred third-turn evaluation (line 4). Her disalignment is further punctuated by her use of his name. Michael, however, challenges her account and provides an excuse to counter hers (lines 5–6). In line 7, Ms. Innis uses a disagreement-implicated, other-initiated repair (Schegloff, 2007) to discern whether Michael came to see her when he had a problem, and rather than responding to this question, Michael treats her question as if she were talking about a future event (line 8). Ms. Innis's subsequent turn treats his prior reply as trouble, as there is a marked silence prior to her turn (line 9). Disalignment piled on disalignment. In line 10, she invokes him by name twice and utilizes multiple pre-sequences to prepare him for her statement. Her first pre-sequence, *Listen* (line 10), utilizes a discourse marker that challenges Michael through a directive (Schiffrin, 1987). Together these pre-sequences prepare Michael for Ms. Innis's statement of advice, *get your shit together. honestly* (lines 11-12), which appears to break away from the institutional-bureaucratic frame and perhaps through colloquial language and a plea of honesty presents a new, perhaps more convincing plea from her personal, emotional self.

Constructions of responsibility resemble those described in Matarese (2012). In line 10, Ms. Innis's *you need* here uses a deontic modal (Coates, 1984; Couper-Kuhlen and Selting, 2018) that she pairs with personal pronoun "you." Line 14 points to a collaborative failure as Ms. Innis uses *we* with the deontic formulation *have not done* and extreme case formulation *anything*. Here the *we* refers to an inertness on both sides, and her repetition presses the point. Here Michael does a sniff-laugh, in which he smiles and does one stressed exhale through his nose while smiling, treating her extreme case formulation as laughable. Ms. Innis does not affiliate with his treatment of her statement, but instead expands on her prior turn, which ends with another extreme case formulation. Her use of *I* pronouns here highlights her emphasis on her own responsibilities and the ways in which his lack of progress impedes her ability to do her job. Lipsky (1980) suggests that "street-level bureaucrats often attempt to involve clients in the difficulties of their jobs in order to gain understanding or sympathy for their position," a bid to gain client compliance though persuasion rather than coercion (64). Her appeal appears to work in some degree as Michael offers some results from a blood test he recently completed with his drug program as an offering of progress.

In this final meeting (ninth month), the initial opening sequence appears to reveal an improvement between Ms. Innis and Michael, as he has complied in having his psychiatric evaluation. This stark contrast of this interaction compared to those prior opening sequences highlights just how compliance and time shape caseworker-client talk in this context.

Excerpt 5.6: Opening Statement, Final Meeting (Meeting 9)

Ms.Innis: Thank you for getting the umm psych evaluation,
Michael: °Ya welcome°. (.) I was gonna leave that day.
Ms.Innis: What happened?
Michael: I was gonna ↑lea:ve.
Ms.Innis: I-yeah- HhUH- [good thing you didn't

Michael: [No, <the reason is> <I'm ↑serious> I was gonna leave
cause I was there- one of the first ones there.
Ms.Innis: Mm-hmm,
Michael: and all of a sudden, (.) they call out everybody else (.) and I'm saying, 'hold on' (.) what
number am I' she goes, 'ah, you're number five' I says,'how can that be?.
((1 minute narrative regarding TB clinic and retrieving wallet from the short-term jail))
But I've been lazy.
(0.5)
Ms.Innis: Okay, Hernandez you gotta start- we gotta start getting you outta here.
Michael: °yeah°
Ms.Innis: Umm, this list (.) and the clients that's on this list (.) and you are ↑ON it,
Michael: A:n:d, what does that mean?
Ms.Innis: You've been here fo:[r
(0.6)
Michael: [January
Ms.Innis: eight months (0.4) alright? A[nd umm,
Michael: [A:n:d what- you gonna kick me out?
Ms.Innis: That's two months past the time you're supposed to be here. Okay? (.) And
ummm (.) it's not kicking you out it's moving you on. ((then discusses public
assistance etc))

This meeting showed marked differences with all those prior, with the exception of the first one. It begins with an overt affiliative move as Ms. Innis acknowledges Michael's completion of his first assigned task. Despite his comment suggesting he nearly left his appointment (line 4), Ms. Innis invites laughter (line 5) and follows her laugh with evaluation in a teasing tone, again affiliating with Michael (Glenn, 2003).

Michael uses *no* and *I'm serious* to shift the tone from nonserious to serious (Schegloff, 2001), and he provides an excuse for his action, using a sequential narrative to supply justification for actions at the psychiatric evaluation (lines 6–11). After discussing personal topics for approximately a minute (line 12), an extended pause (line 13) between Michael's final utterance and Ms. Innis's next turn highlights her disaffiliation with Michael's previous talk. Ms. Innis then uses the discourse marker "okay" to simultaneously acknowledge his story while again not evaluating. "Okay" additionally signifies a topic shift and reentry into talk about his responsibilities (*you gotta*) in the shelter (line 14), which Ms. Innis recasts as a joint effort (*we* talk) in a moment of affiliation.

While her affiliation returns, the benchmark and therefore constructions of responsibility are still present. His compliance is rewarded with friendliness, but ultimately, he has pushed his shelter stay beyond the allowable deadline. Ms. Innis uses deontic formulation *gotta* to construct a collaborative obligation to move him from shelter to housing. She then uses hesitation marker *umm* and a pause to soften her release of potentially damaging or embarrassing information: Michael has been put on a list of clients who have overstayed the now six-month benchmark. The list, developed by the shelter administration in collaboration with the city government, empowers Ms. Innis to put pressure on Michael vis-à-vis the shelter policy. Ms. Innis's utterances in lines 18, 21, and 23-24 contrast the shelter timescale (the benchmarks established by the policy) with his timescale at the shelter (how long he has stayed thus far). Ms. Innis's hesitations and pauses (line 21) potentially show an attempt to gently convey delicate information. However, when Michael reformulates her statement (line 22), he disaffiliates with her and recontextualizes what she is conveying as *kick[ing] me out*. Ms. Innis reformulates his stay according to the shelter policy timescale, and offers a revisioning of his utterance: *moving you on*. Ms. Innis's stance positions Michael in a moving process rather than as one being jettisoned from the shelter.

It is difficult to extricate Michael's lack of compliance from the benchmark. However, it is clear that Ms. Innis persists in constructing responsibility notwithstanding his compliance. We know, moreover, that benchmarks, progress, and timing are referenced often, even when clients are being compliant, particularly if they are, or are perceived as being at risk of becoming long-term stayers (Matarese, 2012).

What Time Tells Us

In order to examine the issue further, I isolated the three longest cases during my fieldwork: Michael, Julio, and Otto. Entering the transcripts into qualitative analysis software (NVivo) and using my previous work on constructions of responsibility to inform the coding, I combed the data for any deontic formulation (*need to, have to, got to, haveta, gotta, supposed to, should have*). I excluded hypotheticals, negatively polarized deontic formulations (e.g., you *don't have to* go there), and directives (e.g., *do* X, *get* your bed). I included separate codes for both the caseworkers' references to their own responsibilities and their references to the client's responsibility. Each number on the x-axis represents a month. Some clients met with their worker several short times in one month.

Michael began his shelter stay in January and stayed nine months, but his interactions with Ms. Innis (from intake to leaving shelter) spanned from April ("1" in Figure 5.1) to September ("6" in the figure). Ms. Innis's constructions of Michael's responsibility are coded black, and her constructions of her own responsibility are coded grey. Instances when she used *we* counted for both categories.

While the *N* is obviously too low to make statistical generalities, it is useful to see the general rise in client-directed responsibility constructions across the data set. The meeting in month 4 was markedly short, occurring just before the nighttime client sign-in deadline of 10:00 p.m.

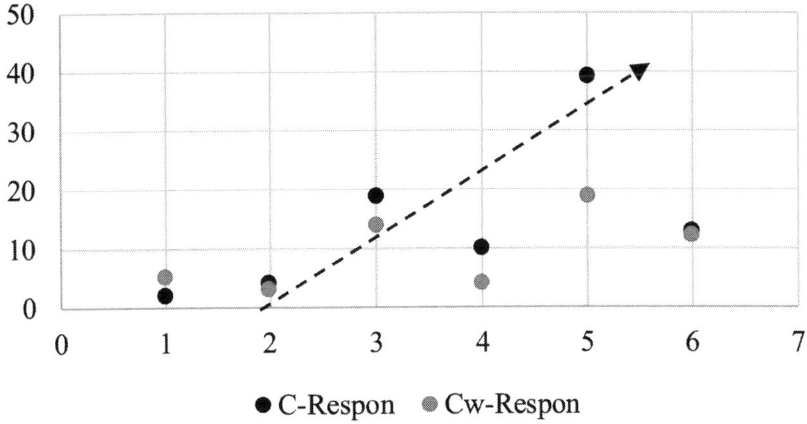

Fig. 5.1. Ms. Innis's Constructions of Responsibility for Michael over Seven Months
This chart shows an upward trend in individual instances of Ms. Innis's constructions of responsibility over the seven months Michael was in shelter.

and totaling less than five minutes in length, by far the shortest interaction, which may explain the dip in client-responsibility talk. Month 6, moreover, included a lengthy meeting but included an intervention by the shelter substance abuse counselor. While he used many constructions of responsibility, I did not include these in the original count because I wanted to focus on the shifts of individual workers' discourse over time. Had I included constructions of responsibility from the substance counselor, the N would be closer to fifty total constructions of client responsibility in that particular interaction. Michael relapsed into heroin use several times during his stay and eventually left shelter of his own volition.

In contrast, Julio was in shelter over thirteen months and was eventually placed successfully in supportive housing. He spoke fluent Spanish and minimal English, and some meetings included a translator, which will become relevant when considering his data. His case with Ms. Innis ran from April ("1" in Figure 5.2) to October (marker "7" in the figure).

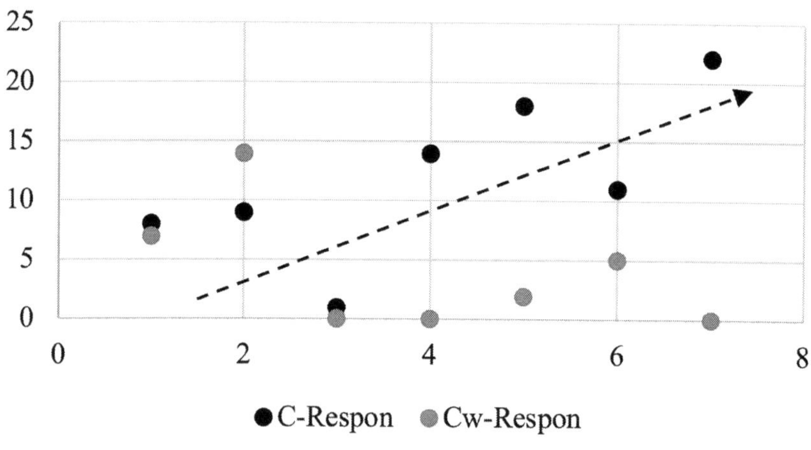

Fig 5.2. Ms. Innis's Constructions of Responsibility for Julio over Eight Months. This chart shows an upward trend in individual instances of Ms. Innis's constructions of responsibility over the eight months Julio was in shelter.

As in Michael's case, Ms. Innis's constructions of responsibility with Julio increased over time. Despite receiving a housing placement in month 7, constructions of responsibility were still high at the end of his case. The meeting in month 3 lasted two minutes and forty-four seconds, which was marked in its brevity. Month 6 included two meetings, the longer one of which, like Michael's intervention meeting, included another participant—a client who translated and conveyed a majority of the constructions of responsibility to Julio in Spanish. Had I included the ad hoc translator's constructions, Month 6 would include far more constructions. Ms. Innis's constructions of her own responsibilities varied and seem without discernible pattern.

Finally, Otto was another long-term stayer, and his meetings with Ms. Clemson began in March and concluded in June. Otto was an older, African American man. He was forgetful and often got lost and had lapses in memory.

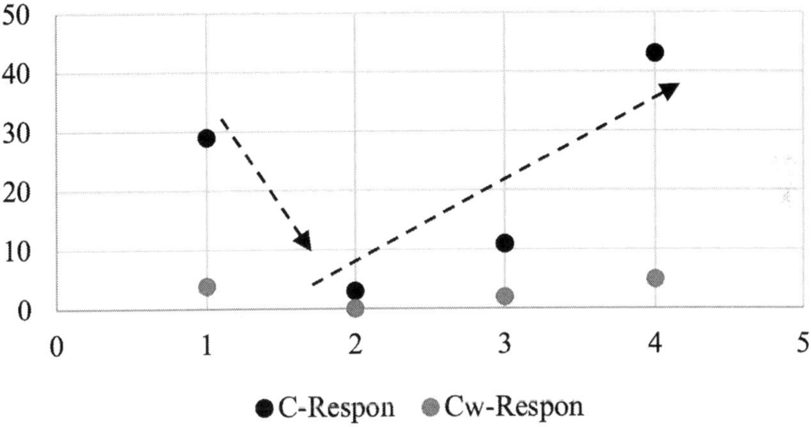

Fig 5.3. Ms. Clemson's Constructions of Responsibility for Otto over Five Months
This chart shows an upward trend in individual instances of Ms. Clemson's constructions of responsibility over the five months Otto was in shelter.

While Ms. Clemson did use constructions of responsibility with Otto, he more often had immediate emergencies that took precedence. For example, the primary topic for the meeting in month 2 consisted of the recovery of lost Social Security checks and lost clothing. Even so, there is some increase of responsibility constructions across his months in shelter.

If we consider all three long-term clients together for the first six months of their shelter stay, there is a trend toward caseworkers increasing the number of constructions of responsibility over the length of a client's shelter stay.

Obviously, given the limited number of cases, these numbers are only useful in prompting further inquiry into how social interaction changes over time. Both Soss, Fording, and Schram (2011) and Lipsky (2010) note how street-level workers may include their own problems and responsibilities in discussion as a means to convince clients to comply. While there is evidence of this across my data, and in particular among long-term stayers, those instances do not appear to necessarily rise over time. It is

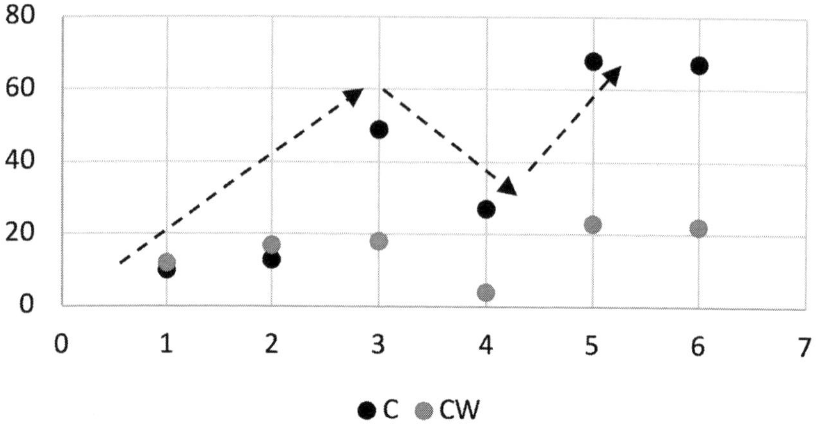

Fig. 5.4. Six-Month Totals for Constructions of Responsibility
This final figure demonstrates an overall upward trend in caseworker constructions of responsibility over time for all thee long-term clients observed.

possible that those instances shift according to how workers experience their job with reference to pressures and discussions with bosses and management, memos with incentives and goal setting, policy shifts, and so on.

Constructions of Responsibility over Time

This chapter captures two ways in which social welfare interaction and the social construction of policy are visible as *talk in flux* and responsive to overall policy timescales and changes in individual cases. This chapter explores how time benchmarks shape practice, revealing how the policy put into practice by street-level workers is constructed with regard to the dynamic ebb and flow of client compliance and progress vis-à-vis established benchmarks. We know that street-level workers adjust to performance benchmarks (Brodkin, 2011), and this chapter helps illuminate what those might adjustments look like both on a discursive level and with regard to constructions of responsibility. At least in the case of Michael, Ms. Innis's discourse quickly lost its affiliative qualities and became more terse, disaffiliative, and responsibility-infused. Soss, Fording, and Schram (2011) note the caseworkers interviewed in their Florida study reported altering interactions with clients based on performance incentives and sanctioning procedures. In describing how one caseworker shifts in her tone over the course of a client's shelter stay and in reviewing tallies for constructions of responsibility over time, this chapter provides support for such a claim.

That said, it is difficult to disentangle the lack of compliance from the approaching benchmark. Did caseworker disaffiliation and constructions of client responsibility increase because the client was nearing the benchmark or because he was noncompliant? Both? Would the client even be approaching the benchmark if he had been continuously compliant? Clients I observed who had fewer co-occurring challenges had a smoother process at the shelter: meeting compliance requirements more easily and spending less time in shelter overall (Matarese, 2008). Therefore, it may be difficult to separate compliance from benchmarks, and the discourse may be responsive to both.

However, as Matarese (2012) found, undocumented clients, who were not yet called "long-term stayers" and who had not even neared the nine-month benchmark for shelter stay, were discursively treated like long-term clients given how difficult it was to find housing for them. In that study, I argued that workers used "imagined time" to discursively project future noncompliance for undocumented clients. Summarizing that finding, I argued:

> Imagined time and space, hypothetical situations that illuminated how Ms. Innis saw the future unfolding, arose vis-à-vis her knowledge and experience, but in writing their future for the clients, they may have been less likely (at that interactional moment) to write it for themselves. (354)

With this study in mind, perhaps the benchmarks matter far less than her awareness of his present or future breaking of the "rules," whether they be noncompliant actions or staying beyond the benchmark for shelter stay. In retrospect, "imagined time" is not dissimilar from Flores et al.'s (2018, 16) "institutional listening subject position" described in Chapter 4. While Flores et al. locate subject position vis-à-vis the institution, both Flores et al. and Matarese (2012) explain how street-level workers treat people with reference to a future-oriented, anxious position. The caseworkers, concerned about the difficulty of placing undocumented people who cannot receive a legal income when the shelter protocols required a proof of legal income to move forward with housing placement, begin these cases with an anxiety that plays out in their discourse. In my data, undocumented, unhoused people were often treated like long-term stayers at the beginning of their shelter stay because the institutional listening subject position of the worker envisions a future time in which the undocumented person outlasts the benchmark for housing placement, which can damage the worker's performance assessments and placement numbers.

This chapter, in considering street-level implementation of policy, also underscores the utility of rethinking methodology and analysis vis-à-vis time. Look what we gain from looking across the data. We need more horizontal studies of street-level work. While have learned more about street-level discretionary action, we know surprisingly little about, for example, whether and how workers' ideologies from their scholastic disciplines find space and traction in their street-level workplaces. We know little about how their identities change and develop over the course of their careers. I know many colleagues who seem wholly burned out, and I often wonder what they were like when they began. Were they spirited and energetic? Did they love their students? What does the erosion of their morale and passion look like? Street-level research needs more longitudinal studies to understand how worker discretion shifts over careers and what instigates such changes. We must press for less static research that considers the *when* of data collection, the *how long* of participants and institutional spaces, and the extent to which data is part of a process that is often overlooked or underdescribed. Adjustments to policy, management, and profession development are discussed in Chapter 7.

In focusing on affiliation and disaffiliation in this chapter I wanted to underscore that even "general niceties" go out the window over time in favor of nastier ways of communicating. Not every worker, not every time, but time matters in these interactions. Performance benchmarks and assessments matter, and compliance matters in how workers communicate. Returning to the references to performance in the gestalt, this chapter underscores that these references to performance are not neutral. Clients' performance is used to assess worker performance, and so these terms carry the weight of not just shelter policy pressures but also caseworkers' anxieties about their own performance. These references, as noted in Chapter 3, are justifications for pressure that transfer responsibility to those who make the benchmarks, and here in Chapter 5 we see how the existence of these benchmarks shapes even social niceties.

The next chapter considers talk over time as well. While there are similar trends in the classroom—constructions of responsibility in talk indeed shift according to performance measurements like college midterms and finals—this next chapter considers the cumulative, vertical heft of a semester of such responsibility talk.

6 | Gestalt of Responsibility Is Not Only Horizontal but Also Vertical

Timescales in the Community College Remedial Reading Classroom

Many of the chapters in this book have asked us to rethink the relevance of time. Chapter 3 explained the gestalt of responsibility—its component pieces including references to time-based performance benchmarks, and Chapter 4 focused primarily on the cultural mythologies facet of the Gestalt, theorizing them as chronotopic—stretching into the past. In that chapter, I argued that we may understand street-level workers as speaking from a particular "institutional listening subject position" that imagines particular futures for those they serve. In this way, street-level discourse stretches both into the sociocultural, historical, and personal past while simultaneously inhabiting a listening subject position in the future. Chapter 5 examined time more literally, exploring how constructions of responsibility shift horizontally over time vis-à-vis performance benchmarks, noting that my earlier work (Matarese, 2012) on "imagined time" in constructions of responsibility among undocumented unhoused men shares some similarities with Flores et al.'s (2018) "institutional listening subject position." While the constructions of responsibility in the classroom context described in this chapter, likewise, shift according to performance benchmarks, in this chapter I focus primarily on the accumulated weight of such constructions. In discourse analysis, researchers often describe the talk used in an institutional encounter without much reference to or interest in how frequently these encounters occurred; how far into this relationship are we looking? Even if these features are representative of trends, the lack of a longitudinal perspective potentially erases valuable information about how those trends *move* and *respond* to institutional pressures.

Not too long ago, I attended a conference that I thought might feel like an academic home. My badge was printed with "Mo" (my gender-affirming nickname at the time) and included he/him pronouns in large block lettering, and I wore a "he/him" pin on my lapel. Every single person, including friends, misgendered me for two days straight.[1] At first, I corrected people, and at some point, I stopped. If one, single interaction was examined, I imagine you might find indications of my discomfort and disaffiliation, but I also wanted to fit in and find an academic home, so perhaps you would also see me "let[ting] it pass" (Firth, 1996, 243). If you saw and analyzed only one encounter, it might be hard to imagine my being so disappointed and frustrated that on the last day of the conference I scrapped my original presentation, instead scripting one that in part investigated the linguistic failures of the conference itself and its attendees. If, however, you had collected and analyzed the data from each and every misgendering experience across the course of the conference, it may be easier to explain my reaction. In this chapter, I argue that it is not simply that the gestalt of responsibility shifts and increases horizontally over time (as established in Chapter 5) that matters—but that those constructions also accrue vertically over time. Like an hourglass, the individual instances of the gestalt accumulate, weighing heavier and heavier on—in this case—the students. They are a type of cumulative microaggression.

I draw on Wortham's (2006) examination of identity formation across an academic year to support my argument. Wortham elegantly describes the ways in which teachers and classmates contribute to individual student identities over time, showing how these individual students, often positioned in negative ways in the classroom, resist and sometimes take up these identities. His book was a clarion call to linguistic anthropologists and discourse analysts, asking them to widen the research lens beyond the interactional events themselves. His work theorizes the ways in which timescales aid in explaining how categorizations of students that fit certain cultural mythologies harken back in time, while the timescales moving forward during the academic year reveal how identities change.

While this is surely an important finding, perhaps even more critical is his argument that the constructions of identity he found were *cumulative* over time. Wortham shows how certain racialized identities are coconstructed in the classroom over time, and that those constructions of identity are repeated like variations on a theme (in fact, several themes), accumulating across the school year. Leander, Phillips, Taylor, Nespor, and Lewis (2010) said of Wortham's study:

> Wortham reminds us that the particularities of the events and settings of repetition matter, and not just repetition as an abstract pro-

> cess. The association (discussed elsewhere as a "lamination," Holland and Leander, 2004) appears to have a particular holding power not merely because it is repeated, but because the repetition happens on a particular sort of occasion when being positioned just so is especially marked or remarkable. The repetition, therefore, is not simply an effect of being located in numerous time-spaces, but an effect of the accrual or accumulation of particularly marked time-spaces that are collected and organized. (341)

Wortham's work shows how repeated, similar kinds of categorizations of students in a particular occasion accrue. For example, some peers take up the teacher's categorizations of individual students, and some students came to demonstrate an adoption of these characterizations through their talk and action. Wortham's work demonstrates how identity accrues; identity formation is cumulative, gathering steam over the course of the academic year. This chapter draws on Wortham's work to consider what the accumulation of constructions of responsibility means for the students and for all those working with street-level workers.

Timescale of the Semester

As established in earlier chapters, the timescale of a spring semester Academic Critical Reading (ACR) course is marked by three events: a departmental midterm (given around week 7 or 8 of the semester), spring break, and the end-of-semester high-stakes exam (the ACT). The performance assessments loom large in the semester and, together with spring break, shape how constructions of responsibility emerge across the semester. The timescale of the course itself followed a general pattern, but each student's ACR timescale was different depending on how many times they had taken the course.

Constructions of Responsibility over Time

Much like the data presented in Chapter 5, the cultural mythologies, deontic formulations, and references to performance used by the professor change with the ebb and flow of semester performance measurements. While I will show some figures that provide simple counts of the frequency of the gestalt, the aim of this chapter is to show how the gestalt of responsibility appears throughout the semester, so that we may consider their collective weight.

The community college data, like the shelter data, were coded for aspects of the gestalt, including deontic formulations, with subcodes that defined which class topics the deontic formulations referred to: Deontic formulations connected to performance measurements and assessments were called "deo test," those related to the class novel or to the goal of being readers-for-life were coded "deo-reading," and those relating to responsibilities in "life" outside of reading were coded "deo-life." Performance assessments and benchmarks were coded with "test taking" and "time," respectively, and cultural mythologies were coded "cultural myth."

Pulling just the codes for constructions of responsibility, performance benchmarks measurements, and cultural mythologies, we can see a trend in *when* the gestalt of responsibility is employed (even given the low total *N*). Spring break that semester was in early April, and the midterm exam was given usually around the eighth week of classes (mid-March). References to the performance assessments, cultural mythologies, and deontic formulations increased prior to the midterm exam and spring break and then increased in preparation for the high-stakes final exam. Given the findings in Chapter 5, it is not surprising that talk in this institutional context also responds to performance measurements and benchmarks. This again confirms Soss, Fording, and Schram's (2011) assertion that workers change their behavior according to institutional demands, demonstrating that these changes are occurring at the discourse level.

In Chapter 4, we explored how cultural mythologies surfaced in the community college classroom, comparing those collecting around performance benchmarks with those around the non-performance-based activity of reading the class novel, *Fahrenheit 451*. As a counterexample, it is useful to consider how constructions of responsibility surfaced when connected to these discretionary topics over the course of the semester.

As demonstrated in Figure 6.2, discretionary topics had an inverse relationship to constructions of responsibility around the topic of performance. The beginning of the semester had ample time to discuss discretionary topics, and with the midterm exam safely behind, the middle of the semester was the calm between performance assessment storms that provided some space for this discretionary topic to thrive. In those moments, constructions of responsibility occurred in relation to those discretionary topics. Rather than discussing responsibilities associated with the performance assessments for the course (midterm / high-stakes final), the professor could discuss responsibilities of readers in general, responsibilities for life, and responsibilities in the present ("deo-now" in the figure) rather that responsibilities for future performance measure-

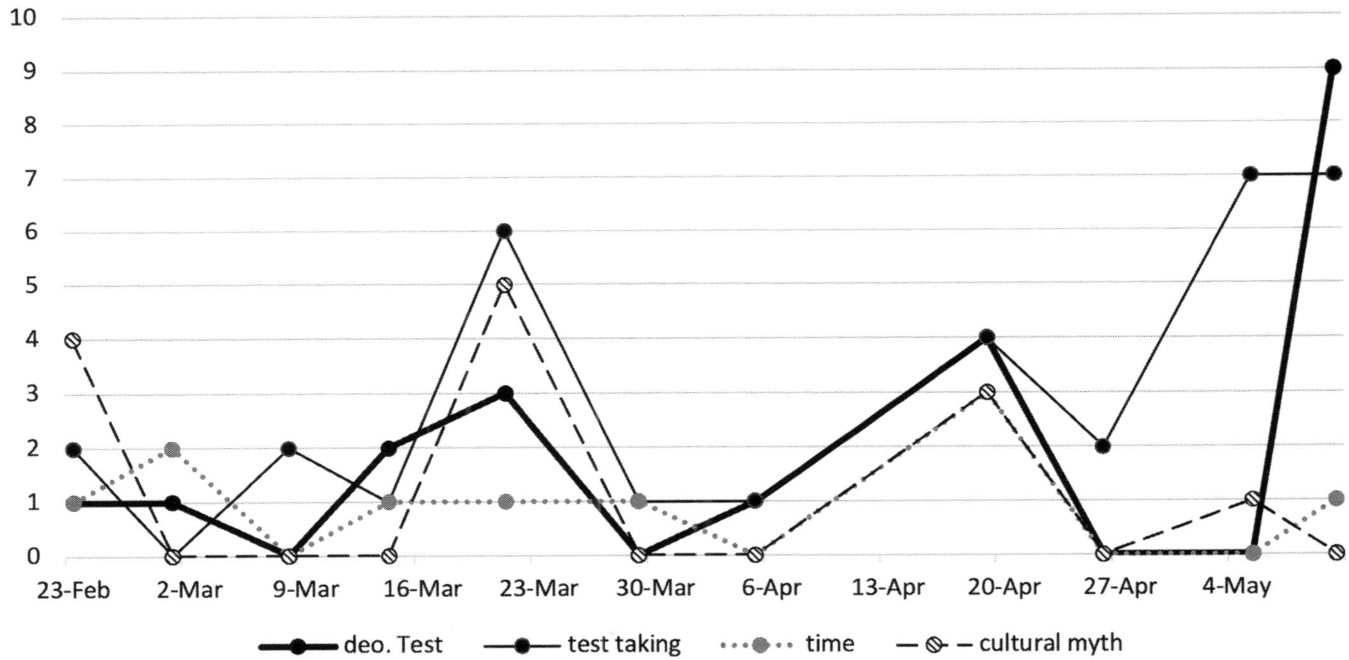

Fig. 6.1. Gestalt of Responsibility Across the Semester Is Shaped by Performance Benchmarks

This figure illustrates how constructions of responsibility are sensitive to performance assessments in the semester, including the midterm and the final.

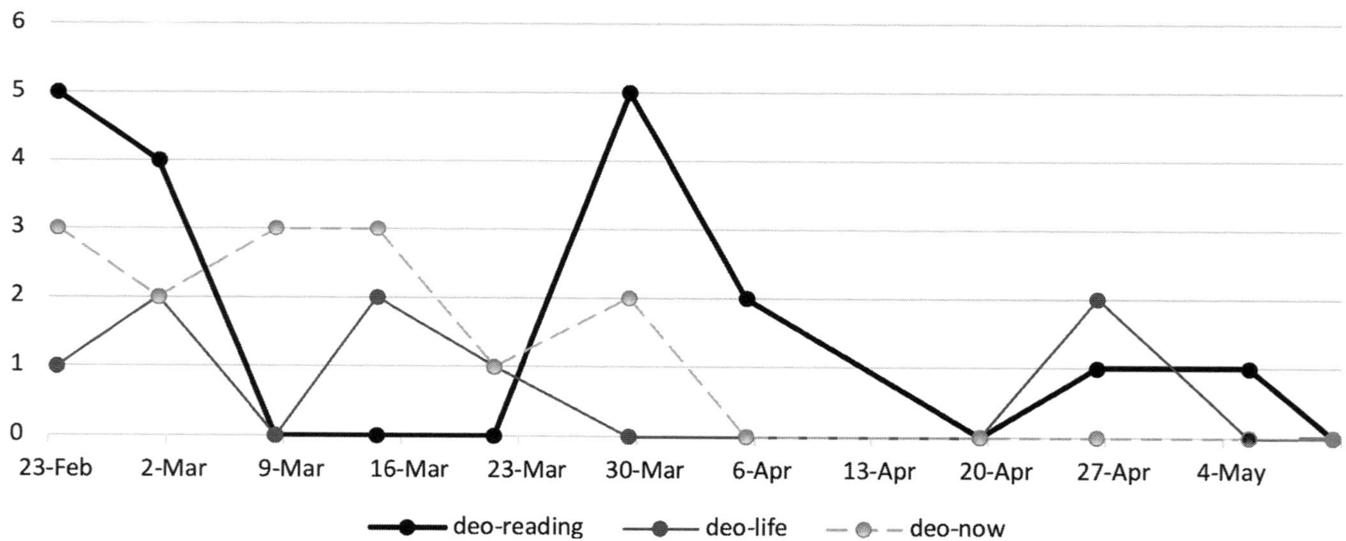

Fig. 6.2. Responsibility for Reading and for Life

This figure illustrates how constructions of responsibilities around a major discretionary course topic function inversely to the gestalt of responsibility vis-à-vis performance measurements.

ments. While these numbers are crude, even I was surprised to see how neatly the frequency of these codes mapped out the dynamic of responsibility talk over the semester.

Although I was tempted to bring you through these shifts discursively over the course of the semester as I did in Chapter 5, I instead want to take this opportunity to move the conversation forward by exploring how these constuctions accumulate. However, first, I want to remind us of the construction of the gestalt of responsibility, so we will look at two examples from the first class we recorded in week 3 in the semester: The first addresses responsibilities relating to the performance assessments, while the second includes constructions of responsibility relating to the main discretionary topic in class—the class novel.

In the first excerpt below, we find the invocation of a cultural mythology that surfaces often in this class: rushing, what I call "the rushed job," which presupposes a slapdash, sloppy, and quick approach to work rather than a slow, deliberate approach. I suggest in Chapter 4 that this cultural mythology aligns with "laziness" mythology, implying a lack of hard work. I use bolded font here to draw your attention to those mythologies. As the focus in each of these transcripts is on what is said (the verbalized mythologies) rather than how they are said, these transcripts do not include underlining for emphasis and overlaps.

Excerpt 6.1: February 23a

Prof: All right. Let's go back even if you haven't finished
with go through it together? Um just a reminder of what's
coming up on Monday the handout that I gave you, **Please
make sure you answer all the questions? And take your time
doing it**. Okay. That's why I gave it to you over the weekend.
Don't rush through it. Give it your best effort not your fastest. Okay?

In this excerpt, the instructor is explaining a homework assignment that he gave to the students earlier that class. Here the polite imperative "please make sure" (lines 3–4) commands the students to complete the assignment with no overt deontic stance. However, there are multiple references to a "rushed job": "all the questions" (line 4), "take your time" (line 5), "don't rush through it" (line 6), and "give it your best effort not your fastest" (line 6). Speed on the test is indirectly equated with doing a poor job. While later in the semester, the instructor provides an alternate reason why the students might rush the assignment (test anxiety), there is no reasoning suggested here. Instead, there is an assumption of laziness signaled by the presupposition that students will indeed rush and value speed ("fastest") over quality.

In the next except from the same session, the instructor invokes a slightly different cultural mythology as he introduces *Fahrenheit 451*.

Excerpt 6.2: February 23b

Prof: Okay. So. A fireman. He doesn't put out fires? He burns books.
So part 1, the title is The Hearth and the Salamander." **Anybody bother**
looking up- a salamander's a little creature, but in mythology,
anybody look up what a salamander is?
(5.0)
All right **we should get into the habit**- particularly, I even put that word
on the board in the list of vocabulary?If you can't figure out what it means,
look it up. **Look it up. Look it up in the dictionary**. Go online. So
in mythology a salamander is a creature that's immune to fire. That
can't burn. So when a fireman wears a shield of a phoenix¿ phoenix,
the bird that- another mythological creature¿(   ) flies out of the fire,
salamander can't be burned. Good thing for firemen to be wearing.
The hearth. What's a hearth.
S: ((raises hand))
Prof: Yeah.
S: It's like the front of the fireplace?
Prof: Front of the fireplace. So both images here, are of fire. If you have your
book, just open it up. I'm gonna read a little bit, with you¿ And then on
your way out, please make sure you leave the summaries with me.
(Make) sure I get them, If you didn't do it, then you have extra work
for Monday, make sure I get the summary on Monday. All right. So this
is the first sentence of the book.
Oh by the way. **Anybody bother looking**
up why this book is called *Fahrenheit 451*? **Does anybody**
care?

In this segment, we see a theme discussed in Chapter 4 wherein the instructor socializes the students as a community of readers. As noted in that chapter, this topic represents a discretionary departure from the test-centeredness of the class, and this instructor often noted that while a particular strategy was good for testing, it may not prove as useful as a reading strategy. As a street-level worker, he was able to create time in class for both exam preparation and legitimate enjoyment of / critical thinking about reading. In line 6, the instructor uses "we" to include himself in the community of readers and "habit," which situates the reading action as a social practice.

However, we also see cultural mythologies surfacing here in lines 2–4 and 23–25. In lines 2–4, the instructor introduces the title "The Hearth and the Salamander." He asks, "anybody bother looking up," at which point he recasts his statement, removing the word "bother," asking "anybody look up what a salamander is." The word "bother" is a presupposition, revealing an assumption that looking up a word may be more trouble than the students are willing to take. It is perhaps because the original question is framed under the assumption of student laziness that the recast of the question is treated with silence from the students who collectively offer a dispreferred response in the form of a long silence (Pomerantz, 1984). This long silence prompts the professor to explain basic reading habits, which functions to socialize the class. He begins this socialization with deontic formulation "We should get into the habit," which collectively encourages the class to engage in a general practice. Winiharti (2012) explains that "should" is perhaps the "weakest" and "politest" of the deontic modals, so it is does not carry the force of "you have to" or "you must." This gentle deontic formulation is, however, followed by a series of commands that direct students to particular actions without explicitly (deontically) obligating them to do so, *look it up, go online.*

"Bother" returns in lines 23–25 when the professor asks students if they looked up the relevance of the novel's title. By including "bother" in "anybody bother looking up why this book is called *Fahrenheit 451*," the instructor again injects cynicism into the question. The word "bother" presupposes the stance of the students who find looking up terminology to be too much work. As such these invocations chime with the cultural mythology of "the rushed job," both of which presuppose laziness through either the sloppiness of rushing through an assignment or through the assumption that students may find looking up words to be onerous. The instructor concludes his question-cum-critique by asking "does anybody care?", a question I have often asked myself in my most cynical moments when only a third of the class turns in homework assignments. In this case, however, when said aloud, this question serves to amplify the presupposition that none of the students care. Heritage and Robinson (2011) argue that "any" prefers, or anticipates, a "no" answer. This statement expects a "no" response, contributing to the overall positioning of the students as unwilling to go the extra mile, students who "rush" the job, lazy students. As the class discusses the relevance of *Fahrenheit 451*, the instructor and the class discuss power, how the novel addresses power, but also how a powerful writer can inspire its readers to question. This class session includes Excerpt 3.6 from Chapter 3, in which the professors equates the students' lack of self-generated research about the novel to "cheating."

I include both of these examples as a reminder that the gestalt of responsibility, while primarily used for institutional, businesslike discussions of performance assessments and benchmarks, is also utilized for discretionary topics that fall outside of institutional requirements.

Responsibility Is Both Vertical and Horizontal

As a linguist and discourse analyst, I have been trained to value the little nuances of language and discourse; even one isolated transcript can uncover important and relevant findings. This book has, in part, demonstrated how responsibility also evolves horizontally over the course of the semester or across an unhoused person's time in shelter. In this chapter, we turn the lens to examine the potential for responsibility to not only evolve over the data collection period but also to accrue vertically. In Table 6.1 I have cataloged every instance of a cultural mythology across the community college data set,[2] most of them in collaboration with deontic formulations and often performance references. I did not include deontic formulations on their own (e.g., "You need to do this assignment by Monday"), and I did not include performance references on their own (references to testing, process of elimination, etc. that exist outside of the gestalt). Cultural mythologies are bolded, deontic formulations are underlined, and performance references are in italics for your analytic convenience. The chart catalogs instances of cultural mythologies coded in NVivo, divided roughly into subcategories; however, it is important to underscore that these are essentially variations on a theme. Thus you may see overlapping and blurring among my imperfect categories. I chose to separate and attempt to differentiate them in order to highlight the frequency of these mythologies, which gets lost in large paragraphs of transcript.

Responsibility, and its construction in talk, has much to do with time. While Chapter 4 suggested that cultural mythologies have a historical legacy, pointing backward in time, in Chapter 5 I illustrated how talk may be shaped by performance benchmarks and assessments, the bookends that constrain institutional time. In so doing, Chapter 5 asks us to consider the progression of institutional time going forward. This chapter, however, examines the ways in which the gestalt of responsibility functions vertically over time: Like grains of sand in an hourglass, the instances of the gestalt accumulate, potentially weighing heavier and heavier on those who endure them.

TABLE 6.1: The Social Construction of a Cumulative Public Identity Around Responsibility

		Rushing	Disengaged/ "lazy"	Easy road	Cheating	Self-appraisal	Hard work / work harder / grit	Deontic responsibility
Feb 23	**Don't rush** through it. (Give it your **best effort**) **not your fastest**. Okay?	✓					✓	
	Anybody bother looking up- a		✓					
	Anybody look up what a salamander is?		✓					
	))**Anybody bother looking up** why this book is called *Fahrenheit 451*?		✓					
	Does anybody care?		✓					
	You hafta keep **going back and asking those *questions***. Even if you don't have *answers to the questions. Cause that's why we're doing this.* It's one of the reasons we're doing this.						✓	✓
	Is that when you come and talk to each other, instead of **just some professor giving you all of *the answers***, you **can get *the answers* among yourselves. (It's) much better**. You'll learn much more that way.			✓				
	Cause I **could just come up here and tell you what the book is about**. But **will you have accomplished anything** if we do it that way? That's **like reading Cliffs Notes. That's cheating**.			✓	✓			
Mar 1	Remember to **take your time** when you do *it*, **don't rush through**.	✓✓						
	Take you time doing *it*, **don't rush though**, and also remember you're also supposed to read the next twenty pages and- of *Fahrenheit 451*?	✓✓						✓
	With autonomy, comes **responsibility**. Right¿ With your boss telling you what to do every day, then **you have to**: make sure you **do it on your own**.						✓	✓
	Or in the vocabulary book. Inane. Okay? But Brad- I'm not trying to embarrass Brad, but Brad fell for the bait. And I put this on *here* as a warning. When you take *your tests, test makers* like to try to trick you. They're not trying to be cruel. (2.0) But they're trying to make sure that you ***take your time and that you think it through*** *and that you* ***don't just look for the quick easy answer***. *Because that can happen especially when you take an important test.* (gesturing) 'cause what did we say yesterday¿ when you take an important *test*, how do you feel? Nervous. Anxious.	✓		✓				
	We tend to rush when we're nervous and anxious. (1.0) an example, that's why I put it here, **to just slow yourselves down**. **Read carefully**. (1.0) Okay?	✓						
Mar 8	Keep working on *that* for another:: say ten or fifteen minutes and then we'll go through *it* together? Very important, **don't rush**,	✓						
Mar 14	Normal eight o'clock time, **please get here on time**¿		✓					
	And before we go, we'll do another chapter in the vocabulary book. So, come in just like any other morning, do: chapter fifteen that we'll be up to tomorrow, and then we'll go over it very quickly, or even if we don't go over it, we still wanna get it done, and we'll follow up next week, and we're gonna go to the reading lab. **If you come in late,** (2.0) go upstairs if you're here after eight thirty. (That's) five hundred, you'll find us up there.		✓					
	But **don't come late**. Be here on time.		✓					

	Also make sure you have your BMCC ID with you. Okay, 'cause they're gonna wanna swipe you in to get you into the system. **You should have that every day, but especially tomorrow**. On Monday¿ um you're going to take a *midterm exam*. I think I spoke to you briefly about it, it's gonna be very *similar to the test we did on the first day of class*, it's a *paper test, it's timed*, (and) we'll use *it* just to see where you are. *Halfway through the semester*, uh ((facial expression)) (will) help us recognize how well you're doing, how much more work you need to do, and I will:- I can't go over the specifics of the test with you, but I will go over your grades with you, a little mini-conference with you next week. After we get the *results*. Please bring a *number two pencil*. Okay, you need that *for your test*, and then, this has been our running assignment, and then Wednesday, next Wednesday this is when this is due.				✓✓
Mar 21	*Treat it like you're taking the test*. Reading three essays **take your time**, read the *questions* first if you need to, read the *answers*, you'll go back and forth with the passage. K?	✓			
	If you rush through this you defeat the purpose. take your time. When I was ((gestures to desk)) speaking to some of you this morning about *the midterm* on Monday?	✓			
	A lot of you said I felt rushed. Well, okay, but on the final exam there's no rush it is un timed. **And good reading doesn't always mean fast reading**. Especially for those of you for whom English is not your first language it takes longer.	✓	✓		
	Well, this is your opportunity even though it's called Timed Readings we're not using it that way. K? **Take your time. Do not rush. You can't do a good job, if you're doing this on the subway Monday morning on your way to school**. **That' just not- you're wasting your time there.** Eh? You have plenty of time between today. And Monday to get this done. The other homework is we're gonna move ahead.	✓	✓		
	The thing you'll have to do not just Olivia, everybody, is you **have to apply the common sense rule here**. You **have to** *plug the word in*, read the sentence again, and see if it makes any sense.			✓	✓✓
	No one can teach you common sense after all. But you have it. You have to use it. Plug the word in.			✓	✓
	When you're sitting here all of you not just Olivia everybody you're sitting here what is one of the main messages I keep telling you? **You need to work harder**.			✓	✓
	I didn't say you need to put in more time necessarily, but some of you need to put in more time but you need to focus more.				✓
	You can't rush through ***exercises*****. If you rush through them they don't really bring you where you want to go, they're not gonna help you they're not gonna give you more confidence**.	✓✓			
	Take your time, but **don't guess. don't guess**. Some of you guessed on the *midterm* you felt the pressure of time, Even though I never said that to you: make sure you finish. I said do the best you can do. **Some of you just rushed through**. That guarantees that those questions are probably going to be wrong. The *final exam is not timed*.	✓	✓		
	Look at the first sentence, listen to the context, "when the company standardized its pay scale the salary for each type of job became Identical throughout all the departments." **So instead of ME repeating it and ME going over it Karina what do we have to do**? . . . No but you need to go over it twice before you do it,		✓		✓
	EVERYBODY, how many times have we seen this we go over it again and we get the right *answer*, hopefully you have learned the lesson of that, that's what I was saying before **if you rush through** you often don't get the results you're looking for but **if you take your time** and you go back through it again chances are you're going to do better, I guarantee chances are,	✓✓			

	and **you have to stop waiting for me to prompt you, you have to do this on your own**, we're *half way through the semester, second half of the semester* you're going to be much more **on your own**, once you have the *skills* you have to start applying them as often as you can. Number 9, stint.			✓		✓✓	✓
Mar 29	n/a						
Apr 5	Want to just go over *them*? Make sure you have the *right answers*? Obviously we don't have a- a full class today? but I think what we will do is after we go over the vocabulary? (then) we can do some more *practice, on the test* and maybe I'll you read a longer piece? *You can read that, answer questions*, and we can call it a morning, okay? **But I appreciate you guys showing up. It says a lot about how hard you work,** so just we'll go through it together					✓✓	
Apr 19	That's good. Ok. But we're all here which is a good thing (1.) today. Some of you are making **a rare appearance** and **uh welcome back** its good to see you again. Umm, we ha:::ve what *three three and a half weeks of class left*. (3.)		✓				
	So *this is the time* your teachers tell you things like, **well you gotta kick it in to a higher gear, you gotta start working even harder than your working,**					✓✓	✓
	so when the teachers tell you that (.) are you paying attention? . . . No, there's an [**honest** answer. Ok (2.) °alright°] **But its good advice** (3.) So now it's that *part of semester*, you *guys are all facing the exact same thing at the end of the semester. You gonna have to take the ACT, sit for the test*, do your best hopefully pass and get to move on. (2.)		✓			✓	✓
	Well this is the time of the semester to when (.) yea **I want you- I hope you all start working even harder than you were working** but it's also the *time* to **assess what you've done so far, to really look yourself in the mirror, HONESTLY, to see how hard you've actually worked**.				✓	✓✓	✓
	Have you done all the assignments, do you go over the work after we finish it, have you gone to the reading lab, have you gone online, worked from home? **If the answer to all those questions . . . is no,** *it's not too late to start.*		✓				
	So I'm not here to criticize you, chastise you, challenge you, I'm here to encourage you **not to stop *at this point*** and *if you haven't really st:::arted* its ok::: to start now, when teachers tell you to **kick it in to upper gear** (4.)					✓✓	
	what they really mean is you got three weeks to **work as hard as you can** (1.) *to accomplish your goal*, **but you're in control of that**.					✓✓	
	Now remember we're at the point of the semester where **simple answers aren't good enough**.		✓				
	You have to **keep** asking why. **Keep digging more and more.** OK? That's what you're going to be *tested* on most. That's what thinking inferences are about.					✓	✓
	Have some knowledge, add what you know, come to a conclusion. **If you're lazy, *it* doesn't happen. If you're satisfied with the surface, *it's* not gonna happen**.		✓✓				
	You can all read and understand on the surface but that's not through challenge. **Challenge is to keep asking questions. You should keep asking them**. Move on to number three.					✓✓	✓
	here are *fi:::ve small passages and a total of fifteen questions*. I'll give you enough time to do that, again if you wanna work with somebody else that's fine, and **take your time don't rush**:::.	✓✓					

Apr 26	I repeat this, I like to repeat. **Do not rush through the homework.** The way to get the most out of it? **Is to take (.) your time and go over it.** I've seen a number of times if you go over something the second time, you correct yourself.	✓✓			
	Take your time. Also for Monday, the next *three timed readings*. And the same assignment I put on the board yesterday, just to repeat, for Wednesday? A short essay, you can write as much as you want but it doesn't have to be lengthy.	✓			
May 03	[lengthy description of the test and what to do] when you take *your final exam* on, *when is it, the 21st of May*, no time limit there's **no reason to rush,** I'm certain you'll have enough time to do this now, ok, so read the *directions* you're gonna look at the *questions* first and then proceed to read through (.)	✓			
	ok there's only EIGHT questions so **don't rush and read them all carefully**, all right as soon as you get *it* you can start.(handing out test papers) And no helping each other this time work on your own please. And if you finish ahead of the other students, review, go back over it.	✓			
May 10	Okay? **so don't rush. Take your time,** and see how you do. Then we'll go over it. No time limit. **You'll have plenty of time to get this done.** ((P distributes the practice test))	✓✓			
	Good, XXXX right? They all require very similar soil and climate conditions. Okay make sure you go back. When *there's factual questions*. This is a matter of *strategy*. **Are you willing to take the time, make the effort, and look for the answer in the test.** *Look at the question, look at the answers, look for the words that match up*, Inferencing you can't do that. Right?		✓	✓✓	
	<u>You have to</u> think larger. <u>You have to</u> read what you have and then connect it. *But factual questions*? just go back to the passage. and also do the *process of elimination* if the answer doesn't get you right away. *eliminate* those that you have a strong feeling are negative? then (.) choose from what's left. How bout number four, Joanie?			✓	✓✓

Constructions of Responsibility as Identity Work

We may remember Hancock's (2004) *Politics of Disgust*, described in Chapter 2. She argues that all-too-common references to "welfare queens" and similar cultural mythologies cultivate a "public identity" for Black people applying for public assistance. Drawing on Hancock (2004), I argue that the cultural mythologies folded into the gestalt of responsibility also do "identity work" (de Fina, 2011).

As described at the outset of this chapter, the cumulative effect of identity work in the classroom is convincingly argued by Wortham (2006), who shows how individual students, often positioned in negative ways in the classroom by the teacher and other students, resist and sometimes take up identities. His integration of timescales encourages a widening of the research lens beyond singular interactional events, explaining how stereotyped categorizations of students point back in time, while also showing how timescales move forward during the academic year as identities are constructed, taken up, and shift. Racialized identities are coconstructed in the classroom over time, repeated like variations on a theme (in fact, several themes). As Leander et al. (2010) remind us: "The repetition, therefore, is not simply an effect of being located in numerous time-spaces, but an effect of the accrual or accumulation of particularly marked time-spaces that are collected and organized" (341). The repetition, then, is central to how identity accrues.

I argue that the professor's use of cultural mythologies of this type is not only identity work but also a kind of microaggression. While occurring individually and often stinging in the moment, part of what makes microaggressions so painful and exhausting is repetition—how often they surface in interaction. Burns (2014) explains that "when students experience microaggressions from classmates and professors on a regular basis, the fatigue and trauma that occur can cause them to become disillusioned about the value of education" and to doubt their academic ability (140). Examining the entire semester at a glance helps us see the repeated instances of these microaggressions.

Pierce (1974) coined the term, and Sue (2010a) further theorized and popularized the concept, defining microaggressions as "the everyday verbal, nonverbal, and environmental slights, snubs, or insults, whether intentional or unintentional, which communicate hostile, derogatory, or negative messages to target persons based solely upon their marginalized group membership" (3). Instances of these often ignore or negate the experiences of marginalized community members. Sue (2010a) describes three different types, the last of which applies best to these findings: microinvalidations, which he defines as "communications . . . that exclude, negate, or nullify the psychological thoughts, feelings, or experiential reality" of marginalized people (37), and it is perhaps this category that best fits these negative cultural mythologies.

There are several studies examining microaggressions from a discourse perspective. Drawing on Sue's (2010b) claim that microaggressions extend beyond race, Di Gennaro and Brewer (2019) use speech act theory[3] to explore microaggressions that surface among faculty with different (and marginal) specializations in an academic department. Also drawing on speech acts, Perez Gomez (2020) suggests using implicature to examine microaggressions in prenatal testing for selective abortion for people with extant disabilities. She states that "medical professionals who promote prenatal testing for selective abortion may sometimes *hyper-implicate*—that is, roughly, *unintentionally* communicate—morally objectionable disability-related beliefs that thereby wrong extant disabled individuals" (90). She argues that hyper-implicatures include values and beliefs that "can be inferred, in part, from what is implicated" (91). Perez Gomez (2021) explores this more deeply, making a case for hyper-implicature. She extends Grice's (1989) work, which argues that statements can have both literal meanings and implicature (implied meanings). Hyper-implicature, she argues,

> refers to a seeming background attitude in a speaker that she does not explicitly state or intentionally imply, but that can nonetheless be deduced from her literal and implied meanings as an inference to the best explanation for why she asserts what she asserts (387).

The attitudes conveyed by the speaker position the speaker vis-à-vis membership in a social group.

While I do not aim to fully theorize microaggressions here, the data presented in this chapter and in this book help to underscore several useful methodological considerations. Namely, if we want to look at microaggressions, then we need to collect data about subtle linguistic and gestural decisions over time to understand how they surface and accrue vertically. An approach mindful of timescales also helps to connect stated cultural mythologies with their historical roots. Moreover, the cultural mythologies invoked in this data, while likely unknowingly invoked, represent a collection of related beliefs about a marginalized cohort of students, nearly all of whom are also from marginalized communities in New York City.

What kind of microaggressions appear in these constructions of responsibility? The cultural mythologies in this data are often connected with deontic formulations around responsibility, and many are aligned with performance measurements and benchmarks. These mythologies fall into several related stances about students: rushing, unwilling/disengaged, lazy, taking the "easy" or "simple" path, and needing to work harder / be gritty. Many of these mythologies connect to what scholars call the "deficit perspective" (Paris and Alim, 2017).

In sociolinguistic circles "deficit perspective" often refers to people who negatively judge speakers of dialects of English that deviate from Standard American English (SAE). Despite ample evidence that dialects outside of Standard American English are legitimate and grammatical (Hudley and Mallinson, 2010, 2011, 2017), many people still hold the inaccurate belief in the supremacy of SAE. Wolfram, Adger, and Christian (1999) explain,

> In terms of language, proponents of the deficit position believe that speakers of dialects with nonstandard forms have a handicap—socially and cognitively—because the dialects are illogical, or sloppy, or just bad grammar. (20)

Lippi-Green (1994) calls this "standard language ideology," which she defines as "a bias toward an abstracted, idealized, homogeneous spoken language which is imposed from above, and which takes as its model the written language" (166). She describes the pervasiveness of this belief system in a variety of institutional domains, focusing on the legal system and language/dialect-based workplace discrimination. Legitimizing the language varieties of marginalized communities has been the work of many sociolinguists for easily half a century.

Despite the fact that these language and literacy ideologies have been fully discredited by half a century of sociolinguistic research,[4] everyday people continue to circulate these destructive, inaccurate, deficit-oriented beliefs and debate them in public forums. Still studying these issues decades later, Rosa (2016) explains how these kinds of deficit perspectives have racist overtones: "What might appear as perceptions of particular nonstandardized practices can in fact racialize populations by framing them as incapable of producing *any* legitimate language" (163). For Rosa, buying into the wholly unfounded mythos that stigmatizes people who speak nonstandard varieties of a language and judges them based on that incorrect belief is a racializing act. (4). Hudley, Mallinson, and Bucholtz (2022) explain:

> Sometimes faculty tell Black and African American students that they must "improve their vocabulary" or "stop using slang," rebukes that can lead students to internalize the false belief that they have some sort of linguistic deficit—that the language they brought to college isn't "good enough." Consequently, Black students may be faced with a dual curriculum, only half of which you earn credit for: Taking your classes and navigating the linguistic expectations of the college classroom. (4)

In fact, they further argue that the "devaluation of [African American English] and Black language practices is a form of *linguistic racism*" (4).

As this data show, language and literacy ideologies are alive and well in the classroom. Statements like "you have to think larger," "Your challenge is to keep asking questions. You should keep asking them," and "simple answers aren't good enough" position the students as small thinkers who have "simple answers" when they "should" be thinking more critically. "Thinking larger" and "simple answers" are part of a long history of deficit perspectives in language and literacy studies.

These perspectives are joined by cultural mythologies relating to perseverance, grit, laziness, rushing through work, and not caring about learning. As discussed in Chapter 2, perseverance and grit are described by Love (2019) as disproportionately expected of Black and Brown children, as part of a "Character Education" approach, one that is part of the neoliberal turn where "hustle" and "grind" are required for success (Spence, 2015).

In the data above, we have the references to "keep": "keep digging" and "keep asking" (perseverance), but we also have multiple references to "working harder." The professor says, "you need to work harder. I didn't say you need to put in more time necessarily, but some of you need to put in more time but you need to focus more." I am reminded of Ms. Innis's words in Chapter 3: "so if they don't put the pressure on then (.) we gonna give you the time to slide. just playing devil's advocate. and that's basically what they look at. regardless of whatever you're doing. you're not doing enough." Similarly, in Excerpt 6.3 from the end of the semester, the professor cites perseverance.

Excerpt 6.3: Whatever (Learning) You're Doing, You're Not Doing Enough

> yea <u>I want you</u>- I hope you all start working even harder than you were working when teachers tell you to kick it in to upper gear (4.) what they really mean is you got three weeks to work as hard as you can (1.) to accomplish your goal, but you're in control of that.

The final line, "you're in control of that" puts students in charge of their success, in effect asking them to pull themselves up by their bootstraps and work harder.

Am I calling out street-level workers on covert forms of racism? Well, not exactly. Although it may feel semantic, I am calling street-level workers *in*. We need to collectively rethink how we talk on the job. Trans activist and writer Schuyler Bailar (2023) said that

> calling something or someone transphobic isn't a condemnation or an erasure of your character. It's a description of an action that that person found harmful. And people need to hear the hurt and the pain they've caused without reacting with offense. The proper response to someone calling someone or something transphobic is to listen and be curious about how and why, and then to apologize when necessary. (110)

I find Bailar's explanation here helpful. Rather than calling these street-level workers "racist," I am identifying racialized language that is embedded in the subtle words they use in institutional spaces that serve marginalized people. Harkening back to Flores et al. (2018), there may be a tension between the professed beliefs of the street-level workers and their actions in the classroom, the latter of which are informed by their listening subject position and socialized implicit biases that inform cultural mythologies. These are linguistic actions that need to be noticed and addressed on an institutional and systemic level. The professor in this data was well liked by his students. The social workers in the shelter data set were also often well liked. Rather than smear their character, I hope to highlight that these individual linguistic actions need attention, change, and potentially apology/amends. As Burns (2014) explains,

> When a microaggression is committed by a professor, the student may feel deeply betrayed and hurt, especially if that professor was held in high regard before the incident. The negative impact of having a respected professor say something discriminatory is much more severe than having a less respected person do it (Sue, 2010: 23). As microaggressions are experienced by members of oppressed groups on a regular basis, negative long-term effects can also occur, such as lower self-esteem, depression, anxiety, and physical health problems (Sue, 2010: 6, 149). As professors, our goal is to facilitate learning, and committing microaggressions and mishandling those committed by students prevents us from succeeding at that task; in

> particular, it reduces our effectiveness with students from oppressed groups. (133)

As a white educator, I have also made mistakes that require investigation and unlearning, and I (and we) have still more to do. This is not the culmination of a finished "me"—this is me right now.

Autoethnography: Ugh. I Am Scrooge.
As I shared in the beginning of the book, *A Christmas Carol* was an influential part of my upbringing, part of a familial liturgical calendar that, like church services, involved the reciting of lines and singing of the film score as a group.[5] While I noted that, like the Ghost of Christmas Present, I ask the reader to reconsider the language used when discussing responsibility, I am, and we are all, also Scrooge, people who are capable of radical change, and as society shifts and grows, we are invited to grow with it. The starting place for our growth is different for each of us, having much to do with the privilege we experience, our awareness of it, and our experience with marginal community members. Despite the challenges I experienced as a young person, I grew up white, middle class, able-bodied, and straight sized, and while aspects of my social actions and forms of dress would later link up with a trans identity, I lived my life looking like a white, cisgender woman.

About ten years ago, the Friday before spring break and late in the afternoon, I was teaching Language and Culture. I was still early in my teaching career and was wrapping up my last class before I was on break myself. I had a stack of books in my arms as I was leaving class, and two students were following me out of class into the hallway, asking questions about an assignment due after the holiday. As I walked out of the room, I turned my head to respond to one of the students, and I inadvertently bumped into a student I did not know in the hallway. I apologized saying, "Oh! Sorry!" She scowled at me, muttering under her breath.

Here's what I should have done: I should have let it go, apologized again, and went on with my evening. Instead, I asked her if she was okay. I cannot remember clearly if my inquiry was genuine and empathetic or whether it was tinged with critique. The latter can have the force of a challenge, indirectly suggesting that her reaction was not "okay," potentially indirectly asking her to change that behavior. This comment escalated the situation, and I deeply regret making it.

At this point, she called me a "bitch," and cursed me out further as she entered her classroom next door to mine. I stood outside her classroom door, and explained that speaking that way to a professor is not acceptable and that I deserved an apology. I was calm but firm. At that point, she started yelling at me. According to my student's account, she said, "Do you think your title means anything to me, you're not going to do anything." She threatened to "kick my ass," and the statement I sent my department chair that evening noted some fear of retribution. I repeated calmly and clearly that her speaking to me this way was not acceptable and that an apology would be appropriate. I remember feeling my heart racing, pounding against my chest, my body shaking. I felt sweaty.

I left the classroom doorway and went back to my office, my students behind me checking in on whether I was okay and commenting on the student's rudeness. "She just flipped out," one of my students said. I helped my students with whatever they needed, and when I was done, I could hear from my office that the student was yelling to her professor about the situation. I decided to reengage, peeking my head in and introducing myself to the professor. The student shouted, "She was harassing me. She was harassing me." I explained my side to the professor, and she kept yelling. I asked the professor to step outside. He did, and we spoke. I heard the student inside the class once again say, "She was harassing me." Another student replied to her, "I was here, she was not harassing you." I asked the professor if he heard that, and he confirmed that he did. I told the professor that if the student wanted a second apology from me, I was happy to give it, but she did not seem willing to listen to me at all. The professor said with a sigh, "Students do not respect faculty" and seemed satisfied with my side of the story, corroborated by the student in the classroom who verbally acknowledged that I was not harassing the student in question.

I then wrote an email to my department chair, including the details above. In that message, I used the following sentence: "The student clearly has no respect for authority or respect for faculty," and I asked my chair what I should do to follow up. Because the student had threatened to come after me, my chair suggested I submit a statement to campus security. I had never interfaced with campus security aside from needing a classroom opened. I did not realize that, after taking my statement, they would show up to her classroom in uniform, ask the student to leave the classroom with them, and interview her. I can only imagine she was mortified, humiliated, and if not scared at least threatened. After giving her statement, she was allowed back in the classroom. I went back to my office to write a follow-up email to my chair, and I left for home. I knew that I had made several huge mistakes—start to finish.

I called campus the next day and asked to retract my statement. I spent much of spring break and the summer thinking about what happened, what I thought students owed me, and what I owed students (and others). I thought about how I had engaged the campus policing system and how that might have felt to the student. This event nearly ten years ago was the last time I called campus security for anything other than a locked classroom door. It was also the last time I called the police. At the time, I simultaneously believed in progressive pedagogies while also hypocritically acting in a way that underscored a belief that my status and authority as a faculty member meant more than student dignity. In short, I thought I was "woke," because I had progressive positions on nonstandard dialect use in student writing, taught from a position of dismantling white supremacy, and was well liked by my students. Instead, I had, and have, more learning to do. I made mistakes, and I knew it.

I needed to learn that my beliefs about my own authority, as well as my assumptions about "rude" behavior, were rooted in privilege, racist stereotypes, white supremacy, paternalism, and colonialist perspectives. These fed beliefs about classroom deference, what students "owe" to faculty, how students "should" act, and what appropriate responses to students should look like. I did not speak to this student from a position of compassion. I spoke to her as "an authority," from a position of entitlement and power. This entire exchange is one that changed how I handle myself, how I view my students, and how I behave at work. Drawing on Givens (2021) and a variety of other resources, I started investigating my internalized racism, radical empathy and vulnerability, nonviolent communication (Rosenberg, 2013, 2015), and pedagogical approaches that shifted authority in the classroom. I also needed to do some deep digging to identify and manage my own personal issues—anxiety, depression, and poor self-esteem, which (although not excusing my behavior) contributed to the problem—feelings of inadequacy feeding overcompensation, perhaps. I should have brought curiosity, empathy, and listening to the situation. There is no way to share

> this story without it being simultaneously read as virtue signaling. I was not perfect before, and I am not perfect now. All I can do is learn, read, listen, be open to hearing feedback, speak from a compassionate place, apologize when I am in the wrong, and actively work to do better, and this is part of what this book attempts to convey.

I want to include this narrative because I would like to highlight that, while I am analyzing this data and while I am critiquing the talk of these street-level workers, I have also been (and probably still am) part of the problem. Charles Dickens offers a story ending with Scrooge's redemption, resulting in joy all around and life for Tiny Tim. For better or for worse, our human stories are rife with mistakes. While we can make radical changes, there will always be new learning to do, new approaches to being and acting better. This unflattering story underscores that these kinds of actions extend beyond the participants in these studies. This is also a systemic issue. I have observed countless classes where faculty demanded unearned respect from students without reciprocating that respect and dignity, where faculty wielded their authority rather than listening to their students. Hancock (2007) discusses the politics of disgust *because* it is widespread. Approaches to solving the problem, therefore, need to be both individual and systemic, both linguistic and action-oriented. The final chapter will briefly summarize findings before exploring what a street-level approach to Applied Linguistics might look like and what recommendations I suggest for street-level practitioners and administrators.

7 | What (Should?) We Do with Our Words

We are judged by what we finish, not by what we start. -Anonymous
—A footer on a BMCC flyer

You've been here for months. *MONTHS*, and nothing's getting done, and what it looks like and what is reflects is I'm letting you skate through the system.
—Shelter caseworker

Responsibility as a Gestalt

Deontic Formulations

This book has outlined what a particular construction of responsibility looks like. While my inclination is to describe what is happening and leave deontic "shoulds" to others, many early readers asked for suggestions. What follows is incomplete and filtered through the lens of this particular white, trans academic. I have ideas, I look to you to help figure out what is best for different areas of professional practice and for different populations. I offer some frameworks that may help us all think differently about institutional discourse analysis, about applying linguistics in professional practice settings. I look forward to the productive dialogue to come!

The gestalt of responsibility in both the shelter context and the community college context included deontic formulations that specifically tie the listener to a responsible action, the shelter more than the community college. This is in part due to the timing of responsible tasks, as well as the difficulty of planning ahead in the remedial reading class. In the community college context, more commands were used, as the professor would give students instructions in the moment for what to do (and relied as little as possible on homework), while in the shelter most assigned responsibilities could only be completed before or after the meeting. Constructions involving commands in the classroom are more authoritarian but less intrinsically tied to obligation and necessity. Someone can order us to do something, and we can simply say no.

I did not consider age in this analysis; however, age might be a factor worth considering in future study. The professor is considerably older than his students, most of whom are eighteen or nineteen years old. It is possible that the paternalism and authoritarianism inherent in directives are more easily wielded in contexts more closely resembling parent-child relationships. I'm not a parent, so I'm not touching that topic, but I have been told there is ample literature on de-paternalizing parenting. In the shelter context, the workers, sometimes twenty or thirty years younger than the unhoused men, cannot be so easily paternal. Telling them that they are responsible hinges on authority, and I wondered if the younger caseworkers may, for example, refer to benchmarks and performance assessments more often to lend authority and institutional weight to their pleas for client action. However, the professor also refers constantly to these performance benchmarks and assessments. That said, there may be more subtle indicators at play that draw out differences between the two contexts, including gender identity of the workers, which is not explored here.

Cultural Mythologies

Working Harder and Not Doing Enough

Stance markers that point to cultural mythologies were also present in both data sets, though they varied slightly between contexts. In the community college context (Chapters 4 and 6), the stances indexed cultural mythologies that focused primarily on a variety of deficit perspectives characterizing the students as needing to be more gritty, autonomous, and individually responsible. The professor made references to students being "lazy," urging them to "work harder" and avoid taking the "easy" and/or "fast" route. As a reminder, consider the excerpt below from Chapter 6. For ease of identification, timing and benchmarks are in italics, cultural mythologies are in bold, and the assignment of responsibility is underlined.

Excerpt 7.1: Work Even Harder (at Community College Reading)

> *Well this is the time of the semester* to when (.) yea <u>I want you</u>- **I hope you all start working even harder than you were working**

> but it's also the *time* to **assess what you've done so far, to really look yourself in the mirror, HONESTLY, to see how hard you've actually worked**. Have you done all the assignments, do you go over the work after we finish it, have you gone to the reading lab, have you gone online, worked from home? **If the answer to all those questions . . . is no,** *it's not too late to start.*

In the shelter context, there was certainly overlap in the kinds of cultural mythologies that were used. Excerpt 3.9 from Chapter 3 underscores a common theme in both contexts: work harder, and however much you're doing, do more.

Excerpt 7.2: You Aren't Doing Enough (at the Shelter)

> Because its *gonna turn into a year*, then it's gonna *turn into fifteen months*, and then it's gonna *turn into*—>you understand what I'm saying?< and *then it adds* ↑ *up*. **So if they don't put the pressure on then (.) we gonna give you the time to slide. just playing devil's advocate. and that's basically what they look at. regardless of <u>whatever you're doing. you're not doing enough</u>**.

In the United States it is not uncommon to be asked to do "more" all the time. As Alec Baldwin's character Blake says in David Mamet's (1992) *Glengarry Glen Ross*, "Always be closing." It is not good enough to get several good sales; one must always be selling more. Unhoused people seeking shelter and students in the reading class described in this book, with significantly less power and privilege than faculty, are also asked to "do more" with far fewer resources. This is the kind of double standard Love (2019) describes, in which marginalized people are disproportionately asked to be responsible.

"System Abuser"

There were also myths that surfaced at the shelter that I did not find in the community college data. Most notably the cultural mythology of "system abuser," which was often mentioned in the shelter data, was not used in this classroom. For example, this excerpt from Chapter 3 includes such a mythology:

Excerpt 7.3: Skating Through the System

> I'm not telling you to get into a program, but what I'm telling you is you're gonna do something. You're not gonna sit here and continue to heavily use drugs the way you used to and and and just come in and work part time off the books and just not doing anything. You know, you know, and like I said befo:re (.) you take a Wednesday off good for you because Wednesday I need to see you getting a psych evaluation. *You've been here (.) for ↑months. ↑MONTHS.* **And nothing's getting done. And then what it looks at and it reflects is (.) I'm getting- I'm letting you skate through the system, and utilize the place just to ha- just to make sure you have a bed every night so you can go do what you need to do**, and I can't do that no more. You understand? I have 40 clients.(.3) and I'm being honest I can't I don't I don't have the patience anymore I'm stressed I just don't have it. **To let you keep skating** because when they need something from me I have to be able to produce it, and if I can't produce it I'm the one that's getting the rap at the end of the day. And so for **on judgment** and being a case manager I have to case manage you. (.) Now you have to help me help you. You understand what I'm saying?

The phrase "skate through the system" and "keep skating" index the cultural mythology of the "freeloader" who "uses and abuses" the system, connecting with Hancock's (2004) description of the public identity of the "welfare queen." Anecdotally, I have heard some faculty complain that students do not "apply themselves" in the classroom because they do not pay for school themselves, using federal funds and Pell grants, though I have no hard data demonstrating such a position. At the same time, the community college generally seems to position students attending school as showing initiative, working to "better themselves" through education, while there is a perception of people seeking shelter as having made mistakes with regard to personal responsibility, mistakes that have moral implications (as Soss et al., 2011 have explained). While not in the data set, in my department at the community college there was a rule that if students missed a certain number of classes, they would be barred from taking the high-stakes final exam. A colleague reading a draft of this book reminded me that the rule is in place in part to ensure that students cannot "skate through" hours of required remediation in the course, expecting to take the final in spite of excessive absences. The assumption of getting through too easily was baked into the rules for the exam.[1]

Meta-Cultural Awareness

There were also mythologies that received less or no attention in the analysis. For example, the "story" of the cultural shift occurring in the shelter system was its own useful mythology in constructions of responsibility, enacted in moments to account for pressure being put on clients. The following excerpts from Chapter 3 may remind us.

Excerpt 7.4: "People started to make this into a home"

> okay. um so (.) the pressure is on now because this is not- (.) what happened is(.)it took(.)people started to make this into a home. [they] started living here twenty-six years, ten years, five years, four years, and it was never supposed to happen. [things fell through the track.] right. things fell through the crack.(.) fine. so now the pressure's on us. yes, the mayor do have a five.hh year plan to bring down homelessness and yes he's on our cases cause he wants to look good. so: heads will ↑roll.

Excerpt 7.5: Ask Bloomberg

> What you really gotta do is go to Bloomberg. Bloomberg is he is the- . . . He's the source of all of this! I'm telling you he's the source of all of this. He's the one that he's sets a budget.

The invocation of the system change here is in line with Lipsky's (1980/2010) finding that workers will involve clients in their frustrations at work in order to gain an alliance and client compliance.

Neoliberal Organizational Mechanisms: Performance over Time

The analyses in this book underscore the relevance of past and future time as constructs that inform present talk, particularly in institutional contexts regulated by strict timelines and among street-level workers whose work is guided by those timelines and benchmarks. Performance benchmarks and measurements were also present in both contexts whether they were references to "that time of the semester" (Excerpt 7.1 above) or references to "months," years, or "five-year" plans (Excerpts 7.2, 7.3, 7.4). Chapter 3 underscored that these performance references, which carry the weight of assessment, potential sanction/failure, and each caseworker's performance record, are not neutral. Likewise, in the community college classroom, student performance and success on the high-stakes final exam gate-kept entry into the broader catalog of college courses.

These weighty references to performance benchmarks and assessments both showed *up* in street-level worker talk (Chapters 3 and 4), while also *shaping* street-level worker talk (Chapter 5). They potentially change *what* is talked *about* and *how* (Chapters 5 and 6). Chapter 5 illustrates how performance measurements shape the pleasantries and dignity offered at the outset of individual meetings. Even when the gestalt of responsibility is not the focus, the general niceties of conversation are lost in favor of disaffiliation and assertion of responsibility over time vis-à-vis these performance indicators. Chapter 6 adds that these performance benchmarks shape talk in both institutionally required and discretionary topic areas. We should consider whether these benchmarks and performance measurements can be altered to lessen the pressure on street-level workers and those they serve, and street-level workers should receive professional development that brings their awareness to how these performance management/timelines impact how they interact with those they serve. It may, as I discuss later, also help for workers to practice nonviolent communication practices, which may help de-escalate difficult moments in interaction (Rosenberg, 2013, 2015).

The relevance of performance benchmarks and assessments draws attention to the importance of time in these contexts. Shelter time and semester time are in part marked by performance benchmarks—tests, tasks. Those timescales are relevant, but so too is the historical past, the places and spaces where cultural mythologies grow and are reproduced, as described by Wortham (2004) and Flores et al. (2018). As demonstrated in these chapters, these cultural mythologies connect to the denigration of enslaved people, Jim Crow–era politics, puritanical positions on work and morality, and Hancock's (2007) *Politics of Disgust*, to name only some. The perpetuation of these cultural mythologies is both identity work (as the people being served are positioned and constructed vis-à-vis the institution and the world through street-level workers' words) and cumulative microaggressions (as these identities, often repeated over months, include damaging cultural mythologies). If these microaggressions do identity work, then future time is also germane, as these identities and damaging perspectives may be absorbed and carried into people's future lives. The gestalt of responsibility functions as a microaggression in which the identities of multidimensional people are interpellated (Althusser, 1971), reduced into morally judged institutional subordinates: "clients who skate through the system," "lazy students."

Moreover, while this book underscores the importance of horizontal time, a linear "over time" understanding of street-level work, it also highlights imagined time (Chapter 3), the way in which street-level workers use hypothetical imaginings, institutional listening subject positions, and future-orientations that shape how they speak to the people they are serving. Time impacts all aspects of the gestalt in some way, making it look more like Figure 7.1.

Personal pronouns refer back in time, stretching back to whom they refer ("you" refers back to "Michael," for example), and the deontic formulations can refer to past responsibilities ("should have," "were supposed to") or future responsibilities ("you need to," "you hafta"). Performance references stretch back to their policies and to when tasks were individually assigned, in addition to stretching forward into the future, as people are assessed on how they perform. The stance markers that point to cultural mythologies stretch backward in time to the myriad uses of these mythologies in our historical past, while also potentially stretching forward as/if participants carry the identities crafted in these institutional spaces into their everyday lives.

The Gestalt Elsewhere and the Problem of Neoliberalism

The 1988 John Carpenter film *They Live* has become a cult classic darling, ideal for teaching ideology. Provocateur and social theorist Slavoj Žižek even used clips from the movie to explain what ideology is and how it works (Fiennes, 2013). In the film, an unhoused man in Los Angeles named John finds a stockpile of sunglasses that enable him to see the ideological messages subtly advocated in city street signs, billboards, and magazines.

Examining the gestalt of responsibility, including constructions of responsibility, cultural mythologies around individual responsibility and work, and performance measurements and assessments, has led to my seeing it everywhere. Much like John in *They Live*, once I saw these ideologies in my data, I could not unsee them. They surfaced everywhere. While institutional effectiveness may rely on the discretionary racism and paternalism of workers, it also surfaces in other aspects of institutional life. I am reminded of the statue of Icarus outside of BMCC, a shining torso that, in my mind, urges students toward paternalistic adherence and qualified, limited ambition.

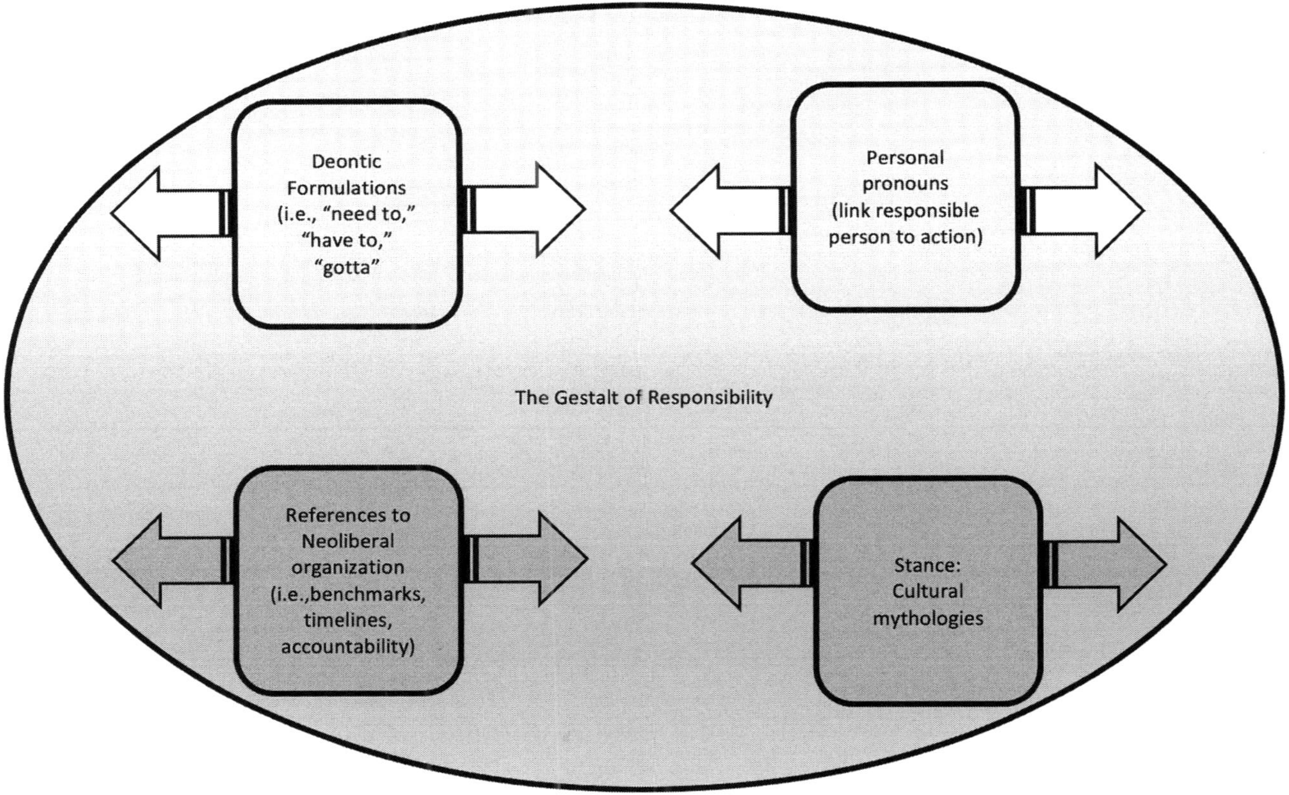

Fig. 7.1. The Expanded Gestalt of Responsibility

This diagram includes four boxes, one for each of the main aspects of discourse that collaboratively construct the gestalt of responsibility. There is a box for deontic formulations, one for personal pronouns, one for references to neoliberal organization (e.g., performance measurements, assessments, timelines, benchmarks), and one for cultural mythologies, which are often identified by stance markers. Grayscale color coding is used to highlight that deontic formulations and personal pronouns tend to be more grammatically oriented and references to neoliberalism and cultural mythological tend to be more lexical. Each of the four boxes has arrows extending to the left and right to demonstrate their connection to both past and future.

In 2016, I happened upon two seemingly mundane signs, one inside a bathroom stall at an elite university and the other in a student bathroom at BMCC. Both were entitled the "Stall Street Journal," which at the time I found somewhat amusing. I took photographs of both and obsessed over the marked difference between the two.

The BMCC sign is spare, having the relatively singular focus of advocating for the "Fifteen to Finish" program.[2] The heading under "The Stall Street Journal" banner sets the tone: "Take Fifteen to Finish!" Under the banner, criteria were clarified in a bulleted list:

Take 15 credits a semester to:

- Graduate in 2 years
- Save money
- Maximize your financial aid
- Start your senior college or career sooner

This is followed by a description of an incentive: "Students who remain enrolled in 15 or more credits/equated credited after the withdrawal date for the fall 2016 semester will be entered into a raffle to win a monthly Metrocard!" Much of the sign is in a dark blue font, and occasional, orange-colored font is used to draw added attention to the items on the bulleted list and the "monthly Metrocard." Fine print includes information for the Transfer Center and the Office of the Registrar, and a small fine-print footer reading, "We are judged by what we finish, *not* by what we start. —Anonymous."

The sign strongly encouraged students through a command ("take fifteen to finish!") to take fifteen credits per semester. The incentive for staying enrolled at the bottom of the sign acknowledges that students taking fifteen credits regularly withdraw, and encourages student persistence (resonating with Isserles's 2021 study) through financial rewards: the possibility of winning a monthly subway card, something many of our students have difficulty securing in order to get to and from campus.

This sign brings together the copresence of several (but not all) discursive features that generate the gestalt of responsibility. Taking fifteen credits is not required to have full-time student status, so we do not see the deontic formulations (such as "have to" and "need to") seen in earlier chapters. Still, the imperatives state the task required: "take fifteen to finish," the latter imperatives ("graduate in two years," "save money," "start your senior college or career sooner") doubling as justification sequences that legitimize the pressure to take more classes. References to timelines/benchmarks ("after the withdrawal date for the fall 2016 semester"), and performance incentives ("remain enrolled . . . will be entered into a raffle to win a monthly Metrocard") reify the connection to neoliberal performance and accountability measures. In the BMCC sign, references to "2 years," "semester," and "withdrawal date" provide a variety of timescales on which student action should take place. This sign emphasizes academic momentum (fifteen credits rather than the traditional twelve required for full-time status) and acceleration, a common tell of neoliberalism in education (Isserles, 2021). Business economic models look to increase production speed and efficiency, and the "fifteen-to-finish" model aims to accelerate students through community college.

An epigraph stands as a coda to the flyer, written at the bottom of the BMCC sign after relevant contact information: "We are judged by what we finish, not by what we start." The personal pronoun "we" inscribes the reader into the generic community of readers who are "judged." Not only does this quotation include a vague reference to the aforementioned benchmarks ("finish") that are so integral to how responsibility is discursively generated, but it also introduces a moral arbiter through "judged," a term commonly used in religious determinations of morality and in legal determination of guilt or innocence—both of which highlight the moral heft attached to constructions of responsibility. Harkening back to "your mother thought you'd pass, and your father thought you'd pass," (see Chapter 1 of this book), shame once again becomes a motivator for student success. These unseen moral judges favor "finish[ing]" over "start[ing]," emphasizing a goal-oriented benchmark that does not value process. Things students do not finish, do not count. As Brodkin (2011) reminds us, determining what "counts" is ultimately a political action that generates de facto laws.

Here the BMCC sign plays "father knows best" with the student body, paternalistically urging students, as Love (2019) has found, to do more, not quit, be gritty, and finish what they started. Current modalities of neoliberalism combine moral categorizations with paternalism in a way that "disciplines the poor" (Soss et al., 2011, 2). I am reminded of Machin and Mayr's (2012) work, which reminds analysts to look not just at what is present, but what is absent, which they call "suppression" or "lexical absence." Although assuredly not intended as such, we might consider whether "We are judged by what we finish, not by what we start" disciplines the student body by implicitly emphasizing school completion over unlisted factors that may also impact their enrollment, including their health, economic security, and emotional well-being (which admittedly the college also strives to support). In this statement, the degree is what ultimately matters, not the individual classes where learning and growth take place. Judgment is determined by grit, a tenacity that is asked primarily of marginalized students, many of whom experience food and housing insecurity, must take on multiple jobs, and sometimes care for children or other family members.

I have not collected data on the differential treatment of marginalized versus more privileged people. That said, in considering parity of treatment and how we might change the way street-level workers talk to those they serve, let us consider the second bathroom-stall sign.

The elite university sign is published by career services and is chock full of information about upcoming career fairs, virtual resume reviews, convocation, and "striking the work-school-life balance." This latter area includes a variety of tips under the headings "Be Where You Are," "Shuffle your Priorities and Set a Schedule for the Week," "Use your Support System," "Learn to Say 'No,'" and "Have some Fun and Reward Yourself." Reconsidering lexical absence, we can think about what this sign advocates when compared to the BMCC sign. The sign from the elite university was authored by Career Services, offering suggestions and encouragement in the "final stretch" of the spring semester. One tip suggested, "Plan segments of time for study, family, exercise, and other tasks that need to get done. Consider which of your endeavors will be the highest priority." Another offered, "Learn to say no. . . . Just meeting your responsibilities at work, school, and home will be enough of a challenge for now. Remember it is only temporary." Still another advised, "Have some fun and reward yourself . . . make time to enjoy yourself and read non-academic books." Last but not least, one suggested, "Remember that you are only human. Nothing will get done if you are emotionally or physically drained. Plan . . . and engage in creative activities." These suggestions appear relatively innocuous and are overwhelmingly supportive. This sign treat students like adults who can determine what is best for them. It acknowledges their lives outside of school, and it supports activities outside of school (e.g., "creative activities"). It is worth noting that even Career Services puts a high premium on student's mental health and encourages them to be kind to themselves and not overextend. Appearing to give equal value to family, work, and school in one piece of advice, and reading for pleasure and reading for school in another, the elite university students are not paternalistically encouraged to be "gritty" or tenacious. Instead, the second Stall Street Journal allows students to determine what is best for them.

These two signs are by no means exhaustive. There are likely others with different content. For all I know, the elite university had other more pedantic bathroom signs, and BMCC had more generous ones. I indeed hope that Stall Street Journals have come further. Rather than arguing that these are exhaustive, I use these as a spring board to remind the reader that that neoliberal ideology and neoliberal managerial approaches corset street-level work. I add my voice to the scores of academics and intellectuals clamoring for a shift away from neoliberalism—an approach that we know creates caste-like division, disproportionately impacts Black people and other marginalized people, and perpetuates paternalistic forms of discipline (see Chapter 2). These neoliberal managerial approaches shape street-level work and talk over time in ways that potentially damage the people they serve. There must be a better way.

Adjusting Our Words, Adjusting Our Worlds

When I began the investigation around this topic, I had not realized it would lead me to explorations of covert racism. In retrospect, it should not have been a surprise. It is useful to briefly situate this book's findings amid research on racializing language. *The Everyday Language of White Racism* (Hill, 2008) is among those most frequently referenced. Hill's work largely falls outside of this study because she is primarily concerned with gaffes, mock-language (e.g., mock Spanish), linguistic appropriation, and slurs. Indeed, much work on this subject focuses on how language varieties are appropriated or mocked, and far less exists that examines subtle words and clusters that index entrenched forms of racism.

Instead, addressing individual responsibility is a subtler form of racism. Some scholars outside of discourse studies have described how references to "individual responsibility" and the like are examples of dog-whistle politics, which Haney López (2014) defines as "speaking in code to a target audience" (n.p.), of which President Reagan's use of "welfare queen" is a prime example. Haney López writes,

> Today, the most powerful racial stereotypes—the ones most generally credited and in widest circulation—dovetail precisely with dog whistle narratives jointly attacking minorities and liberalism. (n.p.)

Explaining that racist statements about interracial relationships have been, in large part, replaced with other narratives like "welfare queens" and "urban" violence, Haney López (2014) argues that "responsibility" is certainly one of the newer dog whistles that, like "urban" and "law and order," are ways of verbalizing racism without the epithets and slurs. Kinder and Sanders (1996), suggest that

> a new form of prejudice has come to prominence, one that is preoccupied with matters of moral character, informed by the virtues associated with the traditions of individualism. At its center are the convention that [Black people] do not try hard enough to overcome the difficulties they face, and that they take what they have not earned. (105–6)

Bobo (2003) calls this "laissez-faire racism," in his chapter with the striking subtitle: "The Crystallization of a Kinder, Gentler, Antiblack Ideology." In Haney López's book, however, these dog whistles are used by conservative politicians to signal in-group racist affiliation while having plausible deniability to outsiders. While subtle, these constructions of responsibility do not seem like dog whistles. Dog whistles are meant to signal political alignment to insiders while not registering as significant to outsiders.

Perhaps Flores et al.'s (2018) "institutional listening subject position" aids in explaining why a person with progressive values may say things that seem out of character in institutional spaces. Their work reminds us that the street-level workers are connected to the institution, and that their level of alignment with the institution may influence how they listen to those they serve. It is possible that people are putting themselves in the position of a future employer or future professor when talking with a student, anxiously viewing the student from a potential future space of rejection.

While this may be true, I wonder if "parts theory" from internal family systems therapy may be helpful (Schwartz, 2021). In that approach (glossing over an entire field of study), it is helpful not to generalize but rather to identify part of you that feels a certain way about a particular thing. Part of us may feel sad about a particular event, for example, while another part of us may be hopeful. While these street-level workers are well intentioned and kind, part of them still has aspects of internalized racism and part of them has not interrogated particular communicative approaches that have a racist history. Parts theory allows us to not paint our street-level workers with too broad a brush, while acknowledging the parts of our workers (and ourselves) that may have internalized unanalyzed and tacit forms of racism.

Rather unfortunately, it is also possible that this approach institutionally *works*, in that it proffers some desired results. Street-level workers are overwhelmed and overburdened, and shaming students into studying harder, or shaming unhoused people into getting into housing, is a strategy that still works. Anger, frustration, sarcasm, shame, blame—workers may believe that these emotions facilitate client performance, and maybe sometimes they do. Brodkin's (2011) argument regarding how administrators infuse new managerialism into street-level work, referred to earlier in this book, resonates: "As long as performance benchmarks are met, it is not necessary to consider how policy work is done (i272)." However, as we have seen, it is critically important to examine how the work is done. Performance-based assessments appear to drive language over time, increasing the frequency of vertically accruing microaggressions that ultimately may, in addition to being hurtful, damage people's ability to successfully complete their assigned tasks. Discretion is at the center of the subtlety of street-level discourse, as workers use language to cajole those they serve into complying within the strictures of performance benchmarks and assessments. In her work on street-level work and performance assessments of workers providing Temporary Assistance to Needy Families (TANF), Brodkin (2011) argues that these performance-based management tools are political choices that in effect generate de facto law. She concludes:

> I argue (as have others) that choosing what to count and what not to count is a fundamentally political matter. When performance metrics are selectively inserted into law, they can undermine, or even virtually negate, those provisions of law that governance instruments effectively ignore. In this sense, performance-based management should be understood as a form of policy politics in that it effectively "makes" law by other (managerial) means, whether through intent or inadvertence. (i273)

If, indeed, street-level workers are using these approaches because they perceive them as a means to successful completion of performance requirements, then negative cultural mythologies (with racist and paternalistic worldviews) and shaming may be baked into the street-level process as a workable strategy that manipulates marginalized people into institutional compliance. These covert forms of racism are, then, not simply unfortunate side effects of street-level overwork but potentially part of a winning discretionary strategy that is conveniently overlooked by institutions because they get desired results. There is a growing and extensive literature on institutional racism, and addressing this one issue will not fix everything. However, in addition to reading what people of color have written on this topic, I do suggest that institutions consider a dramatic reframing of institutional talk that acknowledges discursive shaming practices, including those associated with negative cultural mythologies. Institutions need to investigate positive approaches to motivation that fully avoid stigmatizing already marginalized people. This may include shifting pedagogical practices away from punitive, disciplinary approaches.

Perhaps the institutional listening subject position generates worker anxiety about the future success of those they serve, motivating them to act in ways contrary to their larger belief systems, *and* street-level workers have aspects of internalized racism that have not been interrogated, *and* these discursive approaches are perceived by workers (consciously or unconsciously) as advancing the goals and meeting the performance requirements of street-level institutions. Institutions, interested in efficiency and meeting goals and benchmarks, overlook untoward and inappropriate behavior because, harkening back to Blake's line from *Glengarry Glen Ross*, workers should "always be closing."

Discourse Ideologies

Future research should explore street-level worker's *discourse ideologies*, their beliefs around discourse practices. In Chapter 6, I briefly describe standard language ideology, which Lippi-Green defines as "a bias toward an abstracted, idealized, homogeneous spoken language which is imposed from above, and which takes as its model the written language" (1994, 166). Language ideologies are beliefs people hold about language. I am reminded of a quotation attributed to Spanish monarch and Holy Roman Emperor Charles V: "To God I speak Spanish, to women Italian, to men French, and to my horse—German" (Chesterfield and Belfield, 1897). This assertion reflects certain ideologies about language: Italian being more "romantic" than German, for example. Language ideologies are evident in stereotypes people hold about dialect speakers, stereotypes that lead people to use statements like "People from X region sound ignorant" and "People from Y region sound snobby."

While this will be explored further in my future work, I argue these street-level workers' discursive choices may constitute *discourse ideologies*: beliefs held about particular discourse practices. Street-level workers aim to complete their work efficiently. Overburdened by their workloads, pressured to perform by administration, and navigating the need to serve each person's individualized needs, street-level workers use routines and other strategies to help them manage their jobs (Lipsky, 1980/2010). Just as people have beliefs about language use, they may also have beliefs about discourse—what "works" and what "doesn't work." As Heritage and Robinson (2011) find when examining "some" versus "any" among doctors, we may remember that doctors were hesitant to use "some" (e.g., "What are some questions you have?"), feeling that opening the door to patient questions (rather than constraining the preference for questions with "any") would extend meeting times beyond what they could handle. However, "any questions," while shutting down conversation, made meetings longer, and meetings using "What are some questions you have?" were on the whole shorter (Heritage and Robinson, 2011). The belief that a particular discourse practice is "better" or "more efficient" is a discourse ideology, and like most language ideologies, their usefulness is ultimately an empirical question that often does not hold up under scrutiny.

Similarly, the street-level workers in the data presented in this book, often relying on discourses that point to historical legacies of slavery, racism, and classism, may (consciously or unconsciously) believe these discourse practices to be the most efficient. Whether they have these beliefs is an empirical question. Future research with street-level workers should explore discourse ideologies as a focus. Those studies investigating street-level workers' professional development, researchers and street-level workers' collaboration, and studies exploring how street-level workers analyze and interpret researcher data and findings should pay particular attention to discourse ideologies. In addition to transcribed social interaction, interviews and focus groups with street-level workers who review transcript data and that offer collaborative, ground-up analysis and interpretation of the data may elucidate discourse ideologies that could be examined further.

A Street-Level Approach to Applied Linguistics, an Applied Linguistics of the Street Level

A street-level perspective (Lipsky, 1980/2010) helps explain why the discourses described in this book may be used intentionally by overwhelmed and exhausted workers and offers a window into discourse ideologies. I argue that integrating a street-level perspective may shed new light in applied linguistic and discourse analytic study.

Applied linguistics is a discipline with contested membership, with some defining the field broadly, including nearly any application of linguistics to professional practice (Sarangi and Candlin, 2010) and others drawing very narrow parameters for inclusion, focusing primarily on second-language acquisition (Agiriga et al., 2019). In truth, attendees at the American Association of Applied Linguistics conference continue to be primarily second-language-acquisition scholars despite Sarangi and Candlin's clarion call for casting a wide net. According to Agiriga et al. (2019):

> The thinking is that with such broadening of perspective, practitioners in the field will lack definite knowledge of the precise tasks that make them applied linguists. The delimitation of AL to all language related social problems does not take into consideration the fact that such problems will continue to broaden, and that human language problems are too complex and large to be handled by a single discipline like AL. The implication of this inclusive view of AL is that both the discipline and its practitioners are in a state of flux as human language-related problems broaden and evolve, and as remarked earlier, this has occasioned the question of what the identity of practitioners in the field is, since precision is the hallmark of identification. (228)

It hardly seems fair to exclude members of the field on the basis of identity crisis and material overload. Applied linguistics, broadly or narrowly defined, is deeply interdisciplinary, and it is its interdisciplinarity that makes it so rich. This book has demonstrated the utility of comparing street-level work at the discourse level, with findings relevant for educators and social welfare workers. Taking a broad view of applied linguistics, I urge the field to explore a "street-level approach to applied linguistics." While the street level is not relevant to all subdisciplines of applied linguistics, research on teachers, language assessment, language policy, and all manner of institutional discourse analysis could gain a new vantage point from taking a street-level perspective.

Street-level research stems from Lipsky's (1980/2010) foundational text, which explores how street-level workers handle decision-making in their workplaces, given generally overloaded workers with ample discretion in the context of whatever organizational rules guide their overall work. He demonstrates how street-level research examines the relationship between workers' values/goals and social/institutional requirements. Discretion, Lipsky argues, is deployed by workers as they ration resources, process people, and control clients. Workers cope by changing how they view their job, finding ways to reduce their workload. A street-level perspective on language policy broadens what counts as language policy, giving space to how teachers' classroom discretion and discourse generate de facto policy and highlighting how non-language-related policy criteria (e.g., performance measurement for teachers and students) shape classroom discourse, thereby shaping the de facto policy that is socially constructed in the classroom.

With so much research in applied linguistics examining testing/assessment and the implementation of language policy, a street-level perspective that folds teacher discretion into the conversation would be useful. Given that the collective discretion of street-level workers becomes de facto policy (Lipsky, 1980/2010), a street-level applied linguistics could shed light on how teachers' classroom action becomes policy, how teacher talk is policy work and therefore political work, how those classroom actions intersect with requirements from administration and, therefore, respond not only to theories of language learning but also to schools of public management thinking. A street-level perspective could connect findings regarding teaching and learning with worker strategies for managing their jobs and with administrative and political demands.

Brodkin (2013) adds that these street-level workers, who must respond on the job to politics, in constructing policy in situ are also "mediators of politics" themselves (7). Applied linguistic research that takes neoliberalism into account (Block, 2018; Block et al., 2013; Duchêne and Heller, 2012; Flubacher and Del Percio, 2017; Holborow, 2015; Rojo and Del Percio, 2020), might consider how street-level workers use discretion and thereby become mediators of neoliberal politics.

In another area of overlap, van Dijk (1997), in defining political discourse analysis, aims to broaden its use in political science. His definition is inclusive of not only political pundits and politicians but also voters, demonstrators, the public, and the institutions of which they are a part. He underscores that inclusion should be based on whether a person is functioning as a "political actor" (14). While he cheerfully acknowledges that this actor may be defined very broadly, he advocates some restraint. While I agree that opening the floodgates could invite all manner of study into the field, I wonder how political discourse scholars might receive Lipsky's street-level research and arguments around street-level workers as de facto policymakers doing ultimately political work.

Finally, most research of applied linguistics and "professional practice" involves the analysis of street-level work, for example, intraoffice talk among workers or between workers and clients. In these contexts, a street-level perspective could make implications for policy and practice far more relevant and meaningful. Social workers, doctors, nurses, teachers, professors, airport Transportation Security Administration workers, prison guards and staff, and police officers (to name a few) are street-level workers, and it is useful to consider the professional practices that, while often fully integrated with the disciplinary work, are the result of street-level constraints and routines that are themselves informed by administrative constraints and policy directives. We need a richer, wider understanding of practice that is mindful of the realities of teaching, policing, practicing medicine, and doing social welfare work. How can our understanding of disciplinary praxis be more mindful of institutional and bureaucratic practice?

We may develop more meaningful professional development for workers that considers not just the ideals of the field but also the real-world constraints of street-level workers. Incorporating street-level research would not only bring new ideas to the applied linguistics table but would also help connect microanalytic work to macro-level policy implementation and politics in a way that is cognizant of institutional demands and limitations.

Radical Empathetic and Compassionate Discourse

In concluding the book, we can now return, at the expense of being a bit saccharine, to Jacob Marley in *A Christmas Carol.* Scrooge comments to Jacob's ghost early on in the story that Jacob was a good man of business, and, in turn, Jacob castigates Scrooge, shouting in reply,

> Mankind was my business. The common welfare was my business; charity, mercy, forbearance, and benevolence, were, all, my business. The dealings of my trade were but a drop of water in the comprehensive ocean of my business! (Dickens, 1843/2006, 34)

It is perhaps time to reconsider our business. Why did we want to work in social services or education in the first place?

Discursive mindfulness (Matarese, 2019) requires being thoughtful about what we say by drawing on compassion, empathy, and an awareness of how discourse works in intercultural and institutional contexts. Givens's (2021) radical empathy

> encourage[es] each of us not only to understand the feelings of others, but also to be motivated to create the change that will allow all of us to benefit from economic prosperity and develop the social

> relationships that are beneficial to our emotional wellbeing. Racial divides can cause us to see economic and societal benefits as a zero-sum game. Empathy allows us to see the humanity in others, and radical empathy moves us to work toward social justice and change that will benefit us all. (n.p.)

She encourages readers to "be vulnerable, [be] grounded in who *you* are, [be open] . . . to the experiences of others, practic[e] empathy, tak[e] action, and creat[e] change and build trust" (n.p.). Bloom (2016) suggests that empathy alone relies on biases: white people putting themselves in the shoes of what they think Black people need/want. He argues, instead, for radical compassion. In making a case for discursive mindfulness, at the expense of playing metaphorically into the "industrial wellness" mindset, I argue here for a radically empathetic and compassionate, listening-oriented, street-level-informed conversational practice. Workers need to be made aware of a wide variety of discourse features: ones that prepare those they serve for success, those that put their interlocutors in difficult or uncomfortable positions, those that are linked to histories of racism, ableism, homophobia, transphobia, those are shaped by the constraints of the institution. We need a street-level pedagogy—one that takes into account not only the theories of practice for a given street-level discipline, but also includes the material and administrative realities of street-level practice, including (but not limited to) discretion. Such an approach asks street-level workers of all stripes to own and be responsible for their discretionary choices on the job, linguistic and otherwise.

Discourse analysts often ask, drawing from Sacks (1992), "Why this, now?" when looking at transcripts of what was said. This question asks us to examine our words and consider alternatives. Why was it said *this* way rather than *that* way? What if we were to stop and ask this question, considering answers from the most generous and compassionate perspective. What if, when I bumped into that student in the hallway (as described in Chapter 6), I had thought, "Why this, now?" when she responded in a less-than-pleasant way? What if I had read that moment from a more compassionate, empathetic perspective?

Earlier in the book I mentioned a study by Heritage and Robinson (2011). Their rigorous study shows that efficiency was actively stymied by words that functioned to limit or shorten conversation; instead, language that opened opportunities for conversation and questions was, in fact, more expedient. This study underscores how institutional assumptions about what works best or what is most efficient are not always correct, and may actively fight against the goals of the institution. I am advocating both for discursive mindfulness that rejects paternalistic responsibility in favor of dignity-driven discourse *and* for rigorous studies examining outcomes. Someone might say, "But if you treat people like this, then they will not do what we want them to do!" This, however, is an empirical question, and what we know about language from the aforementioned study is that small changes in language can have surprising consequences. Efficiency doesn't have to be brief and cold; it can be open and generous.

In answer to the question "How should street-level workers talk?" I have multiple answers. I am editing a book that will cull relevant results of studies into a functional support volume for street-level workers. Moreover, the answer to this question, as established above, is an empirical one that would require additional research. Outside of those next steps, I have some suggestions with where to start.

1. **Street-level workers should have verbal curiosity and verbal compassion.**
   a. Consider asking open-ended questions that do not lead and give space for broad answers. Questions beginning with *how* and *why* provide more openness for response than yes/no questions that begin with *is/are/do/does/was/were.*
   b. Avoid rhetorical questions that shut down conversation.
   c. Give people time to think. Research suggests that teachers often do not give students enough time to think between a teacher's question and a student's answer. Rowe (1972) found in a foundational study that many teachers wait 1.5 seconds or less for students to answer questions, but if teachers waited upwards of 3 seconds, results were far better (Stahl, 1994). Consider leaving more time for people to respond to your questions.
   d. Other phrases can also open conversation (Creider, 2016), like "Tell me about . . ."
   e. Anger and frustration can be met with curiosity. Consider asking yourself questions like "What does this person need? What does this person fear?" (Brach, 2003). "What is this person responding to in me?" "Is their anger justified?" Sometimes it is we who have done something wrong, and we need to listen and apologize. Other times we need to learn not to take other people's feelings personally and let it go. How can we give people the most generous interpretation or response?

   f. We need to be curious about the assumptions we are making about those we serve. Again, street-level workers may believe they get better results with vinegar than honey; however, I would suggest that kindness and respect does not need to be saccharine.
      i. Assume and verbally treat people like responsible adults, giving them the benefit of the doubt wherever possible.
      ii. Assume that, and verbally treat people as though, they are honest and their claims are legitimate. Do not treat people like they are out to swindle you, "abuse the system," or cheat you. People with privilege are, more often than not, given the benefit of the doubt in conversation. When I am sick and call out of work, no one suggests I am lying to get out of teaching, but many professors require doctor's notes and physical death certificates from students as proof of their need to miss class.
   g. Read and include the discourse work of scholars of color to ensure that intersectional approaches to discourse and communication are being considered and drawn upon.
2. **SLBs should receive professional development, as part of culturally sustaining street-level work, that specifically addresses cultural tropes that surface in conversation with ties to classism, racism, homophobia, misogyny, ableism, and the like.**
   a. There are various forms of linguistic racism:
      i. Street-level workers should learn about English-language learners, see multilingualism as an asset, and consider their relationship to deficit-oriented thinking versus difference-oriented thinking. English-language learners should not be yelled at or criticized for their language skills. As a reminder, English is *not* the official language of the United States, and every state (and Washington, DC) has some kind of language access law (Youdelman, 2019) that requires that people not proficient in English receive access to government paperwork in their language of choice, and many cities have access to translation services. Institutions have specialized terms and ways of speaking that people with limited English proficiency may not understand.[3]
      ii. Workers should also learn about American Sign Lan-

guage, what D/deaf and hard-of-hearing people experience, and their linguistic rights. The US American Disabilities Act and the Individuals with Disabilities Education Act have requirements for access to interpreters and translation.

iii. Street-level workers should be aware of dialect differences in American English and how differences of meaning may impact communication. Everyone speaks a dialect of English, and negative beliefs people have about dialects are based in prejudice.

iv. Workers should learn where translation services are a legal right and use them rather than including ad hoc translators who are not specialists. This should go without saying but enlisting the help of security guards potentially heightens tensions and creates a disciplinary climate. Enlisting other students or clients may pull focus from the person who needs help (I once heard a client-cum translator say to his friend's caseworker, "Can you be my caseworker?"). Most people who speak a language are not experts in its use. Please use certified specialists for translation. When translation services are not a legal right, please ensure that translators are available who represent the client and their interests without bias, malice, or special interests.

b. Street-level workers should be taught about stance markers, presuppositions, cultural mythologies, and categorizations, noting how those are communicated in real work settings. There are many ways that prejudices can be communicated, and street-level workers should be made aware of these (some of which are discussed in this book), and they should be mindful of avoiding them.

3. **Street-level workers should, in the practicum/training they receive, be taught about how street-level challenges surface in their job.** Be honest with teachers, social workers, police officers, and others about the tension between the discipline/field and the administration pressures common to the job. This includes understanding how performance measurements and assessments can negatively surface in and shape conversation over time, as demonstrated in this book.

4. **Rethink discipline.** Have we lost our way? Sometimes I wonder if we street-level workers have lost our way. Given the documented shift between the 1970s and 1990s away from care and toward a managerial approach to welfare, workers are responsible for sanctioning clients who are not compliant, and worker and client performance is assessed to ensure that workers are doing their job. Caswell and Høybye-Mortensen (2015) found that workers sometimes celebrate sanctioning clients.

   Likewise, many faculty assert their authority and want discipline. "Students who are late will not be allowed into class." "Students on their phones will be asked to leave." "I will collect any phones that I see during class." "Students cannot eat during class." "Deadlines are for students' own good." My own words, "You cannot talk to me like that." At some point we need to ask ourselves: Do I teach my subject or do I teach discipline? Do I teach English/linguistics/history/psychology/math/education/science, or do I teach some other "hidden curriculum"? (Feinberg and Soltis, 2009). Which do I care about more? Does it serve my students to discipline them? Who does it serve? Does the "real world" actually have these standards? Am I inhabiting an institutional listening subject position that views students in terms of their future absences/timeliness/failures? How can I be sure that these students will have jobs where those things matter? Is my behavior preparing students for minimum-wage, entry-level positions? Should I be preparing them for something greater? Is preparing students for disciplinary jobs consistent with culturally sustaining pedagogy (Ladson-Billings, 1992; Paris and Alim, 2017)? Is it my job to police my students? Do I have to police them? If I am choosing to, what does that suggest about how I view them? Do I get something out of disciplining my students? Do I want that to be my job? Are there alternatives?[4] Similar questions may be asked in a variety of street-level contexts.
5. **Street-level workers should have professional development that comes from the inside.**

   There are many vehicles for integrating practitioner reflection into the discourse research itself and using collected data for internal professional development (Caswell and Dall, 2022; Stokoe, 2014). While some approaches require that street-level workers have a more extensive knowledge of discourse analysis, it is perhaps easiest to simply look at wording and other interactional moments and ask "Why this, now?"

a. Did that phrase/question/sentence open up conversation or close it down?
b. Did the person respond in a way that signaled offense? How did I have a hand in offending them?
c. Is the person acting grouchy/disagreeable/terse? Is there any reason you can think of why they might feel so frustrated? Can you help them explain their feelings and then mirror back their feelings to confirm the problem?
d. What words/phrases/moments signal potential biases/problems in my thinking?
e. Where did I exhibit compassion and empathy?
f. Do I see lapses in empathy and compassion, and if so, where?
g. In what ways have I communicated respect?
h. Do I see lapses in understanding and comprehension, and if so, where?
i. What communicative alternatives might make people feel more seen/more empowered/more in control of their own life/more respected/more humanized?
j. How do I think the person being served feels right now? Have I asked? What words/phrases/moments in the discourse indicate those feelings? If I ask about these feelings, are they different from I expected?
k. How do I feel in this moment? When have I felt angry or frustrated in a meeting? What would happen if I talked about those feelings in this meeting? Is there a way for me to bring my own vulnerability to this? Sometimes caseworkers would plead with noncompliant clients when they needed to push them along in the process (often when the client was close to or had surpassed benchmarks, using their personal difficulties and performance pressures to motivate clients). If we were candid with clients about the relationship we have with them from the beginning, mindful that as street-level workers we have power and privilege not often accessible to those we serve, we might be able to develop a more honest dialogue about how we can help each other.
l. Do we see the requirements of the institution shaping this conversation, if so, how?
m. What would I want to change about this dialogue, and can I

rewrite this dialogue from a perspective that comes from a place of curiosity, compassion, honesty, and trust?

n. What is gained by an empathetic/compassionate approach, and what is lost? Is adherence to "standards" worthwhile— for us, for those we serve? Which standards matter more? Do we choose standards that come at the expense of other equally important standards?

Working in small groups with examples like those below (from earlier in this chapter), practitioners can consider questions like this. How might you say these in more culturally sensitive, discursively mindful ways?

Classroom Example

> *Well this is the time of the semester* to when (.) yea I want you- **I hope you all start working even harder than you were working** but it's also the *time* to **assess what you've done so far, to really look yourself in the mirror, HONESTLY, to see how hard you've actually worked**. Have you done all the assignments, do you go over the work after we finish it, have you gone to the reading lab, have you gone online, worked from home? If the answer to all those questions . . . is no, *it's not too late to start.*

Shelter Example

> I'm not telling you to get into a program, but what I'm telling you is you're gonna do something. You're not gonna sit here and continue to heavily use drugs the way you used to and and and just come in and work part time off the books and just not doing anything. You know, you know, and like I said befo:re (.) you take a Wednesday off good for you because Wednesday I need to see you getting a psych evaluation. You've been here (.) for ↑months. ↑MONTHS. And nothing's getting done. And then what it looks at and it reflects is (.) I'm getting- I'm letting you skate through the system, and utilize the place just to ha- just to make sure you have a bed every night so you can go do what you need to do, and I can't do that no more. You understand? I have 40 clients.(.3) and I'm being honest I can't I don't I don't have the patience anymore I'm stressed I just don't have it. To let you keep skating because when they need something from me I have to be able to produce it, and if I can't produce it I'm the

one that's getting the rap at the end of the day. And so for on judgment and being a case manager I have to case manage you. (.) Now you have to help me help you. You understand what I'm saying?

6. **Timelines and benchmarks should be clearly and visually shared for workers and those they serve**. Often, I heard questions from caseworkers at the shelter like, "What are you doing to get out of shelter," and afterward in interviews clients would share that the entire process of moving from shelter to housing felt confusing and obscure to them. The process toward housing in the shelter system was relatively straightforward, but it was never discussed holistically and procedurally among my participants. A graphic/flow chart showing the steps would be tremendously helpful, but in addition to that, workers need to be fully honest and verbally clear (while also compassionate) about the steps and have an open conversation about what parts of the steps feel difficult or insurmountable for the clients. This would be helpful in a variety of street-level contexts. Give people practical, simple diagrams that elucidate the process.
7. **Administration and workers together need to work on developing strategies that help street-level workers cope with institutional demands (performance assessments, benchmarks, etc.), with the realization that these demands can impact how street-level workers make decisions and communicate**. Administrators and street-level workers may want to collect their own internal data and/or collaborate with a discourse analyst to identify how their organizational requirements shape their everyday practices.
8. **Administration needs to extend the community of care to overwhelmed street-level workers**. While street-level contexts may vary widely, worker overwhelmedness is an intrinsic commonality that cuts across organizational differences (Lipsky, 1980/2010). Management needs to communicate to street-level workers that they are on their side and back this statement up with action. Administration should communicate transparency, honesty, trust, compassion, and curiosity to and for the street-level workers, particularly those who are marginalized. These need to be *fully threaded* through institutions, not just as mission statement jargon or lip-service but in action and in communicative practice. Workers also need reliable access to therapy and support groups that do not add to their workload. As Brach

(2003, 223) observes, "Compassion for ourselves naturally leads to compassion for others."

Overall, I argue for street-level professional development that teaches discursive mindfulness in order to facilitate street-level workers' awareness of discourse-level discretionary actions that we make. If the choices of street-level workers become policy (Lipsky, 1980/2010), and if street-level workers are mediators also of politics (Brodkin, 2012), then how might our discursive choices at the street-level change how people experience both policy and politics in institutional spaces? While we can address institutional mission statements espousing inclusion, diversity, equity, and access through hiring, supporting diverse faculty, curricula, and administration, we should also consider how these values surface through our words.

We need a shift toward discursive mindfulness (Matarese, 2020) with radically empathetic discourse, particularly toward people who are most at risk of receiving censorious talk. Isserles (2021), in her study also conducted at BMCC on community college persistence and retention, advocates a care model:

> Care is both a disposition and a practice, something we do and something we experience, and always demands self-reflection and rational thought as well as emotional attention. Care theory places labor and practice around care at the center of all our human interactions and activities. It is a deeply relational construct presuming that fundamental to human existence is the universal need to be cared for and to care for others. At its very core, care theory presents an alternative notion to that of the autonomous, rational individual that has been the basis for most Western political and social thought, and has a strong reemergence in the hyper-individuality of the neoliberal ascendancy. In fact, care theory challenges all that has come to be considered not only normative but virtuous—individuality, efficiency, rationality, and autonomy—suggesting that such socially identified virtues are only possible through good, supported care practices and values. (261–62)

Aligning with Isserles, care is indeed something we "do," and I suggest that it is also something we do with our words. I echo calls for empathetic spaces and practices where accountability and action can coexist with compassion and care. Treat people with dignity. Treat students as competent adults, researchers, respected community members, and responsible humans. Create spaces that give students and people seeking shelter dignity, respect, and the benefit of the doubt. There are pleas for empathy across so many social and institutional domains. Spade's (2011) work on administrative violence in the transgender and gender-nonconforming community resonates with this work. This book joins hosts of others in recommending empathy, curiosity (Zurn, 2020), gentleness, and not assuming the worst of already marginalized people.

When I talk about this book project with friends outside academia, many of them mention Marshall B. Rosenberg's work on nonviolent communication (2013, 2015). I received the books and initially scoffed. "These suggestions aren't empirical," I thought to myself. However, these best-selling books have made great strides in helping people communicate compassionately. In fact, Satya Nadella, CEO of Microsoft, assigned Rosenberg's *Non-Violent Communication* as required reading to improve workplace culture (Abadi, 2018). In wholly practical books that convey communication in laypersons' terms, Rosenberg offers an alternative for how we can speak and listen to others. He says,

> [Nonviolent communication] guides us in reframing how we express ourselves and hear others. Instead of habitual, automatic reactions, our words become conscious responses based firmly on awareness of what we are perceiving feeling, and wanting. We are led to express ourselves with honesty and clarity, while simultaneously paying others a respectful and empathetic attention. In any exchange, we come to hear our own deeper needs and those of others. NVC trains us to observe carefully, and to be able to specify behaviors and conditions that are affecting us. We learn to identify and clearly articulate what we are concretely wanting in any given situation. The form is simply, yet powerfully transformative. As NVC replaces our old patterns of defending, withdrawing, or attacking in the face of judgment and criticism, we come to perceive ourselves and others, as well as our intentions and relationships, in a new light. Resistance, defensiveness, and violent reactions are minimized. When we focus on clarifying what is being observed, felt, and needed rather than on diagnosing and judging, we discover the depth of our own compassion. Through its emphasis on deep listening—to ourselves as well as to others—NVC fosters respect, attentiveness, and empathy and engenders a mutual desire to give from the heart. (Rosenberg, 2015, 3–4)

Rosenberg contends that there are unsatisfied needs that generate our feelings, listing a wide variety of feelings that may derive from people having their needs met (including enthusiastic, calm, comfortable, eager, energetic, helpful, and hopeful) and an equally long list of negative feelings that stem from people's needs not being met (such as apprehensive, disaffected, depressed, exasperated, impatient, indifferent, irate, nervous, numb, perplexed, reluctant, tired). Street-level workers would likely rather serve people who are cheerful and eager than those who are irate or despondent. Unhoused people, students, and other people served by street-level workers, likewise, would rather be treated with respect and compassion.

Rosenberg's (2015) conflict resolution overview may be helpful. He suggests:

> First, we express our own needs.
>
> Second, we search for the real needs of the other person, no matter how they are expressing themselves. If they are not expressing a need, but instead an opinion, judgment, or analysis, we recognize that, and continue to seek the need behind their words, the need underneath what they are saying.
>
> Third, we verify that we both accurately recognize the other person's needs, and if not, continue to seek the need behind their words.
>
> Fourth, we provide as much empathy as is required for us to mutually hear each other's needs accurately.
>
> And fifth, having clarified both parties' needs in the situation, we propose strategies for resolving the conflict, framing them in positive action language. (164)

It occurs to me that the Heritage and Robinson (2011) case specifically involved patient unmet needs leading to some resistance and low patient satisfaction. Patients hesitated, which made meetings longer, and meetings were, therefore, less efficient and less helpful because patients were unable to address additional concerns. The "some" in "What are some questions you have?" opens up space for patients to describe their needs. Street-level workers should consider how more compassionate listening and responding may get them the results they wanted in the first place.

Rosenberg (2013, 2015) suggests that we should avoid negative moral judgments, and while I have criticized those moral judgments surfacing through the cultural mythologies in the homeless shelter and classroom contexts, I am making them too as I negatively evaluate the language used by street-level workers. This book is not meant to condemn the words and actions of a few street-level workers, however. Still, they may feel evaluated, and I can envision how that may sting. I could not be more grateful for their participation, which helps us all understand how workers and institutions must grow. Their words have helped illustrate how neoliberalism, both ideologically and in managerial approach, can structurally change the conditions and discourse of street-level work, and I encourage institutional administration to seek the assistance and direction of discourse analysts who are committed to helping solve these kinds of structural problems. Still, there is work to be done by individuals as well; street-level workers should absolutely and unequivocally eliminate the use of negative moral judgments, including racist and classist language, shaming, and blaming. They should likewise practice active, compassionate listening. Me too. As I think back on the moments when I failed or responded poorly, I find lessons in my mental transcripts of those moments. This book is a call for all us to consider our subtle uses of language on the street-level and collectively do better.

> *Autoethnography: What Are You Excited About?*
> Rainbow flags lined the check-in desk, and the staff person cheerfully greeted me. On this day I was consulting with my doctors at the local LGBTQ medical center regarding gender-affirming hormone therapy (for me, that means the possibility of taking testosterone). I sat in an examination room in a chair facing my doctor, who was herself seated and typing on the computer in front of her. As she filled out forms, she looked at me and said, "What excites you about taking T." I started to rattle off a list—"I'm excited to sing songs that will finally be in my range. I'm really excited to try to grow a mustache. I want to look like a hot, Brooklyn bartender at a speakeasy. Can we make that happen?" I laughed. As she relayed my thoughts onto the computer form in front of her, I stopped myself and said, "Huh, this is for insurance purposes isn't it?" I had read Dean Spade's *Normal Life*, I knew how much medical documentation was needed for trans people. She paused, "Well, yes, but I also *want* to *know*." She explained the regulations and prohibitions that insurance companies have that stand in the way of gender-affirming care, including patients being aware of "risks." I demonstrated my awareness of what T could do to my body by talking about my own anticipation and enthusiasm for those changes.

Sitting in her office, I thought "Why this, now?" She could have asked me for this information in a variety of ways. I mentally listed them:

- I need to tell the insurance company why you want T, so tell me again why you want it for the insurance record.
- Why do you want to go on T?
- Do you know the risks of going on T?
- Are you sure you want to go on T?
- You need to tell me why you want to go on T.
- You have to be clear about the attributes and risks of T. Do you know them?
- Why aren't you comfortable without T?
- Aren't you worried about "male-pattern baldness"?

I imagine there might be other ways of making the same inquiry, including some with more obvious prejudice like "Testosterone—are you trying to cheat in athletics?" Many authors have written about this radically ill-informed and transphobic set of beliefs (Bailar, 2023; Buzuvis, 2010; Karkazis, and Jordan-Young, 2018; Sánchez-García, 2021). It is noteworthy that marginalized people of many stripes experience the baseless categorization: "cheaters of systems."

In this meeting with my doctor, what struck me was that her phrasing combined curiosity, positivity, and acceptance. Her phrasing allowed me to feel comfortable, positive, accepted, and informed. "What excites you?"—an open-ended question with positive polarity (i.e., no "nots"), a question that does not question my own self-knowledge but takes for granted that I have done my own internal work, that I am making a decision that works for me, and that takes a positive stance toward my transition. I *am* excited. Let me tell you about the first song I'll sing with a lower voice![5]

A Closing

Through this book I offer a unique contribution to the fields of street-level bureaucracy, applied linguistics, education, and social welfare. I endeavored to share these thoughts:

1. What constructions of responsibility look like in spaces serving marginalized people
2. Why they can be problematic
3. How neoliberally informed performance measurements themselves shape the talk of street-level workers
4. How references to performance management highlight neoliberal pressures of workers and clients alike
5. How cultural mythologies surface in these moments
6. How these cultural mythologies serve as both microaggressions and moments of identity work that accrue over time
7. How the experiences of more privileged people differ by comparison with these trends
8. How people's individually racist behavior is reflective of systemic and institutional forms of racism
9. How those forms of racism may be used because street-level workers believe that those discursive strategies (shaming, etc.) generate desired results
10. And how we might start addressing these issues

Finally, I would like to remind readers that while I extend the research to which I refer in this book, what I have written about is not wholly new, and those studies deserve to be read in their own right. Community college research is overwhelmingly conducted by (1) faculty outside of community colleges, (2) organizations like the Community College Research Center situated within elite, ivory-tower institutions, and (3) administrators at community colleges and in higher education. These scholars and institutes should, in keeping with methodological recommendations emerging out of postcolonial theory and participatory action research, collaborate with research faculty teaching in community colleges (Fine & Torre, 2003). Consider reading scholarship generated by community college faculty like Sullivan, Isserles, and Levin. Studies among unhoused people should, likewise, include data collected and analyzed by (currently or formerly) unhoused people, social workers, and caseworkers who may also benefit from publication.

There are plenty of prominent Black scholars, academics of color, queer scholars, and trans scholars who have explored related issues. Many of those scholars are in the bibliography. Although my list is admittedly very incomplete, I encourage you to read the work of scholars who are speaking on these issues in various ways already, including H. Samy Alim, Arnetha Ball, John Baugh, Renée Blake, Mary Bucholtz, Christian Chun,

Elaine Chun, Aris Moreno Clemons, Jennifer Delfino, Norma Mendoza Denton, Waverly Duck, Nelson Flores, Ofelia Garcia, Terri Givens, Lisa Green, Ange-Marie Hancock, Jane Hill, bell hooks, Anne H. Charity Hudley, Celia Kitzinger, Paul Kroskrity, Sonja Lanehart, Lorette LeMaster, Wesley Y. Leonard, Adrienne Lo, Gabriela Spangero Lotta, Bettina Love, Ceil Lucas, Christine Mallinson, Flávio Eiró de Oliveira, Ricardo Otheguy, Django Paris, Geneva Smitherman, Dean Spade, Arthur Spears, Steven Talmy, Shirley Anne Tate, Angela Reyes, John Rickford, Jonathan Rosa, Celeste Watkins-Hayes, Bernardo Zacka, Ana Celia Zentella, Lal Zimman, and Perry Zurn, to name a few.

Appendix: Methodology

Autoethnography

Autoethnography is much maligned as an approach, negatively characterized as navel-gazing, narcissistic, "nonanalytic, self-indulgent, irreverent, sentimental, and romantic" (Denzin, 2013, 69). Admittedly, the approach is not without problems. As Denzin (2013) observes, "Experience, lived and otherwise, is discursively constructed. It is not a foundational category. There is no empirically stable I giving a true account of an experience. Experience has no existence apart from the storied acts of performative-I" (2). The performative dimension links autoethnography to its literary forebears and the requirements of "good" storytelling, while also including a level of self-awareness and critique that provides commentary on such storytelling. Did the stories in my autoethnographic writings "happen?" Yes, I had a sister who died of muscular dystrophy, which shaped my growing up substantially. Yes, I got divorced, and about ten years later realized I was trans. My writing on the subject of my growing up, my first marriage and divorce, and my experiences thereafter involve descriptions of memories, and it is always worth acknowledging that these memories are continually contextualized and recontextualized by the passage of time and my own interpretations of my experiences, and that the writing on this subject only identifies events I distinctly remember and my feelings in those areas (not the experiences or feeling of my family, my ex-husband, or others). I have discussed these events with colleagues and other advisers, though for a variety of reasons not with those referenced in the narratives.

If autoethnography is so fraught, why include it? Denzin (2013), paraphrasing Jones, Adams, and Ellis (2013), defines autoethnography as

> the use of personal experience and personal writing to (1) purposefully comment on / critique cultural practices; (2) make contribu-

> tions to existing research, (3) embrace vulnerability with purpose, and (4) create a reciprocal relationship with audiences in order to compel a response.

My story around responsibility is immeasurably different from those described in the two interactional ethnographies, but it does comment on the influences of family and religion in my own experience with responsibility. In being honest, I intentionally embrace vulnerability in the hope that my story, even some of my worst moments, will resonate with some of you. It is worth clarifying for the reader how my privilege as a white person generated a radically different relationship to responsibility, and it is useful to model reflective practice in an academic book.

Many scholars have positioned autoethnography as a feminist methodology (Behar, 1996; Naples, 2003). Ruth Behar (2022) attributes the preferences for quantitative research and the avoidance of personal and vulnerable ethnography to Western, white, patriarchal roots. In responding to critiques of an essay written by Renato Rosaldo that combined his research with expressed grief over his wife's death during fieldwork, Behar said,

> My interpretation is further complicated by the fact that Renato is a literary father who is self-consciously taking on feminist, even "feminine" positions. He is cross-dressing as it were. . . . Daring to speak of his sorrow, of his loss, his rage, daring, yes to privilege sentiments, he dares to be "feminine"—that is, feminine in the terms of our cultural logic and the way we ascribe genders to our writing. And immediately the [critics] come along to chastise him for not being *macho* enough. (170)

Naples (2013) frames it similarly: "I believe that the process of critical reflection informed by the theoretical insights of feminist standpoint epistemologies can help uncover the complex dynamics involved in the production of everyday life" (44). In *The Vulnerable Observer: Anthropology That Breaks Your Heart* Behar states, "The critics of the kind of anthropology that matters to me claim that the price anthropology must pay to survive into the next century is to become science, or risk becoming nothing" (163–64). Including autoethnography in this book points to my skepticism of lab-coat social scientists while reifying my desire to align myself with critical reflection, purposeful vulnerability, and a hope that my story adds another layer to the discussion of what responsibility can look like. My autoethnographic contributions draw on Behar's and Naple's critiques of the patriarchal and misogynistic underpinnings in positivistic social science.

Collecting Data in Two Research Contexts

A New York City Shelter

Prior to my data collection, I worked as a summer intern at New York City's Department of Homeless Services, conducting mixed-method research investigating supportive housing availability for unhoused men who were also level 3 sex offenders. The shelter where I spent much of the time conducting that study was welcoming to me, and the staff seemed relatively happy to have me back when I began my dissertation research. My dissertation fieldwork spanned a full year. During the first three months, I became acquainted with the staff, administration, and the unhoused men, and I collected data for the next nine months between 2005 and 2006.[1]

I used convenience sampling, as I selected caseworkers based on availability and their interest in the project, and I selected unhoused men who were assigned to with those caseworkers based on their interest. Many of them came to me originally thinking I worked with Coalition for the Homeless, an advocacy organization where they could vent complaints. Per the request of the former Department of Homeless Services, all participating clients were given a mini-mental status exam by a shelter social worker prior to signing consent forms,[2] and consent forms and study information were also available in Spanish. While I spoke to many of the men at the shelter about the study, final approval of participants was left to the participating caseworkers and social workers, as clients with schizophrenia and paranoia, clients who have untreated psychological disorders, and clients with a history of stalking were not viewed as appropriate participants for this study due to institutionally imposed restrictions for my safety.

During the data-collection phase of my fieldwork, I conducted interviews with the unhoused men at the beginning, middle, and end of their time in shelter, and interviews with caseworkers were also conducted at the beginning, middle, and end of my time working with them. However, some participating unhoused men, and even one caseworker, left unexpectedly during my fieldwork. I also audio-recorded all caseworker-client interactions each man experiencing homelessness had from the first meeting with his caseworker to the last. In total, I worked with eighteen "homeless clients"[3] and six caseworkers; however, the five clients who spent the most time in shelter from my data set worked with two caseworkers, so the data regarding how responsibility is constructed over time (Chapter 5) focus on those who spent the most time in the shelter. Field notes were taken in each data-collection session (interview or caseworker-client meeting), including sketches of the space. All data were transcribed after collection and uploaded to NVivo. Consent was acquired from all participants.[4] Pseudonyms were used throughout for this data and the community college data.

A New York City Community College

I had already been working as a professor at BMCC, CUNY, for four years prior to data collection. Given our teaching load, it was often more convenient to conduct research at the college, which also supported the mission of a teaching-focused college. After obtaining consent from professor and students and IRB approval, two colleagues and I videotaped and audio-recorded a semester-long college-level remedial[5] reading class at BMCC in the spring of 2013. This class typically meets six hours a week and provides developmental reading instruction to students who have not yet passed the CUNY-wide standardized reading test.[6] The course is designed to help students master a full range of college-level reading and related skills, including critical comprehension, vocabulary, writing, flexible rates of reading, and study strategies. We generally recorded once a week, and we avoided days fully devoted to taking practice exams. We began a couple weeks into the semester, as initial weeks include a departmental diagnostic exam and shuffling students around courses (some students register late, and some are misplaced and required a higher- or lower-level course). While the shelter data is entirely audio-recorded, we received approval to video-record this classroom data, with some students opting not to have their faces shown at all or for blurring of their faces if the videos were used. All eleven recorded sessions were videotaped to give the researchers the opportunity to examine the evolving nature of classroom talk. Three video cameras were positioned in the room (two in front and one in the back) to get different angles. While the video data have been shown and analyzed (Jacknick, 2021), this study does not take video data into account. Classroom diagrams and field notes were utilized to provide a complete picture of what was occurring in class at any given time.

All students, who came from a wide range of cultural and linguistic backgrounds, were asked to complete a brief background questionnaire regarding their age, national origin, native language, and exposure to English (educational background and number of years living in an English-speaking country). The class was an equal combination of ESL, generation 1.5, and native English-speaking students (nonstandard American English dialect speakers). The researchers surveyed the students at the beginning of the semester to ascertain their course goals and at the end regarding perceived benefits of the class. Students were not interviewed. The instructor was interviewed twice to reflect upon his teaching strategies, and the end of many classes included postsession chats between whichever researcher was present and the professor. In addition, classroom artifacts such as the textbook, workbook, teacher's manual, handouts, homework, and lesson plans were scanned as needed and returned to participants.

The Professor

The professor teaching the course I observed was my mentor when I started at BMCC. He is a man in his sixties. He had been teaching this course for decades. His office has a sign in it with the word THINK written upside down. Early in my career, he once observed my teaching on a day when I wasn't at my best. It was springtime, and for some reason the heat had turned on across the building, and my classroom, on the top floor, was an oven, the air was thick and heavy with heat. It must have been over ninety degrees. Sweat beads rolled down my back and dampened my hair. I had worn a suit for my observation. Despite my attempts to be upbeat, the students were languishing in their chairs like wilted flowers. I imagine most students knew they "had" to attend this course, but today few of them legitimately wanted to. Today, they wanted to go home, exit the building, and cool off, but I was a relatively new teacher at the time, and I was floundering, grasping at straws to making learning happen. Nowadays, I would have let my class go and rescheduled the observation, but I was green and far less confident. The observer was so generous with his review of me that day. How do you teach in a room with no windows when it's ninety degrees, when all the students are looking longingly at the door in the desperate wish that they be allowed to leave early? How do you teach a convincing lesson when you should really let everyone go?

We had different teaching styles, for sure. He was more traditional, including using a more formal reading textbook favored by many, if not most, of the department's college reading teachers. He loved the Ray Bradbury book *Fahrenheit 451* and taught it every semester with his ACR students. The message of the book about the transformative power of reading and education as resistance seemed ideal for ACR, and this professor worked hard to instill a love of literature and reading while teaching the skills needed to break down and critically think about college-level readings. The room was most alive when he and the students were discussing the novel, working in groups to share what they had learned, developing critical questions that would pave the way for making inferences.

The Classroom and the Class

When you enter the room from the hallway, the wall shared with the hallway has a long coatrack where students hang soppy umbrellas and jackets. The room is small and rectangular, with a chalkboard and a large "teacher's desk" and open space occupying the front fifth of the room; the other four-fifths of the room is organized in a teacher-fronted style with rows of student desks facing the blackboard. There was a computer in the corner that we were allowed to unplug for our recording equipment because it was never used. There are windows on the far side of the room that overlook the Hudson River. While many of the rooms in the newer building are almost uncomfortably white and fluorescent, this room was the yellowing cream color of an older building in need of renovation.

The class was diverse in gender, mother tongue, and ethnic background. Students were young, most of them between eighteen and twenty years old. Professors ran their classes differently. This professor generally began with students doing about thirty to forty minutes of silent vocabulary work in a vocabulary textbook with fill-in-the-blank and multiple-choice answers. This allowed students who were late to show up begin when they arrived without missing the teaching for that day. The class then turned to whatever the topic was for that day. The vocabulary assignment was written on the board along with what they were working on that day and other upcoming announcements.

Analysis

To analyze these two interactional ethnographies, initial (basic) transcription, qualitative coding through NVivo, discourse-level transcription, discourse analysis, qualitative/thematic analysis, and autoethnography were used. The primary method I use analyze the data is discourse analysis.

Transcription: Where Analysis Begins

Discourse analysts favor the analysis of naturalistic speech. As Ochs (1979) observes in her foundational paper "Transcription as Theory,"

> An area of considerable interest and controversy within linguistics concerns the nature and adequacy of data for positing linguistic rules and norms (Chomsky, 1965; Hymes, 1972; Labov, 1970, 1972). Should the linguist base generalizations on what speakers say they do (i.e. native speaker intuition) or on what they actually do (naturalistic speech behavior)? (43)

For many researchers, transcribing is something that can be farmed out to a graduate student or to a transcription service, but for those of us who study discourse, transcription is part of analysis. Ochs indicates that transcription "reflects theoretical goals and definitions" (44). When we transcribe, we make certain choices about how to portray the data (Psathas and Anderson, 1990; Jenks, 2011), so whenever we transcribe we are choosing what might be relevant to include.

Often discourse analysts go through waves of transcription. We might transcribe just the words or words and light intonation on the first pass through the data. Transcribing an hour of social interaction can take upwards of ten hours to capture the words and modest detail, and the process of transcription fosters an intimate understanding of the data, listening to portions over and over again. It is during this wave that we might begin noticing something of interest.

After this wave of transcription is completed, discourse analysts often create collections, instances of a particular discourse practice or word. With both of these studies, I put initial transcriptions into NVivo, a qualitative coding program and created collections of discourse features of interest using the coding tool (more on coding in the subsequent section). However, after making collections, discourse analysts often have to return for a second round of transcription that represents not only what is said but *how* it is said, using a variety of standard symbols commonly used among discourse analysts (see Table A.1). Transcription symbols signal speed of speech, words that are emphasized, shifts in pitch, the intonation used at the end of phrases and sentences. However, as Mondada (2018) notes, not all symbols are necessarily important to each study, and so

> transcribing is always a selective activity . . . depending on the objectives of the analysis, the granularity of the transcript, the private in-progress versus publicly edited status of the version, the recipient oriented/reader-friendly character of the final version, and so on (88).

For example, while I have video for the community college study, I am not including multimodal notations (symbols and notations relating to body movement, gesture, eye gaze, etc.) in my transcripts because they fall outside the purview of this particular study. This process creates an intimacy with the data not necessarily present in other kinds of methodologies. These transcripts are attentive to the *what* and the *how* of social interaction, including symbols that help articulate the *how* (see Table A.1 for the Hutchby and Wooffitt (2008) transcription conventions that were used in this book). This book presents data from fifty-four caseworker-client interactions (of varying lengths, many upwards of an hour) and ten classroom interactions (each class was one hour and forty minutes long), resulting in over twelve hundred pages of transcripts and approximately five hundred listening hours.[7] In essence, an iterative data analysis began with transcription, in which the focus of the data analysis became increasingly narrowed in the recursive waves of the first basic transcription, NVivo coding, and enhanced transcription.

Field Notes

Folding ethnographic methods into interactional analyses, Scollon and Scollon (2004) suggest that a researcher include interviews with participants, conduct observations, and write field notes and that the observations and field notes should focus on the interactions themselves. They call this observing "the interaction order," a concept that they derive from Goffman's (1983) work, which provides the linguist with an opportunity to ethnographically and richly describe the interactional events taking place. Brodkin's (2008) methodology for applied street-level research advocates for the inclusion of ethnographic study. In so doing, interview data can be compared with ethnographic data in order to "probe for differences between 'what they say' and 'what they do.' Although in interviews caseworkers may portray themselves as 'tough' or 'soft' in applying the rules, their day-to-day practices may be inconsistent with what they preach" (329–30). Although I am primarily interested in "what they do," the interview data and field notes triangulate findings when needed.

TABLE A.1: **Transcription Conventions** (adapted from Hutchby and Wooffitt, 2008)

(1.8)	Pause. The number represents duration of the pause in seconds, to one decimal place.
(.)	A pause of less than 0.2 seconds
[ ]	Overlap with a portion of another speaker's utterance.
=	Latch: no time lapse between two utterances, used when a second speaker begins their utterance just at the moment when the first speaker finishes
::	Extended sound
(hm, hh)	Onomatopoetic representations of the audible exhalation of air
.hh	Audible inhalation of air. The more h's, the longer the in-breath
?	Rising intonation
.	Falling intonation
,	Continuation of tone.
-	Abrupt cutoff, speaker stops speaking suddenly.
↑↓	Sharply rising or falling intonation. The arrow is placed just before the syllable in which the change in intonation occurs.
Under	Speaker emphasis on the underlined portion of the word.
CAPS	Higher volume than the speaker's normal volume.
°	Utterance is much softer than the normal speech of the speaker. This symbol will appear at the beginning and at the end of the utterance in question.
> <, < >	Noticeably faster (>faster talk<), or slower (<slower talk>) than the surrounding talk.
(would)	Transcriber has guessed as to what was said, because it was indecipherable on the tape. If the transcriber was unable to guess what was said, nothing appears within the parentheses.
(XXXX)	Indistinguishable speech

NVivo Coding

An iterative data analysis allows for an analytical sharpening and narrowing over time, each iteration adding clarity and specificity. When I first entered my shelter data into NVivo, a qualitative software analysis program, I was looking for keywords from the city shelter policies, assuming that similar language would be in the caseworkers' interactions with their clients. I surmised that words and phrases from the shelter policies would be present in the data, but when I searched for words like "accountability" and "responsible" (and related variants), I found not one usage of these policy terms. I must admit that at the time I was shocked. In interactional ethnographic terms, this was a "rich point" that abductive logic enabled me to find. I decided to read through the data once again, all one thousand-plus pages, searching for other words that might communicate similar ideas. This is how I stumbled onto deontic formulations, words that communicate responsibility and obligation like "must," "need to," "have to," "gotta," "should," and "supposed to." I developed codes for these based on that discovery, and I combed the data once again with these new codes. Looking at the collection of deontic formulations, I noticed other language that frequently surfaced nearby and in conjunction with these terms: references to time, which led to another iterative comb through the data looking for references to time. This, in turn, led to discovering a relationship between how responsibility is constructed and performance benchmarks and measurements. The collection of those were then richly transcribed and then analyzed in depth using discourse analysis.[8]

At the time, I had not considered the existence of cultural mythologies in my shelter data, and I did not code for them when I conducted my initial dissertation analysis. It was only when I had finished collecting the community college data set, after my team and I had finished transcribing, and a colleague and I were reading through the data, thinking about what we might write about next, that I noticed the presence of constructions similar to my dissertation data. I coded the community college basic transcripts for responsibility, time and performance benchmarks, and performance measurements, and I found something new: cultural mythologies indexed through lexical stance markers. After coding for all of these, creating a collection for the community college data, and embellishing the transcripts within the collection, I analyzed them using discourse analysis.

I then went back to the original shelter data and recoded for the presence of lexical stance markers that contributed to cultural mythologies. Revisiting the data recursively and iteratively allowed me to find what I had not noticed the first time through the data: Constructions of responsibility were not just related to time and performance but also included cultural mythologies that positioned both students and unhoused men vis-à-vis beliefs around laziness, working hard, and so on. The final codes for each data set focused on deontic formulations, references to time (benchmarks) and performance assessments, and lexical and affective stances that indexed cultural mythologies and emotional states. While ultimately the process is interpretivist, extensive familiarity with the data and continuous revisioning of the coding, along with triangulating results with ethnographic field notes and interview data, supports a reliable and valid analytic approach.

Generalizations

The studies in this book combine ethnography with analysis of interaction, using, in part, an ethnographic case study approach. Accordingly, this study makes no claims to generalize to all caseworkers, all clients, or policy implementation across the NYC shelter system. Nor does it claim to generalize to all professors in the department, in the college, or at CUNY. Rather, this methodology shines by displaying depth and rich descriptions of complicated processes, in its descriptions of "local knowledge" (Marshall and Rossman, 2014, 100), in its investigation of policy implementation by a small number of caseworkers and one professor on a practice level. The value of this research lies not in positivistic claims to "established fact" but in the interpretive desire to describe locally situated practices and posit propositions for understanding those practices (Crotty, 2003, 41). According to Goetz and LeCompte (1993), "Establishing conventional validity depends on demonstrating that the propositions generated, refined, or tested match what occurs in human life" (341). Although it is difficult to generalize much qualitative work due to the timeliness and context-based nature of the data, Goetz and LeCompte also suggest that ethnographic research has much to offer to those seeking valid research. They suggest that internal validity of qualitative research stems from its data collection and method. The authors emphasize that qualitative researchers often collect data for long periods of time, particularly using participant observation, and are therefore able to become intimately familiar with the data in ways in which quantitative researchers cannot. Moreover, while single case studies are not broadly generalizable, case study research is able to generalize from the case to theory more generally, what Yin (2003) terms the "analytically generalizable" (Yin, 2003, 32). Within this perspective, cases are not viewed as "sampling units" but as mini-observational experiments that support or refute existing theory (Yin, 2003).

Reliability and Validity

This book comprises an impressive amount of discourse analytic data, over fifteen hundred pages of transcript data, including fifty-four caseworker-client interactions (many of which are over an hour long) and thirteen classroom recordings (each one hour and forty-five minutes long). Given Seedhouse's (2004) claim that between five and ten lessons in classroom discourse research constitutes a "reasonable database," the sixty-seven interactions analyzed in this book present a nearly unprecedented window into talk over time in institutional contexts, more than enough to convincingly posit trends in street-level interaction around responsibility based on extensive collections developed for each data set.

Discourse analyses offer a unique window into reliability and validity. Readers have the unique opportunity with discourse analysis of reading the "hard data" for themselves and making determinations. Moreover, data sessions where a working group analyzes the data together, conference presentations, and article publications provide ample opportunity to review the data analyses. Having presented these data at a wide variety of conferences, having published many articles, and having discourse analysts read this book, I feel confident in presenting these findings to you. Moreover, when possible, I refer not only to what is said by the street-level worker, but to how the recipient (unhoused client or student) responds, which aids in confirming interpretations of analysis (Woofit, 2005). Interpretations of the data are also supported by references to the literature, by other data collected, and the length of time spent in the ethnographic field site. Given my intern research position at Department of Homeless Services, I spent fourteen to fifteen months in that shelter, and I had worked for five years prior to my dissertation in a supportive housing facility connected to the shelter system. I had been at BMCC five years when we collected data, and I have now been teaching there sixteen years.

Notes

CHAPTER 1

1. These were policies active in 2006–2008 and may no longer be active.

2. For information on autoethnography, specifics of data collection, and explanations of reliability, validity, and generalization, please see the appendix.

3. This poor law is not the one to which Scrooge refers, though the Poor Laws of the 1800s espoused similar values.

4. This housing was a kind of halfway house for individuals and families experiencing homelessness. People had individual apartments, and social service workers were available on site to work with individuals on everything from job seeking to connecting clients to outpatient drug rehabilitation programs.

5. I use "caseworker" and "case manager" interchangeably. The social welfare literature often says "caseworker," but the shelter and workers more often said "case manager."

6. Families that do not include street-level workers likely enjoy a significant amount of privilege.

7. Social work has owned up to this far more than education evidenced by the significantly greater inclusion of Lipsky's (1980/2020) work in social work research.

8. During the writing of this book, the high-stakes exit exam for the course disappeared, and spring of 2022 was the last time a stand-alone version of the course was taught.

9. I use the term "client" in the phrase "caseworker-client interactions," as the term most closely links to similar kinds of other institutional pairings in discourse analytic literature (i.e., "teacher-student"). Moreover, because I am interested in these street-level workers and those they serve vis-à-vis their institutional positionality, I sometimes use the organizational nomenclature when discussing individual people's institutional positions and when discussing larger institutional dynamics. However, I also acknowledge that the use of these terms interpellates (Althusser, 1971) people into their institutional roles and into academic parlance, an action I actively critique in the book. I really struggled with how to resolve this without the language getting clunky, and I may not have found the best option. I tried to balance these choices with broader references to individual personhood and the use of appropriate pseudonyms. Needless to say, all participants inhabiting institutional positions (workers and those served) are people with full, rich lives that are not represented in this book. All participants, and all people, are deserving of kindness, dignity, respect, and generosity.

CHAPTER 2

1. Findings later published by Matarese and Caswell (2017, 2018)

2. Neoliberalism should not to be confused with "liberal" as a term of political affiliation.

3. Sometimes "neoliberalism" is referred to by the alternate term "advanced liberalism," which, while referring to the same political movement, avoids the politicized connotations that have been applied to "neoliberalism."

4. For more analysis of this sentence see Chapter 3.

5. As an example, the utterance "When you had intercourse with her, you said something to her, didn't you?" includes the presupposition, or assumption, that the sexual context was "intercourse" and not "rape" or "sexual assault." However, Ehrlich (2010) notes, that the "intercourse" portion of the sentence is difficult to deny or amend given the constraints of the question formation, particularly in court where responses of "yes" or "no" are the primary options with very little wiggle room. Lawyers will infuse questions with presuppositions that serve their angle to sway the jury (Ehrlich, 2010).

6. "Categorizations" in discourse-based social welfare research are often analyzed similarly, although generally this term is generally reserved for studies using membership categorization analysis (MCA) (cf. Hall et al., 2007; Mäkitalo, 2014). While the studies for this book do not use MCA, I do sometimes use the term "category" to describe how certain stances position people according to social categories that circulate in the social milieu.

7. This timescale shifted from nine months to six months during my fieldwork.

8. The semester was used despite many students taking the course multiple times in order to pass.

CHAPTER 3

1. Rather confusingly, "accounting" in discourse analysis is distinct and different from "accountability" as defined in public policy, social work, and educational organizational management literature.

2. I would be remiss to not mention Hill and Irvine's (1993) edited volume *Responsibility and Evidence in Oral Discourse*, which addresses in part the extent to which individuals take or avoid responsibility; however, they do not explore how responsibility is discursively constructed. In that volume, Hill and Zepeda (1993) discuss strategies used to avoid being held personally responsible and devices that "diffuse" or account for responsibility (197), but, much like the literature on accounting, the work in this volume does not reveal how responsibility itself is constructed in street-level talk.

3. Mayor Bloomberg's words; see full quotation below.

4. Exceptions to ILP violations and sanctions are made by DHS for those clients who have mental or physical impairments that prevent compliance.

5. "Appropriate" housing is a shelter term used often in the discussion of ILPs.

6. This section is adapted from field notes.

7. As I have mentioned previously, I use "caseworker" and "case manager" interchangeably.

8. I generally try to use the term "unhoused person," but the caseworkers used the term "clients," and its business tenor is not lost on me.

9. This section is adapted from field notes.

10. All participants took and passsed a required mini mental status exam.

11. For descriptions of these features, please see Chapter 2.

12. Examples in this book are intended to be demonstrative of larger patterns, emically identified across the two data sets.

13. The audio recorder did not work for this interaction, so this transcript was typed verbatim as heard in the moment and included as field notes.

14. Several security guards who translated, including this one, consented to being participants in this study, signing required IRB documents in English or Spanish.

15. The shelter requirements for undocumented, unhoused people may have changed since data collection.

CHAPTER 4

1. For a background on time and timescale, please see Chapter 2.

2. Since data collection, ACR was first integrated into content courses and then was eliminated entirely at BMCC and CUNY.

CHAPTER 5

1. These were policies active in 2006–2008 and may no longer be active.

CHAPTER 6

1. Pitcher (2017) explains that misgendering transgender people is a commonly experienced microaggression, even in academia.

2. This class met three times a week for an hour and forty minutes per session, and we generally recorded once a week, so this is a snapshot of this shift without being fully inclusive of all class sessions.

3. Speech acts explore the relationship between what is said, what is intended, and what is received.

4. See the work of Renee Blake, John Baugh, Anne Charity Hudley, Lisa Green, Christine Mallinson, John Rickford, Arthur Spears, Walt Wolfram, and so many others.

5. This narrative is taken from my own memory of an event that occurred nearly ten years ago, as well as a written statement I sent to my department chair, and I cross-checked that story against a statement a student of mine made for the record.

CHAPTER 7

1. As a reminder, this course no longer exists.

2. The Community College Research Center at Teachers College, Columbia University conducted several studies examining the merits of the "fifteen-to-finish" program, and found positive results in Tennessee (Belfield et al., 2016), Colorado, Hawaii,

West Virginia, and New Mexico (Klempin, 2014). While we may debate whether results from these states are applicable to such a different population of students, anecdotally I can say that many of my students in Linguistics and Criminal Justice courses over the years had a very difficult time maintaining fifteen credits and often had to drop a class midsemester to maintain their GPA.

3. Recently, a White House Executive Order has made English the official language of the United States; however, this ruling has yet to be tested in the courts (The United States Government, 2025).

4. I understand that it is a privilege to think beyond minimum wage jobs. That said, a minimum wage job in New York City is not a living wage. I think we can dream bigger for our students.

5. My voice has dropped, and I can tell you now that the song was "Wichita Lineman," the Johnny Cash version, on Jerry Lee Lewis's piano in Memphis, and it was awesome.

APPENDIX

1. I am aware that this was some time ago. However, the discourse features that arise through analysis continue to persevere in other institutional spaces, as well as among the public. So, while the policies have seen slight adjustments in the shelter system, the linguistic findings are still relevant. I am not claiming that current shelter workers use this particular language, rather that this language is pervasive in social institutions and should be examined and discussed.

2. The mini-mental status exam (MMSE) was available in English and Spanish. After consulting with professors at the Mailman School of Public Health in Clinical Psychology and Clinical Sociomedical Sciences who work with people experiencing homelessness (and with DHS in particular) as well as consulting literature on thresholds on the MMSE, I determined that the threshold score of 27 would be used to determine the ability of a client to give informed consent (Folstein, 1975). The MMSE was administered to each and every client to ensure informed consent, and although it is critiqued by many as an inadequate tool (cf. Crum et al., 1993), the participation and expert knowledge of the clinical social worker increases the validity of the test in ensuring informed consent. As such, the clinical social worker evaluated each person who met or exceeded the threshold (27 or above) in order to understand where points were lost and to ensure that there was not some other factor that should be considered in evaluating the client's ability to provide informed consent.

3. Current terminology prefers "unhoused" over "homeless." This language might have also changed in the shelter system itself. That said, this language was not used at the time of data collection, when all caseworkers used the word "homeless" (i.e., for a "client's" intake evaluation caseworker's asked, "Why are you homeless" or "How did you become homeless?"). I try to maintain current language, "unhoused," for my own current thoughts while keeping to "homeless" and "client" when talking about how they were referred to in the shelter.

4. I would like to thank Department of Homeless Services and in particular Martha Kenton for their helpful feedback during the development of my study, and I extend my greatest gratitude to the caseworkers and clients with whom I worked.

5. In my department, this Academic Critical Reading course was called a "developmental" reading class. The term "developmental," however, is often used to refer to a broader category of dis/abilities. While "developmental" was preferred as a department, in practice "remedial" was often used interchangeably and students (mine and other's) often called it a "remedial" course.

6. The course has recently been eliminated from CUNY's curriculum, and the placement test is no longer used for assessing reading level.

7. The community college data transcriptions were divided among the three principal investigators for the study, which reduced the number of transcription hours for me individually.

8. Because an understanding of discourse featured analyzed is so vital to the argument in the book, information on how I am analyzing the discourse is included in Chapter 2.

References

Abadi, M. 2018. When CEO Satya Nadella took over Microsoft, he started defusing its toxic culture by handing each of his execs a 15-year-old book by a psychologist. *Business Insider*, October. 7. https://www.businessinsider.com/microsoft-satya-nadella-nonviolent-communication-2018-10

Abramovitz, M., and Zelnick, J. 2015. Privatization in the human services: Implications for direct practice. *Clinical Social Work Journal* 43(3), 283–93.

Agar, M. H. 1986. *Speaking of Ethnography*. Sage. https://doi.org/10.4135/9781412985895

Agha, A. 2007. Recombinant selves in mass mediated spacetime. *Language & Communication* 27(3), 320–35.

Agiriga, J. C., Uche, I. A., Ezike, C., and Noke, U. C. 2019. Current trends in applied linguistics. *RUJMASS* 5(1), 227–36.

Alim, H. S. 2016. Who's afraid of the transracial subject. In Alim, H. S., Rickford, J. R., and Ball, A. F., eds., *Raciolinguistics: How Language Shapes Our Ideas About Race*, 33–50. Oxford University Press.

Alim, H. S., and Smitherman, G. 2012. *Articulate While Black: Barack Obama, Language, and Race in the U.S.* Oxford University Press.

Althusser, L. 1971. Ideology and ideological state apparatuses. In Althusser, L., *Lenin and Philosophy and Other Essays*. Monthly Review Press.

Antaki, C., ed. 2011. *Applied Conversation Analysis: Intervention and Change in Institutional Talk*. Springer.

Anyon, J. 2014. *Radical Possibilities: Public Policy, Urban Education, and a New Social Movement*. Routledge.

Apple, M. W. 2019. On doing critical policy analysis. *Educational Policy* 33(1), 276–87.

Atkinson, P. 1999. Medical discourse, evidentiality and the construction of professional responsibility. In Sarangi, S., and Roberts, C., eds., *Talk, Work and Institutional Order: Discourse in Medical, Mediation and Management Settings*. Mouton de Gruyter.

Austin, J. L. 1975. *How to Do Things with Words*. Oxford University Press.

Baier, K. 1970. Responsibility and action. In M. Brand, ed., *The Nature of Human Action*, 100–116. Scott, Foresman.

Bailar, S. 2023. *He/She/They: How We Talk About Gender and Why It Matters*. Random House.

Bailey, T., Jaggars, S. S., and Jenkins, D. 2015. What we know about guided pathways:

Helping students to complete programs faster. Research overview. Community College Research Center, Teachers College, Columbia University.

Bakhtin, M. 1981. *The Dialogic Imagination: Four Essays by M. M. Bakhtin*. Ed. M. Holquist. Trans. M. Holquist and C. Emerson. University of Texas Press.

Banks, S. 2007. Between equity and empathy: Social professions and the new accountability. *Social Work & Society* 5(3), 11–22.

Bartlett, L. 2007. Literacy, speech and shame: The cultural politics of literacy and language in Brazil. *International Journal of Qualitative Studies in Education* 20(5), 547–63.

Beckmann, A., and Cooper, C. 2004. Globalisation, the new managerialism and education: Rethinking the purpose of education in Britain. *Journal for Critical Education Policy Studies* 2(2), 1–32.

Behar, R. 2022. *The Vulnerable Observer: Anthropology That Breaks Your Heart*. Beacon Press.

Belfield, C., Jenkins, P. D., and Lahr, H. E. 2016. Momentum: The academic and economic value of a 15-credit first-semester course load for college students in Tennessee. CCRC Working Paper no. 88. https://ccrc.tc.columbia.edu/publications/momentum-15-credit-course-load.html

Berger, P., and Luckmann, T. 1967. *The Social Construction of Reality*. Doubleday.

Bhabha, H. 1994. *The Location of Culture*. Routledge.

Biber, D., and Finegan, E. 1989. Styles of stance in English: Lexican and grammatical marking of evidentiality and affect. *Text: Interdisciplinary Journal for the Study of Discourse* 9(1): 93–124.

Block, D. 2018. *Political Economy and Sociolinguistics: Neoliberalism, Inequality and Social Class*. Bloomsbury.

Block, D., Gray, J., and Holborow, M. 2013. *Neoliberalism and Applied Linguistics*. Routledge.

Bloom, P. 2016. *Against Empathy: The Case for Radical Compassion*. Ecco Publisher.

Bloomberg, M. 2004. Homeless policy address by Major Michael Bloomberg: Ending chronic homelessness in New York City. Association for a Better New York. Retrieved May 1, 2006 from http://www.ci.nyc.ny.us/html/dhs/html/press/sp062304.shtml

BMCC Office of Institutional Effectiveness and Analytics. 2004. *Facts and statistics*. Borough of Manhattan Community College: Institutional Research and Data Analytics. https://www.bmcc.cuny.edu/iea/institutional-research-and-data-analytics/facts-and-statistics/

Bobo, L., Kluegel, J. R., and Smith, R. A. 1997. Laissez-faire racism: The crystallization of a kinder, gentler, antiblack ideology. In Tuch, S. A., and Martin, J. K., eds., *Racial Attitudes in the 1990s: Continuity and Change*, 15, 23–25. Praeger.

Brodkin, E. Z. 1997. Inside the welfare contract: Discretion and accountability in state welfare administration. *Social Service Review* 71(1), 1–33.

Brodkin, E. Z. 2007. Bureaucracy redux: Management reformism and the welfare state. *Journal of Public Administration Research and Theory* 17(1), 1–17.

Brodkin, E. Z. 2008. Accountability in street-level organizations. *International Journal of Public Administration* 31(3), 317–36.

Brodkin, E. Z. 2011. Policy work: Street-level organizations under new managerialism. *Journal of Public Administration Research and Theory* 21(suppl. 2), i253–i277.

Brodkin, E. Z. 2013. Street-level organizations and the welfare state. In Brodkin, E. Z., and Marston, G., eds., *Work and the Welfare State: Street-Level Organizations and Workfare Politics*. Georgetown University Press.

Brodkin, E. Z., and Marston, G., eds. 2013. *Work and the Welfare State: Street-Level Organizations and Workfare Politics*. Georgetown University Press.

Brown, W. 2015. *Undoing the Demos: Neoliberalism's Stealth Revolution*. MIT Press.

Burns, K. A. 2014. Minimizing and managing microaggressions in the philosophy classroom. *Teaching Philosophy* 37(2), 131–52.

Buttny, R. 1993. *Social Accountability in Communication*. Sage.

Buzuvis, E. 2010. Caster Semenya and the myth of a level playing field. *Modern American* 6, 36.

Canagarajah, S. 2017. *Translingual Practices and Neoliberal Policies*. Springer International.

Carver-Thomas, D., and Darling-Hammond, L. 2019. The trouble with teacher turnover: How teacher attrition affects students and schools. *Education Policy Analysis Archives* 27, 36. http://dx.doi.org/10.14507/epaa.27.3699

Caswell, D. 2019. Talking policy into being: How street-level bureaucrats and vulnerable unemployed talk about labor market participation. *European Policy Analysis* 6(1), 23–37.

Caswell, D., and Dall, T. 2022. Using conversation analysis to develop reflective practice in social work. *Qualitative Social Work* 21(6), 1290–307.

Caswell, D., and Høybye-Mortensen, M. 2015. Responses from the frontline: How organisations and street-level bureaucrats deal with economic sanctions. *European Journal of Social Security* 17(1), 31–51.

Character Lab. 2023. Character. https://characterlab.org/character/

Chesterfield, P. D. S., and Belfield, H. H., eds. 1897. Lord Chesterfield's letters to his son and godson. Maynard, Merrill, & Co. Retrieved May 2, 2025, from https://www.loc.gov/item/11034601/

Chun, C. W. 2017. *The Discourses of Capitalism: Everyday Economists and the Production of Common Sense*. Taylor & Francis.

Chun, C. W. 2021. *A World Without Capitalism? Alternative Discourses, Spaces, and Imaginaries*. Routledge.

Clarke, J., and Newman, J. 1993. The right to manage: A second managerial revolution? *Cultural Studies* 7(3), 427–41.

Clayman, S. E. 2001. Answers and evasions. *Language in Society* 30(3), 403–42.

Coates, J. 1983. *The Semantics of Modal Auxiliaries*. Croom Helm.

Cohen, P. 1969. Theories of myth. *Journal of the Royal Anthropological Institute* 4(3), 337–53.

Collins, P. 2009. Modals and quasi-modals in world Englishes. *World Englishes* 28(3), 281–92.

Conley, R. 2015. *Confronting the Death Penalty: How Language Influences Jurors in Capital Cases*. Oxford University Press.

Couper-Kuhlen, E., and Selting, M. 2017. *Interactional Linguistics: Studying Language in Social Interaction*. Cambridge University Press.

Creider, S. C. 2016. *Encouraging Student Participation in a French-Immersion Kindergarten Class: A Multimodal, Conversation Analytic Study*. PhD dissertation, Teachers College, Columbia University.

Crotty, M. J. 1998. *The Foundations of Social Research: Meaning and Perspective in the Research Process*. Allen & Unwin.

Crum, R. M., Anthony, J. C., Bassett, S. S., and Folstein, M. F. 1993. Population-based norms for the Mini-Mental State Examination by age and educational level. *JAMA* 269(18), 2386–91.

Curl, T. S., and Drew, P. 2008. Contingency and action: A comparison of two forms of requesting. *Research on Language and Social Interaction* 41(2), 129–53.

Daykin, J. B. 2006. "They themselves contribute to their misery by their sloth": The justification of slavery in eighteenth-century French travel narratives. *European Legacy* 11(6), 623–32.

De Fina, A. 2011. "We are not there. In fact now we will go to the garden to take the rain": Researcher identity and the observer's paradox. In Angouri, J., and Marra, M., eds., *Constructing Identities at Work*, 223–45. Palgrave Macmillan.

De Montigny, G. A. 1995. *Social Working: An Ethnography of Front-Line Practice*. University of Toronto Press.

Deem, R., and Brehony, K. J. 2005. Management as ideology: The case of "new managerialism" in higher education. *Oxford Review of Education* 31(2), 217–35.

Del Percio, A., and Flubacher, M.-C. 2017. "Language, Education and Neoliberalism." In Flubacher, M.-C., and Del Percio, A., eds., *Language, Education and Neoliberalism: Critical Studies in Sociolinguistics*, 1–18. Multilingual Matters. https://doi.org/10.21832/9781783098699-003

Department of Homeless Services (DHS). 2002. *The Second Decade of Reform: A Strategic Plan for New York City's Homeless Services*. Retrieved March 2005 from http://www.ci.nyc.ny.us/html/dhs/downloads/pdf/stratplan.pdf

Department of Homeless Services (DHS). 2004. *Uniting for Solutions Beyond Shelter: The Action Plan for New York City*. New York City Department of Homeless Services Presses.

Deresiewicz, W. 2015. The neoliberal arts. *Harper's*, September.

Desjarlais, R. 1994. Struggling along: The possibilities for experience among the homeless mentally ill. *American Anthropologist* 96(4), 886–901.

Desjarlais, R. 1996. The office of reason: On the politics of language and agency in a shelter for "the homeless mentally ill." *American Ethnologist* 23(4), 880–900.

Desjarlais, R. 2011. *Shelter Blues: Sanity and Selfhood Among the Homeless*. University of Pennsylvania Press.

di Gennaro, K., and Brewer, M. 2019. Microaggressions as speech acts: Using pragmatics to define and develop a research agenda for microaggressions. *Applied Linguistics Review* 10(4), 725–44.

Dickens, C. 1843/2006. A Christmas carol. In *A Christmas Carol and Other Christmas Books*, 5–83. Oxford University Press.

Drew, P., and Heritage, J. 1992. Analyzing talk at work: An introduction. In Drew, P., and Heritage, J., eds., *Talk at Work: Interaction in Institutional Settings*, 3–65. Cambridge University Press.

Drew, P., and Walker, T. 2010. Citizens' emergency calls: Requesting assistance in calls to the police. In Coulthard, M., and Johnson, A., eds., *The Routledge Handbook of Forensic Linguistics*, 95–110. Routledge.

Dubois, J. W. 2007. The stance triangle. In Englebretson, R., ed., *Stancetaking in Discourse: Subjectivity, Evaluation, Interaction*. John Benjamins.

Duchêne, A., and Heller, M., eds. 2012. *Language in Late Capitalism: Pride and Profit*. Vol. 1. Routledge.

Duckworth, A. 2016. *Grit: The Power of Passion and Perseverance*. Scribner.

Duneier, M. 1999. *Sidewalk*. Farrar, Strauss, and Giroux.

Ehrlich, S. 2010. Rape victims: The discourse of rape trials. In Coultard, M., and Johnson, A., eds., *The Routledge Handbook of Forensic Linguistics*. Routledge.

Erickson, F. 2004. *Talk and Social Theory: Ecologies of Speaking and Listening in Everyday Life*. Polity Press.

Feinberg, W., and Soltis, J. F. 2009. *School and Society*. Teachers College Press.

Ferguson, C. A., Reilly, J. S., ter Meulen, A., and Traugott, E. C. 1986. Overview. In Traugott, E. C., ter Meulen, A., Reilly, J. S., and Ferguson, C. A., eds., *On Conditionals*, 3–20. Cambridge University Press.

Fiennes, S., director. *A Pervert's Guide to Ideology*. Zeitgeist Films.

Fillenbaum, S. 1986. The use of conditionals in inducements and deterrents. In Traugott, E.C., ter Meulen, A., Reilly, J. S., Ferguson, C.A., eds., *On Conditionals*, `79–95. Cambridge University Press, New York.

Fine, M., & Torre, M. E. 2019. Critical participatory action research: A feminist project for validity and solidarity. *Psychology of Women Quarterly*, 43(4), 433–44.

Firth, A. 1996. The discursive accomplishment of normality: On "lingua franca" English and conversation analysis. *Journal of Pragmatics* 26(2), 237–59.

Flores, N., Lewis, M. C., and Phuong, J. 2018. Raciolinguistic chronotopes and the education of Latinx students: Resistance and anxiety in a bilingual school. *Language & Communication* 62, 15–25.

Flubacher, M. C., and Del Percio, A., eds. 2017. *Language, Education and Neoliberalism: Critical Studies in Sociolinguistics*. Multilingual Matters.

Folstein, M. F. 1975. A practical method for grading the cognitive state of patients for the clinician. *Journal of Psychiatric Research* 12, 189–98.

Fortier, I., and Therrien, M. A. 2018. The public sector challenged by acceleration. *Canadian Public Administration* 61(3), 462–66.

Foucault, M. 2008. *The Birth of Biopolitics: Lectures at the Collège de France, 1978–1979*. Ed. M. Senellart. Trans. G. Burchell. Springer.

Fraser N., and Jaeggi, R. 2018. *Capitalism: A Conversation in Critical Theory*. Polity Press.

Fredman, N., and Doughney, J. 2012. Academic dissatisfaction, managerial change and neo-liberalism. *Higher Education* 64(1), 41–58.

Freire, P. 1970. *Pedagogy of the Oppressed*. Trans. M. B. Ramos. Continuum Press.

García, R. S. 2021. The testosterone barrier in sport. *Sociología del deporte* 2(2).

Gewirtz, S. and Ball, S. 2000. From "welfarism" to "new managerialism": Shifting discourses of school headship in the education marketplace. *Discourse: Studies in the Cultural Politics of Education* 21(3), 253–26.

Giroux, H. A. 2014. *Neoliberalism's War on Higher Education*. Haymarket Books.

Givens, T. 2021. *Radical Empathy: Finding a Path to Bridging Racial Divides*. Policy Press.

Glenn, P. 2003. *Laughter in Interaction*. Cambridge University Press.

Goetz, J. P., and LeCompte, M. D.. 1993. *Ethnography and Qualitative Design in Educational Research*. Academic Press.

Goffman, E. 1959. *The Presentation of Self in Everyday Life*. Doubleday.

Goffman, E. 1981. *Forms of Talk*. University of Pennsylvania Press.

Goldrick-Rab, S., Richardson, J., Schneider, J., Hernandez, A., and Cady, C. 2018. Still hungry and homeless in college. Wisconsin Hope Lab. https://hope4college.com/wp-content/uploads/2018/09/Wisconsin-HOPE-Lab-Still-Hungry-and-Homeless.pdf

Goodwin, C. 2007. Environmentally coupled gestures. In Duncan, S. D., Cassell, J., and Levy, E. T., eds., *Gesture and the Dynamic Dimensions of Language: Essays in Honor of David McNeill*, 195–212. J. Benjamins.

Grice, P. 1989. *Studies in the Way of Words*. Harvard University Press.

Hall, C., Juhila, K., Matarese, M., and van Nijnatten, C., eds. 2014. *Analysing Social Work Communication: Discourse in Practice*. Routledge.

Hall, C., Morris, L., and Juhila, K. 2017. Negotiation risks, choices and progress in case-planning meetings. In *Responsibilisation at the Margins of Welfare Services*. Routledge.

Hall, C., Slembrouck, S., and Sarangi, S. 2020. *Language Practices in Social Work: Categorisation and Accountability in Child Welfare*. Routledge.

Hancock, A. M. 2004. *The Politics of Disgust: The Public Identity of the Welfare Queen*. NYU Press.

Haney-López, I. 2014. *Dog Whistle Politics: How Coded Racial Appeals Have Reinvented Racism and Wrecked the Middle Class*. Oxford University Press.

Hargrave, C. P. 2019. *Analyzing University Exploitation of Diversity to Legitimize Hiring Discrimination: A Black Woman Professor's Narrative*. IGI Global.

Harlow, E. 2003. New managerialism, social service departments and social work practice today. *Practice* 15(2), 29–44.

Harmon, M. M. 1995. *Responsibility as Paradox: A Critique of Rational Discourse on Government*. Sage.

Harvey, D. 2006. Neo-liberalism as creative destruction. *Geografiska Annaler: Series B, Human Geography* 88(2), 145–58.

Harvey, D. 2007. *A Brief History of Neoliberalism*. Oxford University Press.

Heritage, J., and Clayman, S. 2011. *Talk in Action: Interactions, Identities, and Institutions*. John Wiley & Sons.

Heritage, J., and Robinson, J. D. 2011. "Some" versus "any" medical issues: Encouraging patients to reveal their unmet concerns. In Antaki, C., ed., *Applied Conversation Analysis: Intervention and Change in Institutional Talk*, 15–31. Palgrave Macmillan.

Heritage, J., ed. Talk at Work: Interaction in Institutional Settings. Cambridge University Press.

Hersey, T. 2022. *Rest Is Resistance: A Manifesto*. Hachette.

Hill, J. H. 2009. *The Everyday Language of White Racism*. John Wiley & Sons.

Hill, J. H., and Irvine, J. T., eds. 1993. *Responsibility and Evidence in Oral Discourse*. Cambridge University Press.

Hill, J. H., and Zepeda, O. 1993. Mrs. Patricio's trouble: The distribution of responsibility in an account of personal experience. In Hill, J. H., and Irvine, J. T., eds., *Responsibility and Evidence in Oral Discourse*. Cambridge University Press.

Hjörne, E., Juhila, K., and van Nijnatten, C. 2010. Negotiating dilemmas in the practices of street-level welfare work. *International Journal of Social Welfare* 19(3), 303–9.

Ho Shon, P. C. 2005. "I'd grab the SOB by his hair and yank him out the window": The fraternal order of warnings and threats in police-citizen encounters. *Discourse & Society* 16(6), 829–45.

Holborow, M. 2015. *Language and Neoliberalism*. Routledge.

Hopper, K. 2003. *Reckoning with Homelessness*. Cornell University Press.

Hudley, A. H. C., and Mallinson, C. 2011. *Understanding English Language Variation in U.S. Schools*. Teachers College Press.

Hudley, A. H. C., Mallinson, C., and Bucholtz, M. 2022. *Talking College: Making Space for Black Language Practices in Higher Education*. Teachers College Press.

Hupe, P., and Hill, M. 2007. Street-level bureaucracy and public accountability. *Public Administration* 85(2), 279–99.

Hurst, B. D., director. 1951. *A Christmas Carol*. United Artists.

Hutchby, I., and Wooffitt, R. 2008. *Conversation Analysis*. Polity Press.

Isserles, R. G. 2021. *The Costs of Completion: Student Success in Community College*. Johns Hopkins University Press.

Jacknick, C. M. 2021. *Multimodal Participation and Engagement: Social Interaction in the Classroom*. Edinburgh University Press.

Jonas, H. 1984. *The Imperative of Responsibility: In Search of an Ethics for the Technological Age*. University of Chicago Press.

Juhila, K. 2004. Talking back to stigmatised identities: Negotiation of culturally dominant categorizations in interviews with shelter residents. *Qualitative Social Work* 3(3), 259–75.

Juhila, K., Raitakari, S., and Hall, C., eds. 2016. *Responsibilisation at the Margins of Welfare Services*. Taylor & Francis.

Karkazis, K., and Jordan-Young, R. M. 2018. The powers of testosterone: Obscuring race and regional bias in the regulation of women athletes. *Feminist Formations* 30(2), 1–39.

Kirkpatrick I. 2006, Taking stock of the new managerialism in English social service. *Social Work and Society* 4(1), 14–24.

Klempin, S. C. 2014. Redefining full-time in college: Evidence on 15-credit strategies. Community College Research Center. https://academiccommons.columbia.edu/doi/10.7916/D83F4N7Z

Koyama, J. 2017. Assembling language policy: Challenging standardization and quantification in the education of refugee students in a US school. In Flubacher, M.-C., and Del Percio, A., eds., *Language, Education and Neoliberalism: Critical Studies in Sociolinguistics*, 163–83. Multilingual Matters.

Kozol, J. 2011. *Rachel and Her Children: Homeless Families in America*. Crown.

Labov, W. 1972. Academic ignorance and black intelligence. *Atlantic Monthly*, June. Retrieved April 30, 2025, from https://www.ling.upenn.edu/courses/Fall_2015/ling001/Labov1972.pdf

Ladson-Billings, G. 1992. Culturally relevant teaching: The key to making multicultural education work. In C. A. Grant, ed., *Research and Multicultural Education*, 106–21. Falmer Press.

Lakoff, R. 2016. Taking "responsibility" from word to discourse. In Östman, J. O., and Solin, A., eds., 2016. *Discourse and Responsibility in Professional Settings*, 10–36. Equinox.

Lance, K., Matarese, M., Friedman, C., Diaz, C., and Coombs, B. 2023. Your health is in your hands. In Ädel, A., and Östman, J. O., eds., *Risk Discourse and Responsibility*, 142–69. John Benjamins.

Latour, B. 1999. On recalling ANT. *Sociological Review* 47(suppl. 1), 15–25. https://doi.org/10.1111/j.1467-954X.1999.tb03480.x

Lave, J., and Wenger, E. 1991. *Situated Learning: Legitimate Peripheral Participation*. Cambridge University Press.

Leander, K. M., Phillips, N. C., and Taylor, K. H. 2010. The changing social spaces of learning: Mapping new mobilities. *Review of Research in Education* 34(1), 329–94.

Lemke, J. 2000. Across the scales of time: Artifacts, activities, and meanings in ecosocial systems. *Mind, Culture, and Activity* 7(4), 273–90.

Leonhardt, D. 2017. America's great working-class colleges. *New York Times*, January 18.

Levin, H. M., and Calcagno, J. C. 2008. Remediation in the community college: An evaluator's perspective. *Community College Review* 35(3), 181–207.

Levin, J., Kater, S., and Wagoner, R. L. 2006. *Community College Faculty: At Work in the New Economy*. Springer.

Liebow, E. 1993. *Tell Them Who I Am: The Lives of Homeless Women*. Free Press.

Lipman, P. 2013. *The New Political Economy of Urban Education: Neoliberalism, Race, and the Right to the City*. Taylor & Francis.

Lippi-Green, R. 1994. Accent, standard language ideology, and discriminatory pretext in the courts. *Language in Society* 23(2), 163–98.

Lipsky, M. 1980/2010. *Street-Level Bureaucracy: Dilemmas of the Individual in Public Service*. 30th anniversary expanded ed. Russell Sage Foundation.

Lotta, G., and Pires, R. 2019. Street-level bureaucracy research and social inequality. In Hupe, P. L., ed., *Research Handbook on Street-Level Bureaucracy: The Ground Floor of Government in Context*, 86–101. Edward Elgar.

Love, B. L. 2019. *We Want to Do More Than Survive: Abolitionist Teaching and the Pursuit of Educational Freedom*. Beacon Press.

Lukes, D., & Cleveland, C. 2021. The lingering legacy of redlining on school funding, diversity, and performance. *Annenberg Institute for School Reform*, 10.

Machin, D., and Mayr, A. 2012. *How to Do Critical Discourse Analysis: A Multimodal Introduction*. Sage.

Mäkitalo, Å. 2006. Effort on display: Unemployment and the interactional management of moral accountability. *Symbolic Interaction* 29(4), 531–55.

Mäkitalo, Å. 2014. Categorisation. In Hall, C., Juhila, K., Matarese, M., and van Nijnatten, C., eds., *Analysing Social Work Communication: Discourse in Practice*. Routledge.

Makri-Tsilipakou, M. 1994. Interruption revisited: Affiliative vs. disaffiliative intervention. *Journal of Pragmatics* 21(4), 401–26.

Mallinson, C., and Charity Hudley, A. H. 2010. Communicating about communication: Multidisciplinary approaches to educating educators about language variation. *Language and Linguistics Compass* 4(4), 245–57.

Mallinson, C., and Charity Hudley, A. H. 2017. The sound of inclusion: Why teacher's words matter. *Salon*, August 17. https://www.salon.com/2017/08/17/the-sound-of-inclusion-why-teachers-words-matter_partner/

Marshall, C., and Rossman, G. B. 2014. *Designing Qualitative Research*. Sage.

Marshall, P., director. 1992. *A League of Their Own*. Columbia Pictures.

Marthinsen, E., Skjefstad, N., Juberg, A., and Garrett, P. M., eds. 2021. *Social Work and Neoliberalism*. Routledge.

Matarese, M. T. 2008. *Practice, Power, Policy, and Participation: A Linguistic Ethnography of Cumulative Caseworker-Client Interactions in a New York City Homeless Shelter*. PhD dissertation, Teachers College, Columbia University.

Matarese, M. T. 2012. "Getting placed" in time: Responsibility talk in caseworker-client interaction. *Journal of Applied Linguistics & Professional Practice* 9(3).

Matarese, M. T. 2020. Discursive mindfulness among practitioners analyzing social work communication. In Grujicic-Alatriste, L., ed., *Language Research in Multilin-*

gual Settings: Doing Research Knowledge Dissemination at the Sites of Practice, 95–123. Multilingual Matters.

Matarese, M. T., and Caswell, D. 2014. Accountability. In Hall, C., Juhila, K., Matarese, M., and van Nijnatten, C., eds., *Analysing Social Work Communication: Discourse in Practice*. Routledge.

Matarese, M. T., and Caswell, D. 2017. Neoliberal talk: The routinized structures of document-focused social worker-client discourse. In Schram, S. F., and Pavlovskaya, M., eds., *Rethinking Neoliberalism: Resisting the Disciplinary Regime*, 119–36. Routledge.

Matarese, M. T., and Caswell, D. 2018. "I'm gonna ask you about yourself, so I can put it on paper": Analysing street-level bureaucracy through form-related talk in social work. *British Journal of Social Work* 48(3), 714–33.

Matarese, M. T., and van Nijnatten, C. 2015. Making a case for client insistence in social work interaction. *Discourse Processes* 52(8), 670–88.

Maynard-Moody, S. W., and Musheno, M. C. 2003. *Cops, Teachers, Counsellors: Stories from the Front Lines of Public Service*. University of Michigan Press.

Mehan, H. 1979. *Learning Lessons: Social Organization in the Classroom*. Harvard University Press.

Menken, K. 2008. *English Learners Left Behind: Standardized Testing as Language Policy*. Multilingual Matters.

Meyer, H. D. 2002. From "loose coupling" to "tight management"? Making sense of the changing landscape in management and organization theory. *Journal of Educational Administration* 40(6), 515–20.

Mondada, L. 2018. Transcription in linguistics. In *Research Methods in Linguistics*, 85–114.

Naples, N. A. 2013. *Feminism and Method: Ethnography, Discourse Analysis, and Activist Research*. Routledge.

O'Malley, P. 2009. Responsibilization. In Wakefield, A., and Fleming, J., eds., *The Sage Dictionary of Policing*, 277–79. Sage.

Ochs, E. 1979. Transcription as theory. *Developmental Pragmatics* 10(1), 43–72.

Olssen, M., and Peters, M. A. 2005. Neoliberalism, higher education and the knowledge economy: From the free market to knowledge capitalism. *Journal of Education Policy* 20(3), 313–45.

Östman, J. O., and Solin, A., eds. 2016. *Discourse and Responsibility in Professional Settings*. Equinox.

Page, E. C., and Jenkins, B. 2005. *Policy Bureaucracy: Government with a Cast of Thousands*. Oxford University Press.

Paris, D., and Alim, H. S., EDS. 2017. *Culturally Sustaining Pedagogies: Teaching and Learning for Justice in a Changing World*. Teachers College Press.

Payne, M. 1997. *Modem Social Work Theory*. 2nd ed. Macmillan.

Peck, J. 2010. Zombie neoliberalism and the ambidextrous state. *Theoretical Criminology* 14(1), 104–10.

Perez Gomez, J. 2021. Verbal microaggressions as hyper-implicatures. *Journal of Political Philosophy* 29(3), 375–403.

Perry, I. 2011. *More Beautiful and More Terrible: The Embrace and Transcendence of Racial Inequality in the United States*. NYU Press.

Pierce, C. M. 1974. Psychiatric problems of the Black minority. In Arieti, S., ed., *American Handbook of Psychiatry*, 512–23. Basic Books.

Pitcher, E. N. 2017. "There's stuff that comes with being an unexpected guest": Experiences of trans* academics with microaggressions. *International Journal of Qualitative Studies in Education* 30(7), 688–703.

Pomerantz, A. 1978. Attributions of responsibility: Blamings. *Sociology* 12(1), 115–21.

Pomerantz, A. 1984. Agreeing and disagreeing with assessments: Some features of preferred/dispreferred turn shaped. In Atkinson, J. M., and Heritage, J., eds., *Structures of Social Action*. Cambridge University Press.

Psathas, G., and Anderson, T. 1990. The "practices" of transcription in conversation analysis. *Semiotica* 78(1–2), 75–99.

Raaphorst, N., and Groeneveld, S. 2019. Discrimination and representation in street-level bureaucracies. In Hupe, P., ed., *Research Handbook on Street-Level Bureaucracy: The Ground Floor of Government in Context*, 116–27. Edward Elgar.

Ravalier, J. M., McFadden, P., Boichat, C., Clabburn, O., and Moriarty, J. 2021. Social worker well-being: A large mixed-methods study. *British Journal of Social Work* 51(1), 297–317. https://doi.org/10.1093/bjsw/bcaa078

Ravitch, D. 2009. Obama gives Bush third term in education. *Huffington Post*, July 14. https://www.huffpost.com/entry/obama-gives-bush-a-3rd-te_b_215277

Reyes, A. 2004. Asian American stereotypes as circulating resource. *Pragmatics* 14(2–3), 173–92.

Reyna, C., Dobria, O., and Wetherell, G. 2013. The complexity and ambivalence of immigration attitudes: Ambivalent stereotypes predict conflicting attitudes toward immigration policies. *Cultural Diversity and Ethnic Minority Psychology* 19(3), 342.

Robinson, J. D. 2016. *Accountability in Social Interaction*. Oxford University Press.

Rojo, L. M., and Del Percio, A., eds. 2019. *Language and Neoliberal Governmentality*. Routledge.

Romaine, S., and Lange, D. 1991. The use of like as a marker of reported speech and thought: A case of grammaticalization in progress. *American Speech* 66(3), 227–79.

Rosa, J. D. 2016. Standardization, racialization, languagelessness: Raciolinguistic ideologies across communicative contexts. *Journal of Linguistic Anthropology* 26(2), 162–83.

Rowe, M. B. 1987. Wait time: Slowing down may be a way of speeding up. *American Educator* 11, 38–43, 47.

Sacks, H. 1992. *Lectures on Conversation*. 2 vols. Ed. G. Jefferson. Blackwell.

Samier, E. 2002. Managerial rationalisation and the ethical disenchantment of education: A Weberian perspective on moral theory in modern educational organisations. *Journal of Educational Administration* 40(6), 589–603.

Sarangi, S. 2010. Reconfiguring self/identity/status/role: The case of professional role performance in healthcare encounters. *Journal of Applied Linguistics & Professional Practice* 7(1).

Sarangi, S. 2011. Role hybridity in professional practice. In Sarangi, S., Polese, V., and Caliendo, G., eds., *Genre(s) on the Move: Hybridisation and Discourse Change in Specialised Communication*, 271–96. Edizioni Scientifiche Italiane.

Sarangi, S. 2016. Owning responsibility actions/selves: Role-relational trajectories in counselling for childhood genetic testing. In Östman, J. O., and Solin, A., eds., 2016. *Discourse and Responsibility in Professional Settings*, 37–66. Equinox.

Sarangi, S., and Candlin, C. N. 2010. Applied linguistics and professional practice: Mapping a future agenda. *Journal of Applied Linguistics and Professional Practice* 7(1), 1–9.

Schegloff, E. A. 1978. On some questions and ambiguities in conversation. In Dressler, W., ed., *Current Trends in Textlinguistics*, 81–102. de Gruyter.

Schegloff, E. A. 2001. Getting serious: Joke→ serious "no." *Journal of pragmatics* 33(12), 1947–55.

Schiffrin, D. 1987. *Discourse Markers*. Cambridge University Press.

Schneider, A., and Ingram, H. 1993. Social construction of target populations: Implications for politics and policy. *American Political Science Review* 87(2), 334–47.

Schwartz, R. C. 2021. *No Bad Parts: Healing Trauma and Restoring Wholeness with the Internal Family Systems Model*. Sounds True.

Scollon, R., and Scollon, S. W. 2004. *Nexus Analysis: Discourse and the Emerging Internet*. Routledge.

Scott, M., and Lyman, S. 1968. Accounts. *American Sociological Association* 33(1), 46–62.

Scourfield, P. 2007. Social care and the modern citizen: Client, consumer, service user, manager and entrepreneur. *British Journal of Social Work* 37(1), 107–22.

Scourfield, P. 2015. Even further beyond street-level bureaucracy: The dispersal of discretion exercised in decisions made in older people's care home reviews. *British Journal of Social Work* 45, 914–31.

Searle, J. 2010. *Making the Social World: The Structure of Human Civilization*. Oxford University Press.

Seedhouse, P. 2004. *The Interactional Architecture of the Language Classroom: A Conversation Analysis Perspective*. Blackwell.

Skukauskaitė, A., and Green, J. L. 2023. *Interactional Ethnography: Designing and Conducting Discourse-Based Ethnographic Research*. Routledge.

Slembrouck, S., and Hall, C. 2003. Caring but not coping: Fashioning a legitimate parent identity. In Hall, C., Juhila, K., Parton, N., and Pösö, T., eds., *Constructing Clienthood in Social Work and Human Services: Interaction, Identities and Practices*. Jessica Kingsley Publishers.

Smith, K. B., and Larimer, C. 2018. *The Public Policy Theory Primer*. Routledge.

Smith, N. 2003. Changes in the modals and semi-modals of strong obligation and epistemic necessity in recent British English. *Topics in English Linguistics* 44, 241–66.

Smyth, J. 2020. The neoliberal toxic university: Beyond no is not enough and daring to dream a socially just alternative into existence. *Educational Philosophy and Theory* 52(7), 716–25.

Snow, D. A., and Anderson, L. 1987. Identity work among the homeless: The verbal construction and avowal of personal identities. *American Journal of Sociology* 92(6), 1336–71.

Soss, J., Fording, R., and Schram, S. F. 2011. The organization of discipline: From performance management to perversity and punishment. *Journal of Public Administration Research and Theory* 21(suppl. 2), i203–i232.

Spence, L. K. 2015. *Knocking the Hustle: Against the Neoliberal Turn in Black Politics*. Punctum Books.

Stahl, R. J. 1994. Using "think-time" and "wait-time" skillfully in the classroom. *ERIC Digest*, May.

Stivers, T., Enfield, N. J., and Levinson, S. 2007. Person reference in interaction. In Enfield, N. J., and Stivers, T., eds., *Person Reference in Interaction: Linguistic, Cultural and Social Perspectives*. Cambridge University Press.

Stokoe, E. 2014. The Conversation Analytic Role-Play Method (CARM): A Method for Training Communication Skills as an Alternative to Simulated Role-Play. *Research on Language and Social Interaction* 47(3), 255–65.

Stonehouse, D., Threlkeld, G., and Farmer, J. 2015. "Housing risk" and the neoliberal discourse of responsibilisation in Victoria. *Critical Social Policy* 35(3), 393–413.

Sue, D. W. 2010a. *Microaggressions and Marginality: Manifestations, Dynamic, and Impact*. Wiley.

Sue, D. W. 2010b. Microaggressions: More Than Just Race. *Psychology Today*, November. Retrieved April 30, 2025, from https://www.uua.org/sites/live-new.uua.org/files/microaggressions_by_derald_wing_sue_ph.d._.pdf

Sullivan, P. 2017. *Economic Inequality, Neoliberalism, and the American Community College*. Springer.

Talking Heads 77. 1977. Don't worry about the government. *Talking Heads 77*. Winchester Pressing.

Thornborrow, J. 2002. *Power Talk: Language and Interaction in Institutional Discourse*. Pearson Education.

Tomkins, P. F. 2018. King hat. *Laboring Under Delusions: Live in Brooklyn*. https://www.youtube.com/watch?v=RG8BEDZPteM

Trattner, W. I. 1999. *From Poor Law to Welfare State: A History of Social Welfare in America*. Free Press.

The United States Government. 2025, March 2. *Designating English as the official language of the United States*. The White House. https://www.whitehouse.gov/presidential-actions/2025/03/designating-english-as-the-official-language-of-the-united-states/

Van Dijk, T. 2008. *Discourse and Racism: A Companion to Racial and Ethnic Studies*. Blackwell.

Vinkhuyzen, E., and Szymanski, M. H. 2005. Would you like to do it yourself? Service requests and their non-granting responses. In Richards, K., and Seedhouse, P., eds., *Applying Conversation Analysis*, 91–106. Palgrave Macmillan.

Vološinov, V. N. 1929. *Marxism and the Philosophy of Language*. Trans. L. Matejka and I. R. Titunik. Harvard University Press.

Watkins-Hayes, C. 2009. *The New Welfare Bureaucrats: Entanglements of Race, Class, and Policy Reform*. University of Chicago Press.

Webb, P. T. 2011. The evolution of accountability. *Journal of Education Policy* 26(6), 735–56.

Weber, M. 2001. *The Protestant Ethic and the Spirit of Capitalism*. Trans. T. Parsons. Routledge.

White, S. 2003. The social worker as moral judge: Blame, responsibility, and case formation. In *Constructing Clienthood in Social Work and Human Services: Interaction, Identities and Practices*. Jessica Kingsley Publishers.

White, S., and Stancombe, J. 2003. *Clinical Judgement in the Health and Welfare Professions: Extending the Evidence Base*. Open University Press.

Wieder, D. L. 1974. *Language and Social Reality: The Case of Telling the Convict Code*. Mouton de Gruyter.

Williams, R. 2015. *Keywords: A Vocabulary of Culture and Society*. Oxford University Press.

Wolfram, W., Adger, C. T., and Christian, D. 1999. *Dialects in Schools and Communities*. Routledge.

Wooffitt, R. 2005. *Conversation Analysis and Discourse Analysis: A Comparative and Critical Introduction*. Sage.

Wortham, S.. 2006. *Learning Identity: The Joint Emergence of Social Identification and Academic Learning*. Cambridge University Press.

Yin, R. K. 2003. *Case Study Research: Design and Methods*. Sage.

Youdelman, M. 2019. *Summary of State Law Requirements Addressing Language Needs in Health Care*. National Health Law Program. https://healthlaw.org/resource/summary-of-state-law-requirements-addressing-language-needs-in-health-care-2/#:~:text=As%20of%202019%2C%20every%20state,at%20least%20three%20such%20provisions

Zacka, B. 2017. *When the State Meets the Street: Public Service and Moral Agency*. Harvard University Press.

Index